New American Plays

Plays by

ED BULLINS

DAVID STARKWEATHER

TOM HARRIS

WILLIAM M. HOFFMAN

ROBERT PATRICK

MARC ESTRIN

BYRD HOFFMAN

Edited and with an Introduction by

WILLIAM M. HOFFMAN

New American Plays

VOLUME THREE

A MERMAID DRAMABOOK
HILL & WANG *New York*

COPYRIGHT © 1970 BY HILL AND WANG, INC.
INTRODUCTION COPYRIGHT © 1970 BY WILLIAM M. HOFFMAN
STANDARD BOOK NUMBER (CLOTHBOUND EDITION): 8090–7252–1
STANDARD BOOK NUMBER (PAPERBACK EDITION): 8090–0745–2
LIBRARY OF CONGRESS CATALOG CARD NUMBER: 65–14530
MANUFACTURED IN THE UNITED STATES OF AMERICA
FIRST EDITION MARCH 1970

2 3 4 5 6 7 8 9 10

For my father

Contents

The Whole Thing

Of increasing interest to literary critics, nuclear physicists, and laymen—amen!—how do you say it in zee English tongue?—is the
    ongoing
         present
              tense.
Lawdy, look at the   blank space on the page
a   moment, if you don't know what I mean, and if you do,
         WHY, HELLO OUT THERE!
I'm talking about   IT,
if you know what I mean. I'm waving a red flag, I'm the man on the tracks trying to make the train stop.
stop stop stop stop stop stop stop stop stop stop stop stop stop
I'm out here in here and it's happening now and it's good now
      NO TIME NO ATTITUDE FREEDOM
                but
it's also impossible to write a "serious" piece about the ongoing present tense in the theatre in the ongoing present tense. But I will provide some metaphors.

• • •

A spaceship from Alpha Centauri lands. It's not at all what we thought it would be: it's not saucer shaped; it's not made of metal or plastic or any recognizable substance. In fact, we find ourselves describing the object-event solely in terms of how it differs from earthly things. Of one point, however, all humanity is sure: it has landed. The ship has unmistakably communicated that to every man in a mysterious nonverbal, nonvisual, nonosmoleptic, nontactile fashion. Greatly disturbed by the landing and responding to public clamor, the World Government sends a committee of experts to the site-time of the object-event. Consisting of the world's greatest politician, scientist, philosopher, and journalist, the committee's task is to bring back a composite portrait of the indescribable spaceship.

The committee returns and shortly afterward is confined to a mental hospital for observation. For when asked if the spaceship is to be considered hostile, the politician replied: "No. I mean yes. No-yes. Yes-no? On one level, of course, ahem, it is obvious that the sharp spikes are a clear indication of some sort of . . . but then the soft pillows. . . ."

The scientist had no comment and a year later he joined the faculty of the California Institute of Advanced Astrology.

The philosopher issued a long statement proving not only the nonexistence of the spaceship but also the probability of a Buddhist plot to contaminate the oceans with powerful mind-bending drugs.

The journalist wrote: ". . . It was an unusually clear day. The wind was brisk as I approached the site. Unusual in shape, the spaceship reminded me of certain Hindu sculptures, of poems by Blake, of a back street in London, or was it New York. Yes, Paris. Paris in the springtime. Shift. Springtime. Lock. Type. Back space. Yes, back space, definitely like a back space the length of an arm, about a yard, an arm, a yard, an arm, a yard-arm, yardarm, yarm yarm yarm yarm. . . ."

A new committee is sent out. The government tried to ignore the ship for a while but new alarms were raised after a second message was broadcast to mankind. When rendered into words the message was, "We are." This time leading members of the arts were sent out to bring back descriptions of the spaceship.

The artists were not intimidated by the ship. They returned with paintings, sculptures, symphonies, movies, novels, and plays—quite conflicting in style and content—all claiming to be the accurate representation of the spaceship. (The sole casualty of this expedition was an actor who returned declaring that he *was* the spaceship.)

After a third unsuccessful attempt was made, this time by theologians, the spaceship was thenceforth ignored. Occasionally messages from it were received, but mankind was told that they were a kind of chronic electronic disturbance and were to be disregarded. No more delegations were sent by the government, which was soon occupied by the third expedition to Jupiter. Once in a while men set out on their own to visit the ship but there remains no record of these ventures.

• • •

If the theatre and its audience are a fishing village and the Whole Thing that we call reality is a huge clever fish, how do we catch it? How does the playwright in the village help catch the fish? How do the actors? The director? The lighting designer? The costume designer? The ushers? The audience?

• • •

If the theatre and its audience are a construction firm and prospective tenants, and the Whole Thing is a building, how do we build it?

• • •

If we are a primitive tribe sitting around a campfire how do we represent the Whole Thing? If we are a tribe with advanced technology sitting in front of a proscenium and standing on a stage behind it, how do we represent the Whole Thing?

• • •

If we are a chef and the Whole Thing is a banquet, how do we prepare it?

• • •

If the theatre and its audience are a hospital and the Whole Thing that we call reality is an epidemic, how do we stop it? Who would be the doctor? The nurse? The surgeon?

• • •

Given that the Whole Thing that we call reality includes the present (the "ongoing present," that is, the present including the moment you decide to communicate your picture of reality), how would you represent the Whole Thing on stage? What would you call the play? How would you cast it? Would it be a tragedy? A comedy? A musical?

• • •

Projects:

1. A play for blind people. (Not a radio play, but a play that utilizes the theatre in an entirely nonvisual manner.) Similarly, a play for deaf people.

2. A play for racists (white, black, whatever).

3. A play about time.

4. A play written by a paranoid.

5. A play written for an audience of dogs. (Also, a play for people in which all the performers are dogs.)

6. A play for an audience of a culture different from your own: Eskimos, Australian aborigines, American Indians, Aztecs. (Also, a play for people of an imaginary culture.)

7. A pornographic play. (Out-and-out.)

8. A play for an audience of concentration camp inmates.

9. A play set in a forest performed in a forest. (The play may change locale, but this would have to be suggested utilizing what is at hand in the forest.)

10. A conventional Broadway play using insights gained from performing the nine kinds of plays mentioned above.

—W.M.H.

BIBLIOGRAPHY

BUWEI YANG CHAO, *How to Cook and Eat in Chinese*. Faber and Faber, London, 1968.

CAMPBELL, JOSEPH, *The Hero with a Thousand Faces*. Meridian, Cleveland and New York, 1956.

CAMPBELL, JOSEPH, *The Masks of God* (4 vols.). Viking, New York, 1959–1968.

CASTANEDA, CARLOS, *The Teachings of Don Juan*. Ballantine, New York, 1969.

CAVENDISH, RICHARD, *The Black Arts*. Routledge and Kegan Paul, London, 1967.

FREUCHEN, PETER, *Book of the Eskimos.* Fawcett, Greenwich, Conn., 1965.

LAING, R. D., *The Politics of Experience.* Ballantine, New York, 1968.

LÉVI-STRAUSS, CLAUDE, *Tristes Tropiques.* Atheneum, New York, 1963.

LEWIS, C. S., *Out of the Silent Planet.* Macmillan, New York, 1965.

LILLY, JOHN CUNNINGHAM, M. D., *The Mind of the Dolphin.* Avon, New York, 1969.

LORENZ, KONRAD Z., *Man Meets Dog,* Penguin, Baltimore, 1964.

PLATT, RUTHERFORD, *The Great American Forest.* Prentice-Hall, Englewood Cliffs, N.J., 1965.

WATTS, ALAN W., *The Book.* Collier, New York, 1967.

The Electronic Nigger

A *Tragicomedy*

ED BULLINS

Doug Harris

E<small>D</small> B<small>ULLINS</small>: "Member of New Lafayette Theatre, Harlem."

Characters

MR. JONES: *A light-brown-skinned man. Thirty years old. Horn-rimmed glasses. Crewcut, and small, smart mustache. He speaks in a clipped manner when in control of himself but is more than self-conscious, even from the beginning. Whatever,* MR. JONES *speaks as unlike the popular conception of how a negro speaks as is possible. Not even the fallacious accent acquired by many "cultured" or highly educated negroes should be sought, but that general cross-fertilized dialect found on various Ivy League and the campuses of the University of California. He sports an ascot.*

MR. CARPENTIER: *A large, dark man in his late thirties. He speaks in blustering orations, many times mispronouncing words. His tone is stentorian, and his voice has an absurdly ridiculous affected accent.*

BILL: *Twenty-two years old. Negro.*

SUE: *Twenty years old. White.*

LENARD: *Twenty-one. A fat white boy.*

MISS MOSKOWITZ: *Mid-thirties. An aging professional student.*

MARTHA: *An attractive negro woman.*

STUDENTS: *Any number of interracial students to supply background, short of the point of discouraging a producer.*

The Electronic Nigger was first produced at the American Place Theatre on March 26, 1968. The production was directed by Robert MacBeth. Sets were designed by John Jay Moore; lighting by Roger Morgan. The cast was as follows:

MR. JONES   Wayne Grice
LENARD   Warren Pincus
MISS MOSKOWITZ   Jeanne Kaplan
MR. CARPENTIER   L. Errol Jaye
BILL   Roscoe Orman
SUE   Hedy Sontag
MARTHA   Helen Ellis
STUDENTS   Ronald A. Hirsch
             Maie Mottus

The Electronic Nigger

Scene: A classroom of a Southern California junior college.

Modern décor. New facilities: light-green blackboards; bright fluorescent lighting; elongated, rectangular tables seating four to eight students, facing each other, instead of the traditional rows of seats facing toward the instructor. The tables are staggered throughout the room and set at angles, making it impossible for the instructor to engage the eye of the student, unless the student turns toward him or the instructor leaves his small table and walks among the students.

It is seven o'clock by the wall clock; twilight outside the windows indicates a fall evening. A NO SMOKING sign is beneath the clock, directly above the green blackboards, behind the instructor's table and rostrum.

The bell rings.

Half the STUDENTS *are already present.* MISS MOSKOWITZ *drinks coffee from a paper cup;* LENARD *munches on an apple, noisily. More* STUDENTS *enter from the rear and front doors to the room and take seats. There is the general low buzz of activity and first-night anticipation of a new evening class.*

7

BILL *comes in through the back door to the room;* SUE *enters by the other. They casually look about them for seats and indifferently sit down next to each other.*

JONES *enters puffing on his pipe and smoothing down his ascot.*

The bell rings.

MR. JONES *(exhaling smoke.)* Well . . . good evening. . . . My name is Jones . . . ha ha. . . . That won't be hard to remember, will it? I'll be your instructor this semester . . . ha ha. . . . Now this is English 22E . . . Creative Writing.

LENARD Did you say 22E?

MR. JONES Yes, I did. . . . Do all of you have that number on your cards? . . . Now look at your little I.B.M. cards and see if there is a little 22E in the upper left-hand corner. Do you see it?

CARPENTIER *enters and looks over the class.*

MISS MOSKOWITZ *(confused.)* Why . . . I don't see any numbers on my card.

MR. JONES *(extinguishing pipe.)* Good . . . now that everyone seems to belong here who is here, we can get started with our creativity . . . ha ha. . . . If I sort of——

MISS MOSKOWITZ *(protesting.)* But I don't have a number!

LENARD *(ridicule.)* Yes, you do!

MISS MOSKOWITZ Give that back to me . . . give that card back to me right now!

LENARD *(pointing to card.)* It's right here like he said . . . in the upper left-hand corner.

MISS MOSKOWITZ *(snatching card.)* I know where it is!

MR. JONES Now that we all know our——

MR. CARPENTIER Sir . . . I just arrived in these surroundings and I have not yet been oriented as to the primary sequence of events which have preceded my entrance.

MR. JONES Well, nothing has——

MR. CARPENTIER *(cutting.)* If you will enlighten me I'll be eternally grateful for any communicative aid that you may render in your capacity as professor *de la classe*.

MR. JONES   Well . . . well . . . I'm not a professor, I'm an instructor.

BILL   Just take a look at your card and see if——

MR. CARPENTIER   Didn't your mother teach you any manners, young man?

BILL   What did you say, fellah?

MR. CARPENTIER   Don't speak until you're asked to——

MR. JONES   Now you people back there . . . pay attention.

MISS MOSKOWITZ   Why, I never in all my life——

MR. JONES   Now to begin with——

SUE   You've got some nerve speaking to him like that. Where did you come from, mister?

MR. JONES   Class!

MR. CARPENTIER   Where I came from . . . *mon bonne femme* . . . has no bearing on this situational conundrum . . . splendid word, conundrum, heh, what? Jimmie Baldwin uses it brilliantly on occasion——

MR. JONES   I'm not going to repeat——

MR. CARPENTIER   But getting back to the matter at hand . . . I am here to become acquainted with the formal aspects of authorcraft. . . . Of course I've been a successful writer for many years even though I haven't taken the time for the past ten years to practice the art-forms of fiction, drama, or that very breath of the muse . . . poesy——

MR. JONES   Sir . . . please!

BILL   How do you turn it off?

LENARD   For Christ' sake!

MR. CARPENTIER   But you can find my name footnoted in numerous professional sociological-psychological-psychiatric and psychedelic journals——

MR. JONES   If you'll please——

MR. CARPENTIER   A. T. Carpentier is the name . . . notice the silent *t*. . . . My profession gets in the way of art, in the strict aesthetic sense, you know. . . . I'm a Sociological Data

9

Research Analysis Technician Expert. Yes, penalology is my field, naturally, and I have been in over thirty-three penal institutions across the country . . . in a professional capacity, obviously . . . ha ho ho.

MR. JONES Sir!

LENARD Geez!

MR. CARPENTIER Here are some of my random findings, conclusions, etc., which I am re-creating into a new art-form——

SUE A new art-form we have here already.

BILL This is going to be one of those classes.

MR. CARPENTIER Yes, young lady . . . Socio Drama——

MR. JONES All right, Mr. Carpentier.

MR. CARPENTIER (*corrects.*) Carpentier! The t is silent.

MR. JONES Okay. Complete what you were saying——

MR. CARPENTIER Thank you, sir.

MR. JONES ——and then——

MR. CARPENTIER By the way, my good friend J. J. Witherthorn is already dickering with my agent for options on my finished draft for a pilot he is planning to shoot of *Only Corpses Beat the Big House,* which, by the way, is the title of the first script, taken from an abortive *novella narratio* I had begun in my youth after a particularly torrid affair with one Eulah Mae Jackson——

MR. JONES Good . . . now let's——

MR. CARPENTIER Of course, after I read it some of you will say it resembles in some ways *The Quare Fellow,* but I have documented evidence that I've had this plot outlined since——

BILL Question!

SUE Won't somebody do something?

BILL *Question!*

MR. JONES (*to* BILL.) Yes, what is it?

MR. CARPENTIER (*over.*) Of course I'll finish it on time . . . the final draft, I mean . . . and have it to J. J. far ahead of the deadline but I thought that the rough edges could be chopped off here . . . and there——

MR. JONES (*approaching anger.*)   Mr. Carpentier . . . if you'll please?

MR. CARPENTIER (*belligerent and glaring.*)   I beg your pardon, sir?

MARTHA *enters.*

MR. JONES   This class must get under way . . . immediately!

MARTHA (*to* MR. JONES.)   Is this English 22E?

MR. CARPENTIER   Why, yes, you are in the correct locale, *mon jeune fil.*

MR. JONES   May I see your card, Miss?

MR. CARPENTIER (*mutters.*)   Intrusion . . . non-equanimity——

MISS MOSKOWITZ   Are you speaking to me?

MR. JONES (*to* MARTHA.)   I believe you're in the right class, Miss.

MARTHA   Thank you.

MR. JONES (*clears throat.*)   Hummp . . . hummp . . . well, we can get started now.

MR. CARPENTIER   I emphatically agree with you, sir. In fact——

MR. JONES (*cutting.*)   Like some of you, I imagine, this too is my first evening class. . . . And I'd——

MISS MOSKOWITZ (*beaming.*)   How nice!

LENARD   Oh . . . oh . . . we've got a green one.

MR. JONES   Well . . . I guess the first thing is to take the roll. I haven't the official roll sheet yet, so . . . please print your names clearly on this sheet of paper and pass it around so you'll get credit for being here tonight.

BILL   Question!

MR. JONES   Yes . . . you did have a question, didn't you?

BILL   Yeah. . . . How will we be graded?

SUE   Oh . . . how square!

MR. JONES (*smiling.*)   I'm glad you asked that.

MISS MOSKOWITZ   So am I.

LENARD   You are?

MR. JONES   Well . . . as of now everybody is worth an A. I see all students as A students until they prove otherwise——

MISS MOSKOWITZ   Oh, how nice.

MR. JONES But tonight I'd like us to talk about story ideas. Since this is a writing class we don't wish to waste too much of our time on matters other than writing. And it is my conclusion that a story isn't a story without a major inherent idea which gives it substance——

MISS MOSKOWITZ How true.

MR. JONES And, by the way, that is how you are to retain your A's. By handing in all written assignments on time and doing the necessary outside work——

LENARD Typewritten or in longhand, Mr. Jones?

MR. JONES I am not a critic, so you will not be graded on how well you write but merely if you attempt to grow from the experience you have in this class. . . . This class is not only to show you the fundamentals of fiction, drama, and poetry but to aid your productivity, or should I say creativity . . . ha ha . . .

MR. CARPENTIER (*admonishing.*) You might say from the stand-point of grammar that fundamentals are essential but——

MR. JONES (*piqued.*) Mr. Carpentier . . . I don't understand what point you are making!

MR. CARPENTIER (*belligerent.*) Why . . . why . . . you can say that without the basics of grammar, punctuation, spelling, etc., . . . that these neophytes will be up the notorious creek without even the accommodation of a sieve.

SUE *Jesus!*

LENARD (*scowling.*) Up the where, buddy?

MISS MOSKOWITZ I don't think we should——

BILL It's fantastic what you——

MARTHA Is this really English 22E?

MR. JONES Now wait a minute, class. Since this is the first night, I want everyone to identify themselves before they speak. All of you know my name——

MARTHA I don't, sir.

MR. CARPENTIER You might say they will come to grief . . . artistic calamity.

MR. JONES Ohhh. . . . It's Jones . . . Ray Jones.

LENARD Didn't you just publish a novel, Mr. Jones?

MARTHA Mine's Martha . . . Martha Butler.

MR. JONES Oh, yes . . . yes, a first novel.

MR. CARPENTIER (*mutters.*) Cultural lag's the real culprit!

BILL (*to* SUE.) I'm Bill . . . Bill Cooper.

SUE Pleased. . . . Just call me Sue. Susan Gold.

MR. JONES Now . . . where were we?——

MR. CARPENTIER In the time of classicism there wasn't this rampant commerce among Philistines——

MR. JONES Does someone——

MISS MOSKOWITZ Story ideas, Mr. Jones.

MR. JONES Oh, yes.

Hands are raised. LENARD *is pointed out.*

LENARD I have an idea for a play.

MR. JONES Your name, please.

LENARD Lenard . . . Lenard Getz. I have an idea for a lavish stage spectacle using just one character.

MR. CARPENTIER It won't work . . . it won't work!

SUE How do you know?

MISS MOSKOWITZ Let Lenard tell us, will ya?

MR. CARPENTIER (*indignant.*) Let him! Let him, you say!

MR. JONES (*annoyed.*) Please, Mr. Carpentier . . . please be——

MR. CARPENTIER (*glaring about the room.*) But I didn't say it had to be done as parsimoniously as a Russian play. I mean only as beginners you people should delve into the simplicity of the varied techniques of the visual communicative media and processes.

MR. JONES For the last time——

MR. CARPENTIER Now take for instance cinema . . . or a tele-drama. . . . Some of the integrative shots set the mood and that takes techniques as well as craft.

MR. JONES I have my doubts about all that . . . but it doesn't have anything to do with Lenard's idea, as I see it.

MR. CARPENTIER I don't agree with you, sir.

13

MR. JONES It's just as well that you don't. Lenard, will you go on, please?

LENARD Ahhh . . . forget it.

MR. JONES But, Lenard, won't you tell us your idea?

LENARD No!

MISS MOSKOWITZ Oh . . . Lenard.

MR. CARPENTIER There is a current theory about protein varia-tion——

MR. JONES Not again!

SUE (*cutting.*) I have a story idea!

MISS MOSKOWITZ Good!

MR. JONES Can we hear it . . . Miss . . . Miss . . . ?

SUE Miss Gold. Susan Gold.

MR. JONES Thank you.

SUE Well, it's about a story that I have in my head. It ends with a girl or woman, standing or sitting alone and fright-ened. It's weird. I don't know where I got *that* theme from! . . . There is just something about one person, alone, that is moving to me. It's the same thing in movies or in photog-raphy. Don't you think if it's two or more persons, it loses a dramatic impact?

MR. JONES Why, yes, I do.

MISS MOSKOWITZ It sounds so psychologically pregnant!

LENARD It's my story of the stupendous one-character ex-travaganza!

A few in the class hesitantly clap.

MR. CARPENTIER (*in a deep, pontifical voice.*) Loneliness! Es-trangement! Alienation! The young lady's story should prove an interesting phenomena—it is a phenomena that we observe daily.

MISS MOSKOWITZ Yes, it is one of the most wonderful things I've ever heard.

MR. JONES (*irritated.*) Well, now let's——

MR. CARPENTIER The gist of that matter——

MR. JONES I will not have any more interruptions, man. Are you all there!

MR. CARPENTIER I mean only to say that it is strictly in a class of phenomenology in the classic ontological sense.

MR. JONES There are rules you must observe, Mr. Carpentier. Like our society, this school too has rules.

MR. CARPENTIER Recidivism! Recidivism!

MARTHA Re-sida-what?

MR. CARPENTIER (*explaining.*) Recidivism. A noted example of alienation in our society. We have tape-recorded A.A. meetings without the patients knowing that they were being recorded. In prison we pick up everything . . . from a con pacing his cell . . . down to the fights in the yard . . . and I can say that the milieu which creates loneliness is germane to the topic of recidivism.

MR. JONES What? . . . You're a wire-tapper, Mr. Carpentier?

MR. CARPENTIER Any method that deters crime in our society is most inadequate, old boy.

BILL A goddamned fink!

LENARD I thought I smelled somethin'.

MR. CARPENTIER Crime is a most repetitive theme these days. . . . The primacy purpose of we law enforcement agents is to help stamp it out whatever the method.

MR. JONES Carpentier!

MR. CARPENTIER Let the courts worry about——

MR. JONES But, sir, speaking man to man, how do you feel about your job? Doesn't it make you uneasy knowing that your race, I mean, our people, the Negro, is the most victimized by the police in this country? And you are using illegal and immoral methods to——

MR. CARPENTIER Well, if you must personalize that's all right with me . . . but, really, I thought this was a class in creative writing, not criminology. I hesitate to say, Mr. Jones, that you are indeed out of your depth when you engage me on my own grounds . . . ha ha . . .

15

MR. JONES *has taken off his glasses and is looking at* MR. CARPENTIER *strangely.*

MARTHA (*raising voice.*) I have a story idea . . . it's about this great dark mass of dough——

BILL Yeah . . . like a great rotten ham that strange rumbling and bubbling noises come out of——

SUE And it stinks something awful!

LENARD Like horseshit!

MISS MOSKOWITZ Oh, my.

MR. JONES Class! Class!

MR. CARPENTIER (*obviously.*) The new technology doesn't allow for the weak tyranny of human attitudes.

MR. JONES You are wrong, terribly wrong.

MR. CARPENTIER This is the age of the new intellectual assisted by his tool, the machine, I'll have you know!

MR. JONES (*furious.*) Carpentier! . . . That is what we are here in this classroom to fight against . . . we are here to discover, to awaken, to search out human values through art!

MR. CARPENTIER Nonsense! Nonsense! Pure nonsense! All you pseudo-artistic types and humanists say the same things when confronted by truth. (*Prophetically.*) This is an age of tele-symbology . . . phallic in nature, oral in appearance.

MR. JONES Wha'? . . . I don't believe I follow you. Are you serious, man?

MR. CARPENTIER I have had more experience with these things so I can say that the only function of cigarettes is to show the cigarette as a symbol of gratification for oral types. . . . Tobacco, matches, Zig Zag papers, etc., are all barter items in prison. There you will encounter a higher incident of oral and anal specimens. I admit it is a liberal interpretation, true, but I don't see how any other conclusion can be drawn!

MR. JONES You are utterly ineducable. I suggest you withdraw from this class, Mr. Carpentier.

MISS MOSKOWITZ Oh, how terrible.

BILL Hit the road, Jack.

MR. CARPENTIER If I must call it to your attention . . . in a tax-supported institution . . . to whom does that institution belong?

LENARD That won't save you, buddy.

MR. JONES Enough of this! Are there any more story ideas, class?

MR. CARPENTIER (*mumbling.*) It's councilmatic . . . yes, councilmatic . . .

MISS MOSKOWITZ My name is Moskowitz and I'd like to try a children's story.

MR. CARPENTIER Yes, yes, F. G. Peters once sold a story to the Howdie Dowdie people on an adaptation of *The Cherry Orchard* theme . . . and Jamie Judson, a good friend of mine——

MR. JONES Mr. Carpentier . . . please. Allow someone else a chance.

MR. CARPENTIER Why, all they have to do is speak up, Mr. Jones.

MR. JONES Maybe so . . . but please let Mrs. Moskowitz——

MISS MOSKOWITZ (*coyly.*) That's Miss Moskowitz, Mr. Jones.

MR. JONES Oh, I'm sorry, Miss Moskowitz.

MISS MOSKOWITZ That's okay, Mr. Jones. . . . Now my story has an historical background.

MR. CARPENTIER Which reminds me of a story I wrote which had a setting in colonial Boston——

LENARD Not again. Not again, for chris'sakes!

MR. CARPENTIER Christopher Attucks was the major character——

SUE Shhhhhh . . .

BILL Shut up, fellow!

MR. CARPENTIER (*ignoring them.*) The whole thing was done in jest . . . the historical inaccuracies were most hilarious . . . ha ho ho . . .

MR. JONES *Mr. Carpentier! ! !*

MR. CARPENTIER *grumbles and glowers.*

MISS MOSKOWITZ Thank you, Mr. Jones.

MR. JONES That's quite all right . . . go on, please.

MISS MOSKOWITZ Yes, now this brother and sister are out in a park and they get separated from their mother and meet a lion escaped from the zoo and make friends with him.

LENARD And they live happily ever afterwards.

MISS MOSKOWITZ Why, no, not at all, Lenard. The national guard comes to shoot the lion but the children hide him up a tree.

BILL (*to* SUE.) I got the impression that it was a tall tale.

SUE Not you too?

LENARD I thought it had a historical background.

MARTHA Can you convince children that they can easily make friends out of lions and then hide them up trees?

LENARD I got that it's pretty clear what motivated the lion to climb the tree. If you had a hunting party after you wouldn't——

MR. CARPENTIER (*cutting.*) Unless you give the dear lady that liberty . . . you'll end up with merely thous and thees!

MR. JONES What?

MISS MOSKOWITZ (*simpering.*) Oh, thank you, Mr. Carpentier.

MR. CARPENTIER (*Beau Brummell.*) Why, the pleasure is all mine, dear lady.

MR. JONES Enough of this! Enough of this!

MISS MOSKOWITZ (*blushing.*) Why, Mr. Carpentier . . . how you go on.

MR. CARPENTIER Not at all, my dear Miss Moskowitz——

MISS MOSKOWITZ Call me Madge.

MR. JONES (*sarcastic.*) I'm sorry to interrupt this——

MR. CARPENTIER A. T. to you . . . A. T. Booker Carpentier at your service.

MR. JONES This is a college classroom . . . not a French boudoir.

MISS MOSKOWITZ (*to* JONES.) Watch your mouth, young man!
  There's ladies present.

MARTHA (*to* MOSKOWITZ.) Don't let that bother you, dearie.

LENARD What kind of attitude must you establish with this
  type of story and do you create initial attitudes through
  mood?

MR. JONES (*confused.*) I beg your pardon?

MR. CARPENTIER (*answering.*) Why, young man, almost from
  the beginning the central motif should plant the atmosphere
  of——

MR. JONES Thank you, Mr. Carpentier!

MR. CARPENTIER But I wasn't——

BILL (*cutting.*) To what audience is it addressed?

SUE Good for you!

MISS MOSKOWITZ Why, young people, of course. In fact, for
  children.

MR. CARPENTIER I hardly would think so!

MARTHA Oh, what kinda stuff is this?

MISS MOSKOWITZ Mr. Carpentier . . . I . . .

MR. JONES Well, at least you're talking about something
  vaguely dealing with writing. Go on, Mr. Carpentier, try
  and develop your——

MR. CARPENTIER A question of intellectual levels is being
  probed here. . . . The question is the adult or the child . . .
  hmm. . . . *Robinson Crusoe, Gulliver's Travels, Alice in
  Wonderland, Animal Farm* can all be read by children, dear
  lady, but the works have added implication for the adult . . .
  in a word, they are potent!

MARTHA You're talking about universality, man, not audience!

MR. CARPENTIER Do you know the difference?

LENARD (*challenges* CARPENTIER.) What's the definition of audience?

MR. CARPENTIER Of course, I don't use myself as any type of
  criteria, but I don't see where that story would appeal to my
  sophisticated literary tastes, whereas——

MR. JONES   Now you are quite off the point, Mr. Carpentier.

BILL   He thinks we should all write like the Marquis de Sade.

SUE   Yeah, bedtime tales for tykes by Sade.

MISS MOSKOWITZ   I think you're trying to place an imposition of the adult world on the child's.

MR. JONES   The important thing is to write the story, class. To write the story!

MR. CARPENTIER   Well, I think that the story was not at all that emphatic . . . it didn't emote . . . it didn't elicite my——

MISS MOSKOWITZ (*confused.*)   Why didn't it?

MR. CARPENTIER   I don't think the child would have the range of actual patterns for his peer group in this circumstantial instance.

MARTHA   What, man?

LENARD   I got the impression that the protagonists are ex-empliar.

MR. JONES   Class, do you think this story line aids the writer in performing his functions? . . . The culture has values and the writer's duties are to——

MR. CARPENTIER   No, I don't think this story does it!

SUE   Why not?

MR. CARPENTIER   It is fallacious!

MISS MOSKOWITZ   But it's only a child's story, a fantasy, Mr. Carpentier!

MR. JONES   Yes, a child's story . . . for children, man!

MR. CARPENTIER   But it doesn't ring true, dear lady. The only way one can get the naturalistic speech and peer group patterns and mores of children recorded accurately——

MR. JONES (*begins a string of "Oh God's" rising in volume until* MR. CARPENTIER *finishes his speech.*)   Oh God, Oh, God, *Oh, God, Oh, God,* OH, God!

MR. CARPENTIER   ——is to scientifically eavesdrop on their peer group with electronic listening devices and get the actual evidence for any realistic fictionalizing one wishes to achieve.

MR. JONES (*scream.*)   NO! ! !

MR. CARPENTIER (*query.*)   No?

MR. JONES (*in a tired voice.*)   Thomas Wolfe once said——

MR. CARPENTIER (*ridicule.*)   Thomas Wolfe!

MR. JONES   ——"I believe that we are lost here in America, but I believe we shall be found." . . . Mr. Carpentier . . . let's hope that we Black Americans can first find ourselves and perhaps be equal to the task . . . the burdensome and sometimes evil task, by the way . . . that being an American calls for in these days.

MR. CARPENTIER   Sir, I object!

MR. JONES   Does not the writer have some type of obligation to remove some of the intellectual as well as political, moral, and social tyranny that infects this culture? What do all the large words in creation serve you, my Black brother, if you are a complete whitewashed man?

MR. CARPENTIER   Sir, I am not black nor your brother. . . . There is a school of thought that is diametrically opposed to you and your black chauvinism. . . . You preach bigotry, black nationalism, and fascism! . . . The idea . . . black brother . . . intellectual barbarism! . . . Your statements should be reported to the school board—as well as your permitting smoking in your classroom.

SUE   Shut up, you Uncle Tom bastard!

BILL (*pulls her back.*)   That's for me to do, not you, lady!

MR. JONES   Four hundred years. . . . Four hundred . . .

LENARD   We'll picket any attempt to have Mr. Jones removed!

MARTHA (*disgust.*)   This is adult education?

MISS MOSKOWITZ (*to* MR. CARPENTIER.)   I bet George Bernard Shaw would have some answers for you!

MR. CARPENTIER   Of course when examining G. B. Shaw you will discover he is advancing Fabian Socialism.

BILL   Who would picket a vacuum?

LENARD   Your levity escapes me.

SUE   Your what, junior?

21

MR. JONES Let's try and go on, class. If you'll——

MR. CARPENTIER (*to* MISS MOSKOWITZ.) Your story just isn't professional, Miss. It doesn't follow the Hitchcock formula . . . it just doesn't follow . . .

MISS MOSKOWITZ Do you really think so?

MR. JONES Somehow, I do now believe that you are quite real, Mr. Carpentier.

LENARD (*to* MR. CARPENTIER.) Have you read *The Invisible Man*?

BILL Are you kidding?

MR. CARPENTIER Socio Drama will be the new breakthrough in the theatrical-literary community.

MR. JONES Oh, Lord . . . not again. This is madness.

MR. CARPENTIER Combined with the social psychologist's case study, and the daily experiences of some habitant of a socio-economically depressed area, is the genius of the intellectual and artistic craftsman.

MR. JONES Madness!

MISS MOSKOWITZ Socio Drama . . . how thrilling.

MR. JONES Don't listen to him, class. . . . I'm the teacher, understand?

MR. CARPENTIER Yes, yes . . . let me tell you a not quite unique but nevertheless interesting phenomenon——

MR. JONES Now we know that there is realism, and naturalism, and surrealism——

MR. CARPENTIER ——an extremely interesting phenomenon . . . adolescent necrophilia!

MARTHA Oh, shit!

MR. JONES I have a degree. . . . I've written a book. . . . Please don't listen——

MISS MOSKOWITZ It sounds fascinating, Mr. Carpentier.

MR. CARPENTIER Yes, tramps will freeze to death and kids, children, will punch holes in the corpses——

LENARD Isn't that reaching rather far just to prove that truth is stranger than fiction?

SUE I have a story about crud and filth and disease——

MR. JONES And stupidity and ignorance and vulgarity and despair——

MR. CARPENTIER I go back to my original point . . . I go back to necrophilia!

BILL And loneliness . . . and emptiness . . . and death.

MR. CARPENTIER Cadavers! Cadavers! Yes, I come back to that! . . . Those findings could almost be case studies of true cases, they are so true in themselves, and that's where the real truth lies. . . . Verily, social case histories of social psychologists——

MISS MOSKOWITZ (*enraptured.*) Never . . . never in all my experience has a class aroused such passionate response in my life!

LENARD I don't believe it!

MR. JONES But I have read Faulkner in his entirety——

MR. CARPENTIER These people in New York, Philadelphia, Boston, Chicago, San Francisco . . . and places like that——

MR. JONES I cut my teeth on Hemingway——

MR. CARPENTIER ——they just get drunk and die in the streets——

MR. JONES ——*Leaves of Grass* is my Bible . . . and Emily Dickinson——

MR. CARPENTIER ——and then they are prone to suffer adolescent and urchin necrophilia!

MR. JONES (*frustrated.*) ——Emily Dickinson has always been on my shelf beside *Mother Goose.*

MR. CARPENTIER It's curiosity . . . not a sickness . . . curiosity!

MR. JONES I don't want much . . . just to learn the meaning of life.

MARTHA Will you discover it here, Ray?

LENARD But how can anybody be so sure?

MR. CARPENTIER (*offhand.*) We happen to own some mortuaries . . . my family, that is . . . and it is our experience that children will disarrange a corpse . . . and if we don't watch them closely——

MR. JONES Booker T. Washington walked barefooted to school! Think of that! Barefooted!

MR. CARPENTIER Once as a case study in experimental methods I placed a microphone in a cadaver and gave some juvenile necrophilics unwitting access to my tramp.

JONES *almost doubles over and clutches his stomach; his hands and feet twitch.*

MR. JONES I'd like to adjourn class early tonight . . . will everyone please go home?

MR. CARPENTIER What I'm saying is this . . . with our present cybernetic generation it is psycho-politically relevant to engage our socio-philosophical existence on a quanitatum scale which is, of course, pertinent to the outer-motivated migration of our inner-oriented social compact. Yes! Yes, indeed, I might add. A most visionary prognosis, as it were, but . . . ha ho ho . . . but we pioneers must look over our bifocals, I always say . . . ha ha ha . . . giving me added insight to perceive the political exiguousness of our true concomitant predicament. True, preclinical preconsciousness gives indication that our trivialization is vulva, but, owing to the

LENARD What's our assignment for next week, Mr. Jones?

MISS MOSKOWITZ I have something to show you, Mr. Jones.

MARTHA Are you okay, Mr. Jones?

MR. JONES Ray . . . just Ray . . . okay?

SUE Do you have office hours, Mr. Ray?

MR. JONES I just want everybody to go home now and think about what has happened tonight . . . and if you want to be writers after this then please don't come back to this class. I've just published an unsuccessful novel, as you know, and I thought I'd teach a while and finish my second one and eat a bit. . . . But I think I'd rather not, eat press of the press our avowed aims are maleficent! True! Yes, true! And we are becoming more so. In areas of negative seeming communications probing our error factors are quite negligible. . . . For instance . . . Senator Dodd getting a pension for someone who has gotten abducted and initiated at a Ku Klux meeting . . . well. . . . It's poesy! . . . Monochromatic! well, that is, so you won't see me next week but if any of you'd like a good steady job I could recommend you. . . . Reading is the answer. It must be . . . cultivating the sensibilities. . . . Plato. . . . Aristotle. . . . Homer. . . . Descartes. . . . And Jones . . . I've always wanted to carry the Jones banner high.

BILL (*to* SUE.) Hey, I've got some pretty good grass that just came in from Mexico.

SUE. Yeah? You have, huh?

BILL It's at my pad. . . . Would you like to stop by?

SUE How far?

BILL A couple of blocks.

SUE Okay. It might be interesting.

MR. CARPENTIER (*to a* STUDENT.) Ubiquitous! A form of reference which exposes . . .

BILL *and* SUE *exit.* STUDENTS *begin filing out.* MARTHA *walks over to* MR. JONES, *though the other students are gathered about* MR. CARPENTIER.

MARTHA You look tired, Ray.

MR. JONES Yeah . . . yeah . . . I've been reading a lot. The classics are consuming.

MARTHA Yes, I've heard. Why don't we stop by my place and I'll fix drinks and you can relax . . .

MR. JONES Okay . . . okay . . . but my ulcer's bothering me. . . . Mind if I drink milk?

MARTHA   It's not my stomach.

She helps him off.

MR. CARPENTIER   Who's that French poet . . . Balu——
LENARD   Bouvier?
MR. CARPENTIER   ——Bali . . . Blau? . . .

MISS MOSKOWITZ *shows* MR. CARPENTIER *a bound manuscript as he deposits his own in his briefcase.*

MISS MOSKOWITZ   Will you please look at my few labors of love when you find time, Mr. Carpentier?

He shoves it in the case beside his own.

LENARD (*gathering up his books.*)   Mr. Carpentier?
MR. CARPENTIER (*snapping clasps of his briefcase.*)   Yes, Lenard.
LENARD (*pushing himself between* CARPENTIER *and other* STU-
DENTS.)   What weight does language have on the contemporary prevalence to act in existential terms?
MR. CARPENTIER (*leads them off.*)   When the writer first named the crow "Caw Caw" it was onomatopoeia in practice, of course . . . but too it became the Egyptian symbol of death.
LENARD   The crow.

MISS MOSKOWITZ *giggles.*

They all exit crowing: "Caw caw caw caw caw . . ."

Blackness.

The Poet's Papers

Notes for an Event

DAVID STARKWEATHER

For the tenth anniversary of the Cino

Michael Sullivan

DAVID STARKWEATHER: "I was born in Madison, Wisconsin, was processed in the usual, and became an Organ of Analysis, an Appetite for Absolutes, and Potential Victim in more or less that order. Petrified by imagined inadequacies, I became a mosaic of cautious habits pretending to be The Compleat Me, keeping me alert and backward-looking as I progressed like Little Eva to what I imagined was a safer shore. Relaxing from such Paranoia I fell to my Senses, said goodbye to Death and came to know the world as Chaos and glory in its changing face. Liquids began flowing outward as all Belief fell by the wayside and I became saints and assassins, rocks and reptiles, polygons and straight lines. I became an Organ of experience and learned to love. But to love like an ocean, without language or direction—with nothing to love against. So facing what I most feared (What's the difference who I am?), I dropped out of Experiencing Myself into Being Myself—and all the buzzing died away. All the billion inner lights and pools of comfort sailed off into the darkness. And I stood up on legs that for the first time were my own. Human legs, responding without pause to human needs; eyes, breathless in their instant subjectivity; hands, at last the only gods of my intangible Wishes, creating and destroying with equal ease and fury. And I began to write as sap flows from a wounded tree, healing with crystals of its exposed essence.

Then, at the age of two . . ."

Characters

PRESIDENT   (KING OF THE ORALS)
SECRETARY OF LOGIC   (KING OF THE ANALS)
SECRETARY OF REALITY   (QUEEN OF THE ANALS)
SECRETARY OF THE ULTERIOR   (QUEEN OF THE ORALS)
POET
POET'S WIFE
TWO ANNOUNCERS
HEAD ENGINEER
MINOR PHARAOH
CHRIST
POPE INNOCENT
POPE SIGMUND
VARIOUS SENATORS, ANIMALS, CONSTRUCTION WORKERS,
   VOICES, a SURVEYOR, and a FOREMAN

The Poet's Papers

An ubiquitous primeval sound arises, filling the darkness. As it fades.

POET'S VOICE And streaming in the manner of light, the Poet was returning from the farthest reaches of the Galaxy where he had been arranging constellations to promote his latest myths, when he came upon that fatal crossroad in the Forest of Walking Fish.

In dim, slanting beams of light, a strange procession is seen to begin. A large effigy of the POET is being carried on by a mass of animals holding poles on the top of some of which are giant three-dimensional letters of the alphabet, and on many others small cubes of single colors. A few giant pencils are visible, but the effect is primitive and pagan rather than comical. Among the animals are bears, giant rats and chickens, a walking fish, a pterodactyl and several extinct life forms still unknown to archeologists. They wind their way through the semidarkness making quiet squeaks and grunts of homage and celebration. After a moment the voice continues.

For in a nearby cranny crouched a frightened she-wolf, long separated from her party. Ravenous, she set upon him and devoured him. But he would not stay down and sprang forth whole anew. Again she devoured him. Seven times she devoured him. And the next day they were married.

A second procession enters from another direction carrying a large effigy of the she-wolf, and the two groups join to briefly re-enact the wedding.

Two by two, delegations from all the major sounds came to do them homage.

An upper and a lower case A followed by an upper and lower case E are approaching them.

Two by two, all colors and their complements came to present themselves. And in a miracle the Poet laid his hand on three confusing hues and for all time defined "Ambrose," "Redolet" and "Flush."

An harmonious buzzing begins filling the air as a golden beam of light falls upon the she-wolf.

And as a wedding gift he gathered bees of different pitch; and coaching them in patterns of restraint, invented music. But when his new bride heard them, in terror she wet upon the ground.

Light and buzzing fades.

And when at last they were alone, upon the mount he whispered "Beware of circles." And in reply she removed his ear.

The procession seems to be moving out, now as one group.

And he shared her bed for seven centuries, but fed her soup of alphabet to no avail.

Then with finality.

Before the beginning there was the Poet.

Suddenly a vision of CHRIST, *nervously trying various postures on a cross, is seen near where the effigy of the* POET *is passing.*

CHRIST Well how's this? Well what about this? I've got it— this is it. Believe me I can do it. Just give me a chance.

His light is dimming as the animals making their inarticulate noises continue carrying the lifeless effigy out, ignoring him.

I'll have 'em eating out of my hand. I'm printing up all new résumés. COME BACK HERE! COME BACK HERE!

All is dark and filled again with the swelling primeval sound, which then slowly fades away.

ANNOUNCER I *(in the darkness, speaking in hushed tones.)* Good evening ladies and gentlemen. We are broadcasting from the chamber of the House of Representatives where Congress is met in joint session. And we are awaiting the arrival of the President. The Speaker of the House is rising. He is . . . yes . . . I believe he is going to give the A.

An A is heard and an orchestra begins tuning.

From here it seems to be a rather good A. The House sounds exceptionally good this year. Due to an influx of freshman trumpets from the Midwest. Midwesterners are of course famous for good lips. The Midwest is, as I'm sure you all know, right in the heart of the Lip Belt. The tuning is finished now. The program is the première of the President's new composition which he calls "Concerto Grosso with Violin Obbligato, Opus 72."

Applause in background.

The President is entering the chamber.

Lights begin coming up on the PRESIDENT *walking on with violin, bowing, and taking a seat.*

The members of the House and Senate are tapping respectfully on their various stands. In the Visitors' Gallery the President's claque is bravoing prematurely. He is smiling, bowing. He will now spend some time tuning his instrument. As you all know he prides himself on having perfect pitch. In fact many commentators believe that was the deciding factor in his rather remarkable election. If you will remember it was just a year ago, at the President's Opus 71, there was not quite the harmony that is apparent here today. The Senior Senator from Kentucky on the cello, who by reason of seniority was second chair, threw a snag into the President's program when during an extended solo he broke his G . . .

33

throwing the entire body into parliamentary staggers.

PRESIDENT (*to three string* SENATORS *near him.*) This violin sounds terrible. I'm only using it for sentimental reasons.

ANNOUNCER I The President seems to be joking with a few colleagues. We can't pick it up from here. Perhaps he is referring to the decision of the Supreme Court this afternoon. In what is taken as a sharp rebuke to the President, the ultra-liberal Court has come out strongly in favor of atonality. The historic ruling said in part, "Freedom of speech is not limited to the diatonic."

PRESIDENT The President has lost his rosin. (*To startled* SENATORS.) I said rosin.

ANNOUNCER I The President seems a bit nervous. Last year if you will remember it took him three-quarters of an hour before he could bring himself to begin. No—no . . . he's raising his bow. Yes he's ready. Opus 72. "Concerto Grosso with Violin Obbligato."

ANNOUNCER II Ladies and gentlemen we interrupt this program for an important announcement. The Poet is dead.

The PRESIDENT *looks ill. Blackout.*

We repeat that. The Poet is no more. From his birth a victim of arcane and mysterious causes, his body was found early this morning missing. Reactions are coming in from all around the world. The President of Bulgaria, the Poet's birthplace, put it most movingly when he said, "We have waited years for this moment. Every night we have prayed, we have entreated, we have bribed the Deity to bring this moment to pass. Now we can all breathe easier." He further proposed that the site of the Poet's home, destroyed earlier this year by a mob of angry children, be turned into a fitting memorial by digging an irregular pit nineteen feet deep and letting it fill with Bulgarian rain water. Echoing his sentiment, the Council of Ireland passed the following resolution, which was forwarded by telegram to the Poet's widow: "May his eyes spin backward and his black brain rot forever in a dark hole stop."

Blast of an Irish jig.

ANNOUNCER I   In what seems to be a related incident, the famous bronze Buddha of Benares, over one hundred feet in length, is no longer reclining but is now half-lotus. The shift occurred this morning when the Buddha rose, with some difficulty, did three push-ups and relieved himself on the nearest bo tree. Returning to his plinth, he pronounced "Om" in a very peculiar manner and assumed the new posture. Fifty bewildered pilgrims had to be treated for inundation. Trained observers, however, see in the incident no significance whatsoever.

ANNOUNCER II   Meanwhile the President, in emergency session with his Cabinet, confronts his Secretary of Logic, Secretary of Reality and Secretary of the Ulterior . . .

Light comes up on scene indicated.

PRESIDENT (*near tears.*)   I could have died. Sitting there looking like an idiot. My violin sticking out of my Adam's apple.

SECRETARY OF LOGIC   It must have been a great embarrassment.

SECRETARY OF THE ULTERIOR (*a pregnant young woman.*)   Would you like some hot milk?

S. LOGIC   But the world is awaiting our response.

PRESIDENT   I know.

S. LOGIC   And we haven't begun to attack the issues.

S. ULTERIOR   We don't need to attack them.

SECRETARY OF REALITY (*a self-assured young woman.*)   Things like this happen all the time. Not a day passes that some era doesn't come to an end. All we need is a fitting monument.

CONSTRUCTION WORKERS *begin assembling colorful geometric units of giant size; cantilevering them over one another, climbing through them; rearranging them; subtracting from them; arriving by the end of the scene at a simple monumental configuration.*

S. LOGIC   How is he to be remembered without some external structure?

S. REALITY   To enforce—to resonate with the structures in our memories?

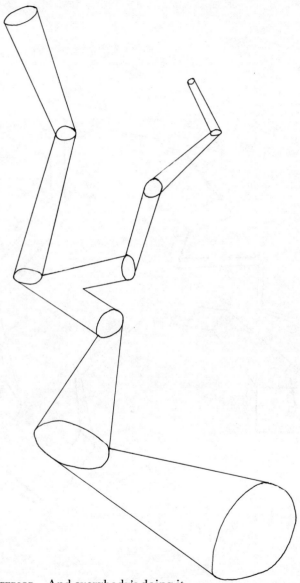

S. ULTERIOR   And everybody's doing it.

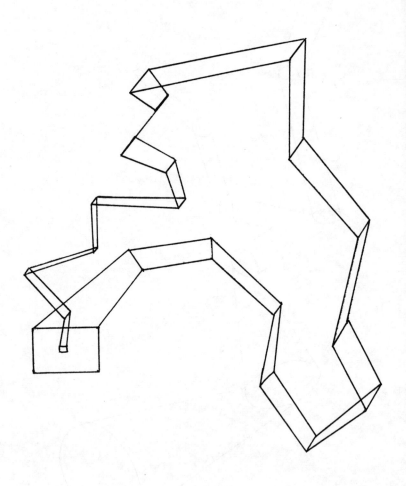

s. LOGIC So we can know forever what he was.

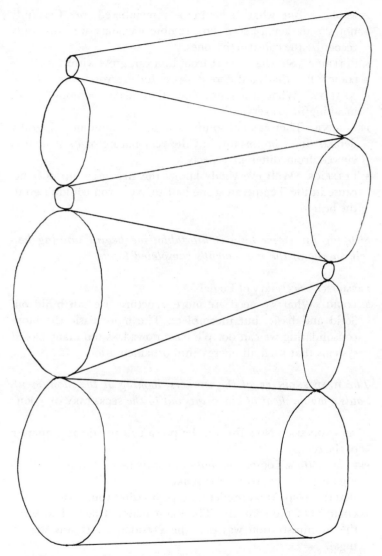

s. REALITY   So we have the power forever to make him real
again.

PRESIDENT But what is he to be remembered for? Certainly not the darker aspects. To promote harmony we must only recognize the constructive ones.

S. ULTERIOR So what we get from him can grow within us.

S. LOGIC But that's a different aspect for everyone.

S. REALITY What difference does that make, so long as it's meaningful to everyone?

PRESIDENT Then it's not so much what the monument literally depicts that's important, but the very nature of its structure, viewed from different aspects.

S. ULTERIOR Well everybody knows the Arts grew up only because in the Temperate Zone half the year you couldn't go to the beach.

Slipping into something comfortable, she begins sunning herself on one of the monument's completed facets.

PRESIDENT Secretary of Logic?

S. LOGIC What we need are more structures we can build on. Solid and basic, but incomplete. The more basic the more consolidating we can do. We have nowadays too many closed systems that turn all energy into ornamentation.

The HEAD ENGINEER *of the workers, looking at the monument, holds a whole sheaf of blueprints out to the* SECRETARY OF LOGIC.

HEAD ENGINEER Now this can be precast in plastic at a quarter of the cost.

PRESIDENT (*to* S. LOGIC, *who ignores* ENGINEER.) Are you criticizing my policy of Art for Art's sake?

S. REALITY No, Mr. President, he's criticizing your Art.

S. LOGIC On the contrary. The main reason I agreed to serve the Administration was that the President's Art was strictly fugal.

PRESIDENT But first of all—if the Poet is worth remembering at all—it must be beautiful.

40

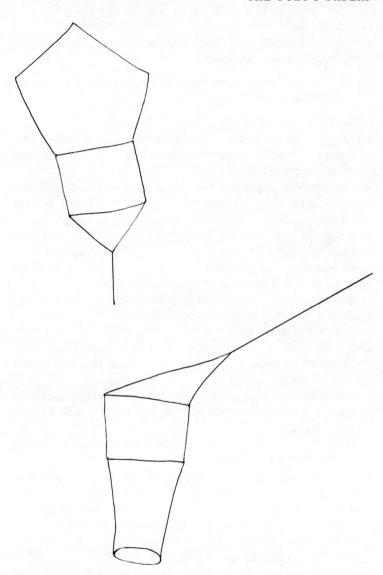

SECRETARIES   Of course.

PRESIDENT Secretary of Reality?

S. REALITY I agreed to serve you not because your Art was fugal, but because it was evocative.

Middle Eastern music is heard and a MINOR PHARAOH *enters with his surveyor and foreman with whip.*

S. LOGIC She means "familiar."

S. REALITY All things that are meaningful to us are reminiscent. Because our Idea of the Past determines the very way we extract meaning from the present.

MINOR PHARAOH (*looking at the monument and casually placing an ancient robe over* S. REALITY'S *shoulders.*) Well I'm sorry fellahs, that is the worst pyramid in the Upper Kingdom.

S. REALITY (*barely noticing him, shakes off the robe and continues.*) And that's why we must be cautious when we turn our machines upon residues, lest we crumble the foundations of the present, leaving us open to future chaos.

PRESIDENT I don't have the vaguest notion what you're saying.

S. REALITY That's just what I was saying.

PRESIDENT Was that it?

S. REALITY We must value first of all structures which help define for us what is real, even if the structures themselves are logically ill-founded.

MINOR PHARAOH (*slipping the robe over* S. REALITY'S *shoulders again, says to his surveyor.*) I wouldn't seal a wife in that if you paid me.

S. LOGIC You know what that means Mr. President. Shady politics. Backroom deals.

S. REALITY Show me a man who knows who he is and I will show you a city with efficient mass transit, adequate housing and verdant parks. With temples to the Sun and Moon, and to the Corn encroaching on the suburbs. (*Throws the robe off his shoulders again, with impatience.*)

S. LOGIC Don't believe her Mr. President.

PRESIDENT Believe her? I can't even find her. Secretary of the Ulterior?

S. REALITY   Show me a man who thinks he knows what he's doing and I will show you a building with adequate plumbing, adequate wiring and laundry facilities——

HEAD ENGINEER (*now showing the blueprints to her.*)   And I can reproduce him at a third the original cost.

S. REALITY *ignores him.*

PRESIDENT   Secretary of the Ulterior?

S. ULTERIOR   You don't look so well. I think you're due for an operation.

PRESIDENT   Oh you're so right. You I can understand.

S. ULTERIOR   What can we take out this time?

PRESIDENT   Anything you want.

S. ULTERIOR (*opening thermos from beach picnic basket.*)   Are you sure you wouldn't like some milk and cookies?

PRESIDENT   Milk and cookies are just what I need!

S. LOGIC   Mr. President, this is no time to malinger. Now is the time to tear down and build anew.

MINOR PHARAOH (*now slipping the robe over* S. LOGIC'*s shoulders.*)   That's what I say. This pyramid has far too many corners.

S. REALITY   Mr. President, the past is schist! The schist on which must rest the present. What we need is strong schist to prevent faults and slippage. Show me a healthy man and I will show you schist without faults!

HEAD ENGINEER (*seconding him.*)   And if it's near the surface I can cut it into slabs and make us all a pile.

PRESIDENT (*falling to one knee.*) Milk and cookies.

MINOR PHARAOH (*with megaphone, calling from the monument over the audience.*)   ALL JEWS BRING YOUR FILES.

S. LOGIC   But Mr. President——

S. ULTERIOR (*pulling monstrous surgical tools out of picnic basket.*)   Scalpel and syringe.

MINOR PHARAOH   ALL JEWS CUT CORNERS.

S. REALITY   But the monument is not finished.

PRESIDENT   The blasted monument. The blasted Poet.

43

MINOR PHARAOH   FOUR EDGES AND ONE CORNER.

Confusion reigns.

PRESIDENT   Why did this have to happen while I'm in office? Why couldn't he hang on another year?

S. ULTERIOR (*about to operate.*)   This won't hurt a bit.

PRESIDENT (*pushing her away.*)   Everybody's picking on me.

SECRETARIES   Mr. President!

PRESIDENT (*threateningly.*)   Did you ever see a President cry! (*Everyone stops working. Calm again.*) Gentlemen. The President is the loneliest man in the world. He's going up to bed. Don't follow him.

Blackout.

During the speech that follows, indeed during all blackouts that follow, the stage is illuminated with ultraviolet light and the structural members of the monument fluoresce in brilliant colors. Open tetrahedrons, whose structural members likewise glow, seem to float into the theatre from behind the audience and attach themselves to the monument, in a manner that suggests nothing so much as the formation of chemical bonds. In such a way throughout the play the monument progressively grows out over the heads of the audience until it spans it completely with a glowing arc of light.

ANNOUNCER I   Within hours of the announcement of the Poet's death the President of Argentina, renowned painter-metaphysician, was thrown from power and sought sanctuary in the Musée des Beaux Arts. The country is reportedly in the control of a junta of greengrocers, who are massing seedlings at the border of potassium-rich Chile.

"Rock-a-Bye Baby" is heard.

In a related incident the Ivory Babies continue. When the first baby of solid ivory was reported yesterday, born in Anchorage to the wife of an Eskimo functionary, the birth was thought an anomaly. Perhaps an occupational hazard. But hospitals around the world report that Ivory Babies are suddenly being delivered at the ratio of one in every three. The Vatican views the phenomenon a miracle. Informed sources report the Pope plans to collect them, and build in honor of them the "Grandest Church in Christendom." Excuse me that should read, "plans to build OF them the 'Grandest Church in Christendom.'" For confused mothers the Department of Health and Welfare issued the caution that new Ivory Babies should be waxed every four hours or they will yellow and become unlovely.

ANNOUNCER II Meanwhile the Poet and his wife enjoy a special morning.

The lights come up and the POET *enters his monument meditating. He is followed by his wife in a sari. Indian music. The* POET'S WIFE *carries two small branches which she holds out to the audience as the* POET *speaks.*

POET What is the oak's idea in being so gnarled? Its branches following the curve of last year's dominant twig like governments with weak constitutions? While the fascist maple sends out its branches in fanatical thrusts, undeterred by splinter groups? Even the leaves suggest the same philosophies. The oak's are lobed, irregular; whereas the maple's always point three distinct directions at the same time. The maple grows faster but dies younger. The oak is more Chinese. (*Looking around as he walks.*) The willow is so maternalistic this morning. The industrious apple. The evergreen is ever green. Speculations in the ivy. Mountains implying strategies. And the sky is . . . full of changes. . . . (*He goes off dreaming.*)

POET'S WIFE (*speaking to us, sadly.*) I am alas not capable of human speech. You understand me only by convention. Because you are intelligent. And because I am using your language. Oh I can speak to a species of the wolf. But I would rather not. We have grievances. They ate my mother. They damaged my father, who then died of remorse. And they turned me—turned my very soul into a wolf. I may appear human to you, but that is only because you are intelligent. To others I am covered with long grey hair. I have yellow teeth and live only for blood. My moods are governed by the phases of the moon. My tracks are studied by apprentice hunters. My voice can freeze the stars into a cage for travelers. It's true . . . I have eaten children. But only because my mother told me. "Eat your child," she said, "or I won't let you curl up in my long grey tail." And we are all victims of needs. I have a telegram with shamrocks. (*Taking it out.*) It smells of cities. What fear and joy in such a smell. It is a message of love I am sure. Oh should he know how much they love him, would an old wolf ever be enough for him? Even now I do not know why we are here away from the cold and snow. These are regions we have never traveled. And there is danger we may meet a human being.

POET (*re-entering.*) How warm the wind is. Like a child's crusade. Yet here all things are warmer I suppose without danger of dissolution. We can expect to see small animals my dear. You'll want to eat them.

POET'S WIFE   Oh look.

POET   Ah yes a rabbit. He's come higher than is wise.

POET'S WIFE   He looks so good.

POET   You're dreaming of your wild mother aren't you? And your packs of relatives. Orgies of flashing teeth, dividing victims. Small final cries. Fluids rich with life and warm as gravy. Gnawing all afternoon.

POET'S WIFE (*to audience.*)   I was thinking of my mother and the midnight family reunions. The banquets we used to have. And afterward we would all sing. Once I ate a whole child all by myself.

POET   There he goes. There'll be others. You'll want to chase them. And you'll have to learn to. They dart and tack like skiffs through the grass. The path itself is easy to compute. But you must learn not to follow the rabbit, but to intercept the path. There are tables I can teach you. The probabilities are three a day which is overkill.

POET'S WIFE   Oh let's go back before it's too late. Why are we here? Was I not enough for you?

POET   You wonder why we are here don't you?

POET'S WIFE   I'm so afraid. The wind is so warm and filled with dazzling odors. Strange memories awake.

POET   You're afraid aren't you? Your tail is quivering.

POET'S WIFE   I was happy alone with you. The ice was nothing. The rocks were friendly to my feet. I love you, do you understand? I love you.

POET   This orchard falls as far as I can see.

The POET'S WIFE *delicately puts her hands on her female parts and howls forlornly.*

Do you smell a mate on the wind? Your ears are up to listen. Do you hear a step beneath your window? He approaches through the orchard like a boy upon a crime of pears.

She howls holding herself again.

He will come. (*Turning away.*) It is so strange to see things growing with my eyes. These minerals are mad with love. And know peace only in the arms of twisted flowers.

POET'S WIFE   Surely he is hungry. We have come a long way. I will feed him and he will see how he needs me. I who taught him how to eat the berries of the snow.

POET   You're hungry aren't you? Well we have berries don't we? And I have something else for you. Your own bowl. (*He fills it.*)

POET'S WIFE   What is that? It looks just like our bowl.

POET (*hands it to her.*)   Now eat. (*And begins eating out of his own. She looks bewildered, then puts down her bowl and tries to eat with him out of his.*) No you must eat out of your own bowl.

POET'S WIFE   What is this? I cannot understand. I will starve.

POET (*handing her bowl to her.*) This is yours. You must get used to it.

They sit and eat separately.

POET'S WIFE (*to audience, sadly.*) Oh this is not nearly half a meal.

POET You must learn to get along without me. We will soon be among men, but you do not need to be afraid. For you are clever, and anything a man can know you can know too. Ideas are the only weapons men possess. I am teaching you now. And all ideas are merely relationships. Established in our minds by contrast and similarity. Your bowl and my bowl are no longer the same. They look the same but are different places. And if all ideas are relationships, all thoughts can be expressed in structures. This is what the Poet knows.

POET'S WIFE (*moving away.*) What wild dreams must live in these red berries. How much more tempting than the breakfast we call "making do." If I could cook a stew of these he wouldn't leave me.

POET Science is the search for meaning thought implicit in the structures found around us. But Man's Art specializes in extravagant hypotheses. For there is nothing we can know of the world beyond the mind save by metaphors in the language of the senses.

The POET'S WIFE puts her hands on her parts and howls mournfully again. She is answered by the sound of a pack of approaching dogs. Terrified, she hides behind the POET as he shoos them away.

Don't be afraid. You must wear this. (*He gives her a bracelet of temple bells.*) Now they will not disturb you. Come. It is getting late.

He goes off. She follows slowly, fascinated with the bracelet. She seems to want to dance, then sadly.

POET'S WIFE   Were I human he would love me.

She follows him as lights fade out.

Majestic "Star-Spangled Banner" by string orchestra plays through "twilight's last gleaming." Light comes up on PRESIDENT *with violin. Seated in a row behind him are the three* SECRETARIES.

PRESIDENT   Ladies and gentlemen, this is your President. You remember me. I'm speaking to you tonight on a matter of some importance. Oh . . . I hope you're not busy. I hope I'm not taking you away from anything.

S. LOGIC (*quietly.*)   Uh Mr. President.

PRESIDENT (*to audience.*)   Excuse me. (*To* S. LOGIC.) Yes?

S. LOGIC   A little more self-assurance.

PRESIDENT   What?

S. LOGIC.   Con brio.

PRESIDENT   Oh yes! Ladies and gentlemen these are the times that try our strings.

S. LOGIC and REALITY (*whisper harshly.*)   Our souls.

PRESIDENT   Our souls. For during this past week one of the significant events of our era has taken place. As you know the Poet is no more. (S. LOGIC and REALITY *break into applause. To them quietly.*) Now stop that. (*To audience.*) We have of course no direct evidence of this. He has simply disappeared. Which is not like him. As a matter of fact give me a moment and I'll check right now. (*Picks up a telescope and looks.*) There's the mountain. There's the top of the mountain. There's his chair. There's his typing table . . . typewriter. Pair of earmuffs. Lots of icicles. And no Poet. Now from here in the pit, all we can logically conclude is that he died and fell off. This of course leaves us with a great vacuum in our foundations.

S. REALITY   Uh Mr. President.

PRESIDENT (*to audience.*)   Excuse me. (*To* S. REALITY.) Yes?

S. REALITY   That's not possible.

PRESIDENT   Well then how did it happen?

s. REALITY   How should I know? I'm just glad I'm not in your shoes.

PRESIDENT *(to audience.)* Uh . . . this of course leaves us with . . . rumors of a vacuum in our foundations. Now the question before us is, now that he is dead———(s. REALITY *and* LOGIC *applaud and are again stopped.)*———how can we best take advantage of this opportunity? Your Administration has of course arrived at a policy . . . which is my Opus 73.

The cabinet members pick up pans, spoons and washboards and with hostility beat rhythm as the PRESIDENT *plays his violin.* s. ULTERIOR, *rather liking the melody, vocalizes dreamily with it.*

ANNOUNCER 1   Ladies and gentlemen we interrupt this program for an important announcement.

PRESIDENT   Oh for Christ' sake.

ANNOUNCER 1   The long-feared war between the Orals and the Anals has erupted in the Urals.

All look stunned. Blackout.

At this moment the only word from the front is that the U.N. has a team of neutral Genitals freely circulating in no-man's-land. Stay tuned to this station. We have reporters on the field, flat on their backs, eager to cover this story from every angle. This crisis has been in the making for nearly a decade. The Phallic Riots of the fifties. The Chain Letters. The Boston Pee Party. But the roots of the division go back a century when the Church, in reaction to the ecumenical spirit, not only reiterated its historic position that sex be void of carnal pleasure and permissible only for procreation, it expressly forbade it entirely. As Pope Innocent put it:

Lights up on POPE INNOCENT.

POPE INNOCENT   If She didn't have to have it, nobody does.

Blackout.

ANNOUNCER I Dogma was further reformed two popes later when it was announced the Church would only recognize marriages between psychologically noncompatible members of the same sex. As Pope Sigmund put it:

Lights up.

POPE SIGMUND It doesn't work. It doesn't work. It doesn't work.

Blackout.

ANNOUNCER I What exactly he was referring to was not quite clear. It later became apparent it was none other than the mixed marriage.

Lights up on POPE, *fondling choir boy.*

POPE SIGMUND Men should be brought up with men to learn what being a man is. The mixed marriage confuses the sexual identity of the child.

Blackout.

ANNOUNCER I Five years later, after the Great Wave of Suicide, sex was again allowed, but only when sanctioned by the New Marriage. (*Voice fading.*) And so, after a half century of papal senility, effeminacy, inbreeding, ineffectuality . . .

ANNOUNCER II Meanwhile the Secretary of Logic, in his private life a successful engineer, in his inner life is secretly King of the Anals, unhappily wed to none other than King of the Orals; the result of an early indiscretion, and all in all a marriage of considerable inconvenience.

Light comes up on KING OF THE ORALS *and* KING OF THE ANALS *seated at a table.* K. O., *in public life the* PRESIDENT, *is dressed like a wholesome undergraduate;* K. A. *wears a leather jacket and boots.* K. O. *is mending socks;* K. A. *is drinking from a mug of beer. He blows his nose in his hand; throws the product to the floor; belches.* K. O. *watches, refusing to be perturbed.*

K. O. And what discriminating thing did you do today?

143951

K. A. We diverted the Ganges. Into the Trans-African Canal. It was a bit of a trick. It goes by aqueduct over the Indian Sea. It's very poor over there—very dry. We hope to make it a little worse.

K. O. I should think you'd try to make it a little better.

K. A. Well it is for the Africans. For a while. What they don't know yet is that when the first monsoon hits Bengal, half the Sahara will wash into the Atlantic. Very bad drainage. We hope to make it a little worse.

K. O. It's not that they have bad drainage. They just can't hold their water.

K. A. Finished the bridge to Hawaii. That was a mistake. Drive all the way out there and what is there to do? There's no parking. You have to make your own with the fill you have left over from Bengal.

K. O. I don't know why you can't just leave things the way they are.

K. A. Well you have to have parking. You build a bridge all the way to Honolulu and just put a loop on the end?

K. O. I don't know why you can't be . . . satisfied with . . . doing things around the house.

K. A. Oh God. You're so . . . passive.

K. O. I have to put up the storm windows, I have to mow the lawn—and what thanks do I get? Spend half the day at the barber and you don't even mention my sideburns. (*Suddenly near tears, he sucks his thumb for comfort.*)

K. A. This house. That's all you ever think of.

K. O. This house is my home. And I am trying the best I can to make it home for you.

K. A. And that is possibly the main reason I can't stand you. And that boy too. That boy that lives with us.

K. O. That boy happens to be our son.

K. A. He's not my son. Not the way he acts. Weeding the garden.

K. O. Max don't you ever say that again. He is ours and don't you forget it. (*Near tears again.*) That night we came together. When they mixed us in that little tube. Before they sent us packed in ice to that little post office——

K. A. Don't get sentimental.

K. O. And someday, if we do our job well, by God he's going to make some man a beautiful husband.

K. A. Beautiful husband! Grow up to be a thumbsucker like you? Oh God if I had only listened to my fathers. I should have been satisfied with contact sports.

K. O. I know you don't like me—you have never liked me Max. I knew it after that disastrous wedding night. But I said to myself, "Shower and forget." "We are legal husbands and tomorrow the shoe will be on the other foot."

K. A. And you got yours didn't you? All around me like a cocker spaniel.

K. O. All I ever wanted was gratuitous praise.

K. A. And all I ever wanted was to deny you everything you ever wanted.

K. O. Oh you make me so mad—so mad I could——

K. A. (*smiles, rising.*) Yeah? What could you do?

K. O. (*sits, mends nervously.*) Nothing, nothing. (*To audience.*) I have to play this well. I have a message I'm sewing in this sock. It must be delivered to my troops before dawn.

K. A. (*with scorn.*) You're all alike. (*Drinks from his mug of beer.*)

K. O. Big day tomorrow dear. (*Quickly puts his arm through* K. A.*'s cocked elbow and loudly sucks his thumb again with apparently an increasingly pacifying effect on himself.*)

K. A. (*to audience, on observing this.*) Oh I tell you humanity it is hell to be married to a man you cannot bear. Nightly the indignities of marital obligations. Bare meaningless gestures.

K. O. Darling, it's getting late.

K. A. *takes a swig of his beer as* K. O. *sighs in subdued ecstasy and begins snoring loudly.*

K. A. (*to audience.*) How I would truly love to beat the shit out of this creep. (*Music begins as spot narrows on him.*)

53

I know it's dreaming. Dreams I don't even dare to dream. But maybe someday I'll find someone made for me. Maybe a kid just getting out of school. A strong kid from a good male home. Maybe in the Golden Gloves. Losing a lot. Fighting beautifully, but not getting the breaks. And a great loser. God how I love a great loser. A kid who needs somebody to LOSE TO. Cause then when I—dare I wish it—when I beat the shit out of him, I'll at least know that the only thing I have to give is appreciated.

Blackout. A great uproar of what seems to be tanks and Gatling guns is heard and fades into background.

ANNOUNCER I It is just past midnight here in the war zone, traditionally the hour of heaviest in-fighting, and reports of atrocities continue to pile up. In the bloodiest encounter so far five hundred motorcyclists were ambushed, their members severed and forced between their lips, which were then sealed. This has added fuel to the rumor that the Oral Army has an elite Seamstress Corps. Which has perfected an instant hemstitch capable of sealing all of a man's orifices in less than thirty seconds.

The sounds come up again, only now we realize they are not tanks and guns but motorcycles and sewing machines. Hysterical battle cries of "Mary" are heard and the KING OF THE ANALS *runs on.*

K. A. I have come my troops, I have come. Our backs are to the wall. We are surrounded on all sides. All we have to protect us is our manhood and that wall. And whatever we do we must never forget even that wall is only a metaphor.

KING OF THE ORALS *runs on.*

K. O. I have come my troops. Victory is at our fingertips. Don't give up the stitch.

Cheers.

K. A. But are we going to let them get our organs? (*Cries of "No!"*) Because a man with his organs in his mouth is a pathetic thing. He cannot speak. He cannot eat. Except of himself.

K. O. (*saluting as he leaves.*) For King and Mother.

Cheers and exit.

K. A. Don't fire till you see the eyes of their whites. (*He runs off.*)

Alarms and excursions.

ANNOUNCER I From California reports are coming in of the costliest pillow-fight ever to hit the San Joaquin Valley. Even in the Midwest, hotbed of provincialism, a great wall of semen is reported to be rising in the headlands of the Missouri. Geologists report that if it ever gets to the Mississippi, it could make the Johnstown flood look like foreplay.

The POET *and his* WIFE *walk on. She has a red cross cap and arm band.*

POET'S WIFE Plasma, Playboy, Cosmopolitan, Vaseline.

ANNOUNCER I The Anal Army at the front, resorting to biological warfare, has perfected a device it calls the Shit Bomb.

Alarms and sorties.

It claims also to have fielded a tactical Shit Bomb, which uses a standard Shit Bomb as a trigger, but is thrown into a very large fan.

Odors and farewells.

POET'S WIFE What interesting people these are.

ANNOUNCER I Unfortunately the new weapon seems to have backfired. For it has a remarkable effect on plant life, turning battlefields in a matter of minutes into teeming gardens.

K. O. *and* S. ULTERIOR *disguised as hippies enter with garlands of flowers chanting "Hare Krishna." Hundreds of voices echo*

55

them. They are followed by K. A. *and* S. REALITY *dragging chains and whipping them with whips of hair.*

One hybrid pansy is reported to have measured twenty feet from cheek to cheek.

Music is heard, and trying to wrap their chains and flowers around one another, the combatants form a ring around the distracted POET *and succeed only in entangling him. They run off leaving him heavily burdened, sinking to the floor. Music fades.*

POET *(dreaming, recites Marvell.)*

> "What wond'rous life is this I lead!
> Ripe apples drop about my head;
> Stumbling on melons, as I pass,
> Insnar'd with flowers, I fall on grass."

POET'S WIFE *(looking off after them, examining flowers and chains.)* What strong and generous people. *(A Shit Bomb falls near them.)* What a bad smell. It reminds me of my mother.

Lights fade out.

ANNOUNCER II   Meanwhile, the Secretary of Reality, in private life a free-lance religious, in her inner life is none other than Queen of the Anals, unhappily wed to Queen of the Orals; the result of a long-standing and laughable confusion involving dead letters and a pair of changelings with false names.

Lights come up on QUEEN OF THE ANALS *and* QUEEN OF THE ORALS (S. ULTERIOR) *seated at a table, plates before them. On* Q. A.'s *plate is an interesting rock which she is tapping at with a small geologist's hammer.* Q. O. *picks up a fork.*

Q. A.   You picked up your fork before your knife.

Q. O. I can't remember all that. And I left the book in the bedroom. Which pea do I eat first?

Q. A. There's only one.

Q. O. Only one!

Q. A. It's Wednesday.

Q. O. (*stands, pregnant.*) I'm eating for two.

Q. A. Split it down the middle.

Q. O. Well do I get something extra to drink? Can I stay up an hour later? There must be some advantage to Wednesday.

Q. A. Wednesday makes you stronger.

Q. O. I'm dying of starvation! Why don't we have a whole week of Wednesday and just get it over with. I could go home to mothers' you know. They loved me. They didn't WANT me strong. They wanted me fat and helpless.

Q. A. Thirty seconds to finish supper.

Q. O. To wolf down a whole pea? It'll take me at least a minute to find it. To say nothing of getting it on my fork.

Q. A. Fifteen seconds.

Q. O. Now stop it Marsha. This pea is swabbed in butter. (*Racing it around the plate.*) It has a very low . . . coefficient of friction.

Q. A. Time's up. (*Throws pea on floor.* Q. O. *aghast.*) I'm sorry Ingeborg, you waited too long. It got stale.

Q. O. I don't understand this. In some basic way I must be imperfect.

Q. A. Jabber jabber jabber. Spend a hard day at the bar. Watching all those judges get drunk. Drunk with power.

Q. O. Where do you work anyway?

Q. A. At the sand bar. We're exposing a culture. And when I come home, after supper I want some peace and quiet.

Q. O. After supper? But you didn't eat a thing.

Q. A. Well . . . for you Wednesday may be only a joke.

Q. O. Marsha? I want a marshmallow. Face it, we're different people. I give up—I can't live up to your standards. I was brought up on marshmallows. Grilled American marshmallows with pickle chips. Roast chicken stuffed with marsh-mallows. (*Becoming terribly excited.*) Oh I die just thinking of it. Broiled marshmallows smothered in mushrooms! Oh God—every morning breakfast of bacon and marshmallows—ham and marshmallows. Served me in my own bed by the four hands of my loving mothers.

Q. A. All right! So you had a rough childhood. Is it my fault you were coddled? That your parents were compatible and not supplementary?

Q. O. I just think about marshmallows and I go into a feeding frenzy. I feel like a school of piranha encircling a swimming class.

Q. A. You are so self-indulgent! And I have had about enough. But someday I warn you I'm going to haul off and start treating you like an adult.

Q. O. What's happening to us Marsha? This whole war thing. It's getting to me.

Q. A. You're about to have your baby.

Q. O. What do you mean?

Q. A. Your eight months are up.

Q. O. It takes nine.

Q. A. No daughter of mine needs nine whole months.

Q. O. Well I need nine whole months! You think it's an easy thing. I've never been so confused in my life. I was awake all last week trying to figure out a collective unconscious. I don't even know what it is, but they say it's there somewhere. I put it in the vagina. But how do I know she's not going to have running dreams? I tell you a woman comes in her own time.

Q. A. Well let's get this straight here and now Ingeborg. I am responsible for my daughter and I want no interference from you. My daughter comes when I call. (*Begins Gregorian Chant.* Q. O. *doubles up in labor pains. Consoling her as other voices take up the chant.*) Nine is an odd number Ingeborg.

Q. O. It's a magic number. It's nature's number. It's divisible by three.

Q. A.   Eight is divisible by two and four.

Q. O.   Nine is a square three on a side.

Q. A.   Eight is a cube two on a side.

Q. O.   Oh God she's right.

Q. A.   Oh you people who would live two-dimensional realities, not taking the extra effort to Define Yourselves.

Q. O.   Marsha what's happened to us? Since that first night. When they scrambled our eggs in that little tube? In that sauce—whatever it was. Sort of a white sauce. Like Eggs Benedict without the marshmallows——

Q. A.   What are you doing overgrowing my daughter? I want none of your manifestations of being without being anything in particular for any particular reason. I want a daughter who can measure and master. Who is a systematic accretion of all the available information from the:

Azoic	
Archeozoic	
Proterozoic	
Paleozoic	Cambrian Silurian Devonian Carboniferous Permian——

Q. O.   Stop it—I can't keep track.

Q. A.   Keep track of what?

Q. O.   The Code. The Genetic Code. What every mother knows. You may not know this but all by myself I have to translate the four-letter alphabet of ribonucleic acid into the twenty-word language of protein. The Code established for three billion years and the same for all organisms from bacteria all the way up to man. And if you rush me and I don't get it right, I could give birth to a cold.

Q. A.

Mesozoic		
Cenozoic	Tertiary: the Age of Mammals—get ready;	Paleocene Eocene Oligocene Miocene Pliocene
	Quaternary	Pleistocene Recorded history Day before yesterday This afternoon NOW!

Q. O. (*giving birth.*) Oh . . . quick—tomorrow.

Q. A. (*holding baby.*) She's beautiful.

Q. O. (*looking at it.*) God no, it's one of those.

Q. A. It's not ivory. It's more like a good whalebone.

Q. O. Eight months of agony and all I have to show for it is an artifact.

Blackout.

ANNOUNCER I Keenly sensitive to world opinion, both Orals and Anals have made overtures in the U.N. A lady Oral from Rio proposed a Stitching Pause, while an Albanian Anal spoke on peaceful uses of the Shit Bomb. The latter speech alluded ominously to the Big Bomb still under development, with the words "the impending increment in the excrement." At which point several delegates became constricted and were asked to leave.

Noise of chattering mob fades in and down.

ANNOUNCER II An unrelated event of considerable human interest occurred yesterday when the entire state of Czechoslovakia burst into flame. At the border of Germany, where the fire stops abruptly, the population is living in a carnival atmosphere. Busloads of picnickers with long sticks are arriving from as far away as Paris, which is downwind. From where I am standing right next to the wall of flame I can see close to a quarter of a million happy faces roasting bratwurst. Slovakian border guards are beside themselves. One cried out to me as I approached, "My country, my country." Our latest satellite, Uruguay, launched by the Army this morning, reports fire storms over Prague reach five miles high. In Prague itself however it is business as usual.

Gypsy music. Red light comes up on the POET *in gypsy costume dancing with finger cymbals as his* WIFE *sings and accompanies on the tambourine.*

POET'S WIFE

> In flaming Prague the Poet sings
> Of transubstantiating things.
> And as the city turns to gas
> The Poet's heart absorbs the mass.

POET *dances a verse.*

> Now heavier than Prague is he
> And dancing in its gassy gale
> The planet wobbles on its nail
> And tides are flashing in the sea.

POET *dances a verse.*

> In flaming Prague the Poet's heels
> Now pound the planet as it reels
> And rolls in routes it should not run
> For epicycles of a sun.

POET *dances a verse.*

ALL except POET
> In flaming Prague the Poet sings
> And as the city turns to gas
> The Poet's heart absorbs the mass
> Of transubstantiating things.

The song ends.

POET'S WIFE   The city I was born in was not like this. I cannot understand these streets alive with fire. The buildings on every side sagging into ashes.

POET   You're afraid aren't you? Stay close to me.

POET'S WIFE   I should be miles away from here. This is exactly what my mother told me to avoid. It is so strange and beautiful. Like walking in a warm blizzard.

POET   There's nothing to be afraid of. See the lovers hand in hand, smiling as the flames approach their legs? See the taxis melting at every intersection? Little dogs lifting their heads in a gust of particles? The children playing at their games; licking one another, running with juices?

POET'S WIFE   There certainly is a lot to see.

POET   For what is oxidation but the affinity certain kinds of denied energy have for one another; the result being the mutual release of certain aspects of the denial?

POET'S WIFE   Here come two apparitions, exploding like a pair of comets.

"Flaming Prague" music is heard and K. A. *and* K. O. *enter as the* POET *puts on a woman's wig and gypsy skirt.*

K. A.   This is the place.

POET *begins dancing.*

K. O.   She's beautiful.

K. A.   She has a body like no woman I ever saw. You watch. She's gonna dance her little ass off and send you right up the wall. (*Opening his Baedeker.*) "These people are the best lays in the world." Three stars and two daggers.

K. O.   What are the daggers?

K. A.   Something to do with risk.

K. O.   I don't know. All I have is a traveler's check.

K. A.   Look at her. She likes you. Go ahead talk to her.

K. O.   Some other time.

K. A.   What do you mean? This is your chance. Nobody'll ever know. (POET *throws* K. O. *a rose.*) Did you see that?

K. O.   She probably likes older men.

K. A.   Oh Jesus.

POET   I speak English.

K. A.   Man what a break!

K. O.   That's a break all right.

K. A.   Will you take a check?

POET   You not Czech. You American.

K. O.   I don't feel very well.

K. A.   No—a traveler's check. Do you understand?

POET (*like a brainless parrot.*)   I speak English.

K. A.   Well will you take a traveler's check for your body?

K. O. (*running off.*)   I'm getting sick. I think it's the water.

K. A.   Where are you going?

K. O.   The water in this place is killing me. (*He is gone.*)

K. A.   Sorry Miss.

POET   Oh don't go. I have rose for you too.

K. A. (*leaving.*)   Uh . . . my hotel is burning down. (*He is gone.*)

The POET *quickly begins changing into some sort of Balkan uniform.*

POET'S WIFE   My husband is shedding early this year. I have never seen his coat so glamorous. Each time he turns, a different facet catches fire.

POET   You must wonder at the poet's protean nature. True I am only a chameleon, but a free chameleon—I can go where

I want. I may change with the landscape, but that is merely my aesthetic sense.

Q. A. *and* Q. O. *enter and* POET *begins marching back and forth.*

Q. A. This is the place.

Q. O. I hope we're not late.

Q. A. (*reading Baedeker.*) Every hour they change the guards at the Royal Bon Fire.

Q. O. Why is that handsome man marching all by himself?

Q. A. He's the Chosen One. Every hour one of the guards actually walks through the flames. Legend has it if there is a virgin present he will be burned alive.

Q. O. Oh we must go!

Q. A. (*reading.*) "This stop is a must. Three stars and two daggers."

Q. O. Quickly.

Q. A. Go? This is your chance of a lifetime. See? He's looking at you. He's got fifteen minutes to live honey and it's all up to you.

Q. O. Oh I couldn't. There are all those people.

Q. A. What do you think those little red booths are for? You don't want to go back to that office responsible for that beautiful young man's death do you?

Q. O. No I want to leave.

Q. A. (*showing her book.*) But it's a must! Look at him. It isn't just his life he wants. He wants you. Maybe he's tired of being a guard. He wants to settle down.

Q. O. Why doesn't he settle down with you?

Q. A. They can only marry virgins.

Q. O. But virgins can destroy them.

Q. A. Well . . . it's touch and go. See how strong he is? Marching in the face of it—willing to die for his Code?

Q. O. I don't understand all these rules. They seem cruel and arbitrary.

Q. A. They're beautiful. If you learn to live with them—submit to them.

Q. O. Well there's nothing *I* can do. I feel sick to my stomach. Why don't you run to him—save him!

Q. A. Me? Save him! You fool. That bonfire is FED by people like me! (Q. O. *runs off, horrified. To* POET.) I'll get you yet. (*Starts to leave. Comes back and says with great frankness.*) I will say this. That nine minutes in booth five was the high point of my life. (*She leaves.*)

POET *begins changing back into his costume.*

POET Come it is getting late. We've been here too long.

POET'S WIFE Let me help you. (*As she touches his hand he lets out a cry of pain and sinks to the floor. She says with amazement.*) My hand . . . went right through him.

POET (*struggles to his feet. Fighting back the pain in his hand, he smiles at her and says.*) Come. I have no more time.

Blackout. Thunderstorm is heard.

ANNOUNCER II And the Poet begins his final journey, walking only by night, along faults thrust up in granite ridges. For a secret known only to himself, now guessed by his hapless wife—the secret that caused him to leave his mountain top —is that his flesh is mysteriously transforming into a substance of no dimension, but incredible density—his total weight already equaling half that of the moon. Already he is responsible for great tidal flooding in the Netherlands. For the opening of a trench across Bavaria. For the sudden dislocation of night and day in a severe wobbling that threatens the concord of the planets themselves. The storms of the atmosphere mass around him, deluging him and the lands he passes. The magnetic pole shifts from its axis to rest beneath his feet, and the aurora showers upon him nightly the ghastly fluids of the quiet sun. Meanwhile in flaming Prague the destruction continues.

Loud gypsy music and great screaming. Light comes up on
Q. A., *dressed in leather and chained to the wall, being beaten
by* K. A., *likewise attired. After inflicting howling damage, he
embraces her passionately, and in a choked voice:*

K. A. My husband would die if he knew we were together.
Q. A. (*nearly expiring.*) When will people learn . . . that
Ingeborg and I . . . just weren't made for each other?
(*Passes out.*)

Blackout. Gypsy music up and out. Lights come up on K. O.
and Q. O. *in flannel pajamas whispering to one another, apparently raiding a refrigerator.*

Q. O. Oh . . . look at the candy eggs. Oh I die.

They begin gobbling voraciously.

K. O. Eggs eggs how I love eggs.
Q. O. I can't get them fast enough.
K. O. I am eating the largest jelly bean I have ever seen.

A very deep voice is heard off.

VOICE Who is down there?

They both stop.

K. O. Did you hear something?
Q. O. Did you? (*They resume eating with more energy.*) Oh
look, chocolate chickens. Chocolate ducks. Chocolate dogs.
K. O. Chocolate soldiers. Chocolate tanks. Chocolate howitzers.

A heavy thumping is heard off.

Q. O. A chocolate Miss America!
K. O. I think somebody's hopping down the stairs.

They listen and indeed someone is, so they eat all the faster.

Q. O. A chocolate playground.
K. O. A chocolate Navy Yard.

Q. O.   A chocolate Welfare Center.

K. O.   A chocolate Police Station.

VOICE   That refrigerator contains goodies for all the world's children.

Frantically:

Q. O.   A vacation in the country.

K. O.   A month in the hospital.

Q. O.   An afternoon at the beach.

K. O.   I think somebody's at the door.

Q. O.   Quiet I'm eating Sunday School.

Loud ominous squeaking of a door is heard and K. O. *and* Q. O. *stand back aghast. A shadow falls on them.*

VOICE   I am the Easter Bunny and you are thieves in a house of goodness.

K. O.   He'll murder us!

Q. O.   We're going to get it now. Look—it's all over us! God!

K. O.   Jump him—jump him! (*Runs and seems to grab him from behind as* Q. O. *wrestles with him from the front.*) I got him behind!

Q. O.   I got his paw!

K. O.   Eat—eat for your life!

They begin voraciously. A moan is heard.

VOICE   Oh . . . help me. I am milk chocolate and vulnerable. (Q. O. *and* K. O. *are eating their way with ecstatic delight through the rabbit, toward and finally upon one another, as lights fade out and the rabbit says weakly.*) Forgive them my children. They know not what they eat.

Thunderstorms again in darkness.

ANNOUNCER II   Fording streams, avoiding all man-made constructions, the Poet approaches the long-forgotten Bottomless Lake out of which once all life emerged; its waters still containing fossil chemicals of that event, and minute life

67

forms that have nowhere else survived. The Poet submerges himself in the waters, knowing gravity will pull him to the center of the earth, restoring equilibrium. But first he bids farewell to his faithful wife.

Lights come up on the POET *submerged in the lake and his* WIFE *with her hands again on her female parts, howling.*

POET   It was early I learned that I could not be touched. I lacked surface tension. And the matter of another could pass right through me with an indescribable one-sided pain. That's why I lived on the mountain. Not because I didn't like the company of men, but to examine the structure of my substance and to seek a cure for all men. But the more I examined the worse it became. Soon the wind itself went through me, but with a pain so slight I called it joy. I do not know why that happened. Perhaps it is in my papers.

POET'S WIFE   Oh if he only understood my native tongue.

POET   I cannot deny the fact my life is a failure. For what I have done to myself has caused calamity to others. I sought to free the hearts of men, but have only further imprisoned myself. I have broken their homes only to realize I cannot build new ones that do not house the same dangers. For there is a denying in the act of building that says, "I am this and nothing else." And that I could not accept. For nothing human must be written off.

POET'S WIFE   If I were blonde he wouldn't leave me.

POET   Already the sky is clearing. It should be a nice day for picnics. My dear wife in these liquids are many common bonds between us. In suspension they exist even today, our relatives who were little more than minerals. What would have become of us if they had said, "I am this and nothing else"? Yet why does it seem all building is dying and even growing is but destroying? Because we are the children of Energy, who achieve our definition only through Matter, which is Energy denied its freedom. And growth is the release of the denial, but the destruction of the definition. (POET'S

WIFE *howls again.*) My dear you must leave now. Do you understand? For I must let go. And Poets do not float. Go away. Go away.

POET'S WIFE   Oh . . . my heart must break. An animal heart cannot bear a human loss.

POET   Go away.

POET'S WIFE   That is the secret of the lemmings. They possess almost human feelings. And an animal inclination to form binding pacts. Oh take me with you—take me with you!

POET   Go—do you understand? Bad! Bad! Go away! (*She leaves in tears.*) Who would believe it if a poet claimed no truer words of love than "bad, bad, go away"? Oh where would we be without the symmetries of thought? That all ideas naturally suggest opposites, and that every value can be extended to absurdity in either direction? (*Turning in the water.*) And what if we had never conceived of "similarity," forever ebbing and flowing with the world around us, never bothering with two and two? Constructing no hierarchies of sensation, which acquire more reality than the sensations themselves? Hierarchies of Ideas which crystallize and kill? I sometimes wonder if it is possible to know anything without limiting your ability to know something equally true.

He sinks out of sight. As the light fades out, a heartbeat is heard growing louder and louder. In the darkness during the following speech an entire second arc is constructed from the monument out over the audience to a different yet analogous destination.

ANNOUNCER I   Ladies and gentlemen at this hour the rhythm continues. The unexplained throbbing, noted yesterday by seismologists around the world, grew louder today, becoming gradually perceptible to everyone. As near as can be ascertained, the source is the very core of the planet. In the last twelve hours the throbbing has accelerated slightly, and now approximates the rate of a frightened human heart. Several confused Parliaments have passed resolutions ordering all responsible citizens to panic. As one man among many observed, "It's as if the earth itself were coming to life." The analogy is perhaps not as farfetched as it seems, for this afternoon were discovered hitherto unnoticed vast arteries moving just beneath the surface of the earth; filled with a liquid of marvelous properties; allegedly capable of both defying gravity and bringing back the dead.

ANNOUNCER II   Meanwhile the President faces an internal crisis.

Lights come up on the PRESIDENT, *moaning, sick to his stomach. It is a cabinet meeting.*

S. REALITY   Mr. President, my figures indicate the earth's crust is expanding at the rate of three feet every hour. Do you realize what that means to our cities? The schisms that will divide families—turn brother against brother?

PRESIDENT   Will you stop talking about expansion.

S. LOGIC   But Mr. President, you're the only one who can save us. With all the world around us transforming in ways we cannot understand, what can we hang onto but the structure of authority?

S. REALITY   Mr. President there are five hundred people downstairs who claim to have just returned from the dead.

PRESIDENT   What do they want from me?

S. REALITY   They're asking about their Social Security. You can't let them get away with it. What's past is past. We must revive the concept of Heresy.

S. LOGIC   Mr. President last night my bridge to Hawaii grew all the way to Japan.

PRESIDENT   Well . . . isn't that good?

S. LOGIC   Good? I'm out of a job. From that one bridge my boss is getting cuttings for bridges all over the world. He could go to the moon if he had a lunar trellis.

PRESIDENT   What do you want me to do?

S. LOGIC and REALITY   Revive the concept of Heresy.

PRESIDENT   Oh leave me alone—I don't understand a word you're saying.

Q. A. (*aside to* K. A.)   I'm so frightened.

K. A.   We should have never done it. Look what's happened.

K. O. (*aside to* Q. O.).   It's that damn rabbit I know it. He's getting back at me.

Q. O.   You were supposed to guard the door. If he hadn't caught us we wouldn't have had to get rid of him.

K. O.   But I can't get rid of him—that's the whole problem.

S. REALITY   What are you saying over there?

S. LOGIC   Speak up so we can hear.

PRESIDENT   It's getting bigger and bigger.

S. ULTERIOR (*listening to his stomach.*)   I can't go along with these doctors who take such a dim view of the cancer cell.

PRESIDENT   Oh God.

S. ULTERIOR   It's so seldom you get a going thing. It is actually a biological triumph. A cell that has conquered genetic inhibition. A free spirit capable of unlimited expansion. In fact who is to say the cancer cell is not the ultimate product of evolution? And Man merely a fantastically elaborate foodstuff?

S. REALITY   Mr. President that is what I mean by Heresy.

S. ULTERIOR   Surely the cancer cell destroys its host and thereby itself. But viewed from the proper distance, can we really say cancer colonies are any more shortsighted in this matter than are the nations of men? Who is to say a new Athens does not flourish in every dying grandmother? An Athens teeming with the freedom to redefine. The breaking down of age-old barriers. And the flooding of each spirit with the new light of infinite possibilities.

S. LOGIC *and* REALITY   Kill her—kill her!

They lock in mortal combat. Lights narrow on the PRESIDENT.

PRESIDENT   It's that damn Poet. Why do the wise men always have to die?

S. LOGIC (*from the darkness.*)   You are responsible now.

S. REALITY (*from the darkness.*)   You must get the answers yourself.

Blackout. The throbbing grows louder and louder.

ANNOUNCER I (*over the noise.*) There will be no news today ladies and gentlemen, for there is too much that is new. Stay tuned to this station for the latest on anything that remains the same.

Blast of strange music in and out.

ANNOUNCER II   Yes our old friends the lemmings are at it again. Or rather I should say our old friends are making a comeback. For it seems millions of these lovable creatures thought drowned for centuries have in reality been crouching on the bottoms of the fiords holding their breaths. And yesterday was L Day. Following is the last communication received from the Mayor of Lefse, a small fishing village on the Norwegian coast.

Great deal of static is heard and a faint and desperate voice.

MAYOR'S VOICE   This is Lefse calling. God save us. We are being smothered by long-lost lemmings.

The throbbing dies away and light comes up on the PRESIDENT *with a knapsack on his back and a violin.*

PRESIDENT   All the people it might have been and I have to climb the mountain. Fortunately I have a snack. Ancient wisdom tells us that Mountain is the spirit of Woman. My entire upbringing tells me I should put my foot on woman. What am I to do, poor artist torn between form and content? (*Shouts from off, "Shake a leg. Get going." He begins climbing.*) I wish there were some way I could know what I was going to find up here.

He passes K. A. *chained to a rock, naked, his stomach covered with gore.*

K. A. (*cries weakly.*)   Help me. I am Prometheus. I gave you fire. I gave you power. I am being eaten by a crow.

PRESIDENT   A crow? (*Shooing it away.*) Nevermore! Nevermore!
(*Passes on, looking back briefly.*) I'll have to do something
for that man's liver. On the way back. (*Smiling to himself.*)
I'm learning selflessness I think. If only somebody could help
ME. Why did I have to grow up to be President? I wanted
to be loved from afar. That's the only reason I auditioned.
Intrapersonal responsibility, as between a man and his moun-
tain, was the very thing I was trying to avoid.

Q. A. *approaches him as seductive belly dancer.*

Q. A.   Help me—help me. I am Circe of legend and I have lost
my pigs.

PRESIDENT   I can give you a ham sandwich. (*In disgust she
moves away. Delighted with himself.*) I'm becoming a very
generous person.

Q. A. (*unchaining "Prometheus."*)   Oh there you are.

They go off, passionately involved.

PRESIDENT   I must be nearing the top. What's that big shadow?
Who are you?

Q. O. *with head of a bull enters.*

Q. O.   I am the Minotaur.

PRESIDENT   That's ridiculous. You're in the labyrinth.

Q. O.   I am the Minotaur.

PRESIDENT   Yes but who are you really?

Q. O.   Oh all right I'm Ingeborg. (*Taking off mask.*) I was just
playing a game. Here are his papers. (*She has been holding
them prominently. As he looks at them.*) You can't read it.
It's all runic. I'll show you mine if you show me yours.

PRESIDENT   I see it on television every night.

Q. O.   It's not the same.

PRESIDENT   Nobody's looking—let's make mud pies.

Q. O.   Do you have babies?

PRESIDENT   Yeah, we get them from the post office.

Q. O.   So do we.

73

David Starkweather • *The Poet's Papers*

PRESIDENT   Special Delivery.

Q. O.   We deliver our own.

PRESIDENT   It's not the same.

Q. O.   God knows. I want to see yours.

PRESIDENT   Why?

Q. O.   We don't have color.

PRESIDENT   Do you realize I'm your President?

Q. O.   Does that mean you don't have one?

PRESIDENT (*slow smile.*)   Watch it Ingeborg.

Q. O.   That's just what I want.

PRESIDENT   Watch it Ingeborg. (*Puts his finger in her mouth.*)

Q. O.   I'm getting a divorce. Marsha is going into politics. And I don't want to sit home alone and try to feed that baby. It doesn't eat. They think they can fool you. They put a little hole in its mouth. And you put the spinach in and it all runs out the other end, but it's still spinach. Marsha says it's very practical. I can use the same spinach. Isn't that just like her? She says it's even better second time around. My child has to grow up under that influence. Three days old and already hard as a rock.

PRESIDENT   Let's play post office. I get to be mailman.

Q. O.   All right . . . I'm mailbox. Though frankly I'm sick up to here with it.

PRESIDENT   Why?

Q. O.   It's the sitting and waiting. And the mailman travels.

PRESIDENT   I'll take you with me.

Q. O.   Do you think you should? That's an innovation.

PRESIDENT (*proudly.*)   I'm the President.

The POET'S WIFE *enters, howling, holding herself.* Q. O. *and* PRESIDENT *run off frightened.*

POET'S WIFE (*in tears, picking up the papers.*)   Oh keen, familiar odor. (*Indian music begins as she looks at them. Sadly.*) Why that's not runic. That's labanotation.

She sets the papers on the floor around her and begins to dance among them. As she dances.

POET'S VOICE   To the alert mind the existence of antimatter suggests that matter exists or can exist only because of its somewhat inexplicable isolation from its own denial. And that matter itself, no matter what the organization it has undergone to make it more or less inaccessible as energy, that process can only be interpreted as the denial of an analogous process, starting from the same energy, that gives precisely analogous antimatter results. The intriguing question is the nature of the analogy.

The Indian music stops, as the POET'S WIFE *thinks about what she has danced. Offstage a well-rehearsed contrapuntal chorale begins.*

K. O.   "In flaming Prague the Poet sang"
K. O. and Q. O.   "Of reuniting yin and yang."
K. A. and Q. A.   "In flaming Prague he sang to us"
ALL FOUR   "Of anima and animus."
POET'S WIFE   No—no that's not what he said. (*The chorale elaborates.*) He only sang that to you. But he sang for everyone.

The chorale fades as the Indian music resumes and she dances again.

POET'S VOICE   For one cannot resist speculating that a universe exists somehow precisely analogous to ours that remains inaccessible only by virtue of our power to deny it. And that universe is not necessarily "another place." Do I, in a far more real sense than I had ever imagined, coexist with my denied possibilities? Or even "all that I am not"? And is it the world of Matter itself, and the confidence one has in the "reality" of Solid Things, that makes it impossible for me to see, or accept, or release from denial the equally real being of my Dreams? The being that I am as truly as my material being? And is not this Unity the frightening secret that all Worship of Matter and Disparaging of Dream seeks to avoid?

The music has stopped. The POET'S WIFE *has picked up the paper and is now reading it intently. Light narrows to a small spot on her. The* POET'S VOICE *continues wearily.*

My hand grows heavy as I write. The danger grows. And in the morning I must leave this place that I have made my home. Oh spare me all that I am not. Define me. Save me from becoming all I wish to be. I cannot bear another miracle.

POET'S WIFE (*slowly putting down the paper.*) Then . . . I was human all along.

POET'S VOICE (*with compassion.*) Oh yes my Beloved.

The intellect bears within itself, in the form of natural logic, a latent geometrism that is set free in the measure and proportion that the intellect penetrates into the inner nature of inert matter.

Intelligence is in tune with this matter, and that is why the physics and metaphysics of inert matter are so near each other.

BERGSON

Thus "matter" is not part of the ultimate material of the world, but merely a convenient way of collecting events into bundles.

RUSSELL

Always with Love

(A Diabolical Comedy)
or Mother's Little Helper
A *Play in Two Acts*

TOM HARRIS

Tom HARRIS was born in New York City, but his theatrical training has been centered in Los Angeles. He received his M.A. degree in theatre arts at UCLA and completed his undergraduate studies at Howard University. He has been associated as writer and director for Studio West and Channel 22 television in Los Angeles and is a member of the Burgess Meredith Acting Group and Actors Studio playwriting unit. Among his other full-length plays are *Fall of an Iron Horse, All the Tigers Are Tame, The Relic, Death of Daddy Hugs and Kisses, Divorce–Negro Style, Who Killed Sweetie,* and *City Beneath the Skin.* He received a citation from the Los Angeles city council for *Always with Love.* Mr. Harris has taught playwriting at UCLA and the Inner City Cultural Center and since 1961 has been a librarian with the Los Angeles Public Library.

Characters

AVERY PANE
ISOBEL PANE
HENRY PANE
ANTHONY PANE
GINGER PANE
ANNIE JONES
FELIX JONES
REMBRANDT
OFFICER CLARK
JUDGE'S VOICE
SECOND VOICE
THIRD VOICE

Always with Love was first produced at the Pasadena Playhouse on February 8, 1967. The production was directed by Mary Greene. Set was by Randy Kone; lighting by William W. Young. The cast was as follows:

ANNIE JONES Isabelle Cooley
FELIX JONES Don Marshall
REMBRANDT Mark Dymally
AVERY PANE Hal Torey
ISOBEL PANE Sondra Rodgers
ANTHONY PANE William Wintersole
HENRY PANE Peter Parkin
GINGER PANE Betty Anne Rees
OFFICER CLARK Karl Lukas

Always with Love

Act One

Scene 1

The action takes place in two large rooms of an estate on Long Island: a well-equipped kitchen with an exit up three steps to the outside, and also three steps up to the servants wing; and a swinging door to the living room-study, which also has a dining area. Off living room, an alcove leading to the hallway down right, and a flight of stairs which are not seen. A pair of French doors upstage overlooking the bay. Five large picture frames sit empty upstage.

The servants, ANNIE *and* FELIX, *both Negroes in their early twenties, sit dejectedly on a big sofa with their little son* REM-BRANDT. *The boy is six. Seated around them in the living room are the Pane family:* HENRY *and his wife,* GINGER, *are in their mid-twenties;* ANTHONY PANE *is thirty-three.* AVERY PANE, *the head of the household, paces the floor. His wife* ISOBEL *sits in an overstuffed chair. She looks very uncomfortable. All wear black mourning clothes.*

AVERY (*stops pacing.*)   Beautiful ceremony. Beautiful! I'm sure wherever she is, she appreciated that eulogy.

ISOBEL   I'm sure she did.

AVERY The nice things people say about you when you're gone. Things they should say when you're around to hear them.

ISOBEL Poor old Alma. With the family for forty years.

HENRY I'm hungry.

They all stare at him.

AVERY Seems like only yesterday Alma was banging around in the kitchen making some magic out of ordinary food.

HENRY She certainly could make great cherry pie.

ANTHONY Knock it off! (*He motions to the servants.*)

HENRY What's with you?

AVERY She was more than a cook to us. More than just a servant. She gave us forty years—a lifetime.

ISOBEL She was sweet.

AVERY She practically raised me from a pup.

ANTHONY All of us.

AVERY We'll miss her.

ISOBEL Yes.

GINGER She was a dear.

ANTHONY Yes.

ISOBEL She was sweet.

AVERY We'll miss her. We'll miss her strength.

HENRY Did you know that when she made cherry pie, she always made an extra one for me alone?

AVERY That was just like her. She was a queen in the kitchen.

GINGER She was a dear.

ISOBEL She was sweet.

AVERY We'll miss her strength.

ANTHONY Yes.

HENRY She used to clean my boots sometimes, too.

AVERY That was just like her.

ANTHONY Yes.

GINGER She was a dear.

ISOBEL She was sweet.

AVERY We'll miss her. After forty years, Alma . . . oh— Alma . . .

ANNIE Mason. Alma Mason.

AVERY Yes, of course.

ISOBEL Mason?

ANNIE That was her name.

ISOBEL Funny, I always thought it was Jones.

ANNIE That's my name. I'm Annie Jones, but I've only been here twenty-three years. My name was Mason, too, but I married Felix Jones.

ISOBEL Yes. I'm not very good at names. They don't really mean anything in the long run. It's the people that count. Take Alma . . . your mother——

GINGER She was a dear.

ISOBEL You can't say it enough. She was sweet.

HENRY I'm hungry.

ANTHONY You're always hungry.

HENRY So?

AVERY Annie, I want you and your family to know that you have got a place in this house as long as I live. I'm speaking for the whole Pane family.

ISOBEL We're with you, dear.

ANTHONY We need you, Annie.

GINGER Be a dear and stay.

HENRY Can you make a cherry pie, Annie?

GINGER If she can't, I can.

HENRY You can't even boil water.

GINGER Would you like boiled water for dinner?

AVERY Chldren, please! This is no time to be fighting among ourselves.

GINGER I'm sorry.

HENRY And how!

GINGER *scowls at him.*

AVERY Well, Annie, have you decided?

83

ANNIE As long as you live? You said I can stay as long as you all live?

AVERY Yes.

ANNIE I grew up in this house. I think of it as my home. After the sweet things you all said and the funeral today, I couldn't tear myself away.

AVERY Wonderful! We're in business again. The queen is dead. Long live the queen!

ANTHONY and HENRY Hear, hear!

GINGER Now maybe we can have some order around here again.

HENRY If you stay out of the kitchen.

GINGER Henry Pane, I'm going to make you a cherry pie no matter what you say!

HENRY I'd better change my will. That's what I say.

ANTHONY Say, Annie, do you know anything about explosives?

ANNIE No, sir.

AVERY Now why would she know about things like that?

ANTHONY It's just that Alma used to help me with my experiments.

AVERY You and your idiotic transistor bombs!

ANTHONY The Army doesn't think they're idiotic. Just think, a bomb no bigger than a cigarette lighter.

ANNIE Have you made one, sir?

ANTHONY Several. I'm talking to the Army about it now. Just think of what this will do to stock in Pane Corporations, Limited.

AVERY We specialize in electrical appliances. We lead the world in our particular field.

ANTHONY But this is new.

AVERY We'll blow ourselves up soon enough without you helping.

HENRY I'm hungry.

ISOBEL *gets up.*

AVERY Where are you going?

ISOBEL I thought I would bathe before lunch.

AVERY You took a bath before we went to the funeral.

ISOBEL (*meekly.*) I know, Avery, but——

AVERY Oh, sit down, Isobel. (*She sits.*) You sit around in that tub all day long. How can anyone possibly be so dirty.

ISOBEL I'm not dirty. I just like to sit in the warm water.

AVERY Every time you get upset you stuff yourself in a bucket of water. That doesn't solve anything.

ISOBEL It makes me feel better. I have some new soap I want to try.

AVERY Today we are on our own, even if that means starving to death. Annie has the day off.

HENRY Who's going to fix lunch?

ANNIE It's all right, sir, I'll do it.

AVERY (*going to her.*) Not today. A girl doesn't lose her mother every day! We expect to keep you around a long time, Annie. That goes for you, too, Felix.

FELIX Thank you, sir.

AVERY (*touching* REMBRANDT'*s hand.*) And you, Rembrandt, you going to help your mother?

REMBRANDT Yes.

ANNIE He always does. He's mother's little helper.

AVERY Good. You help Annie in everything now.

ANNIE He will, sir, he will.

GINGER He's such a dear.

ISOBEL He's sweet.

AVERY We're in your hands now, Annie.

ANNIE I feel better already. Alma would want it that way.

ANTHONY Good! Well, I think I'll go down to my shop. (*He gets up.*)

HENRY I'm going out to lunch before I become food for the ants.

GINGER (*getting up.*) Thanks for the invite.

AVERY Wait a minute! We're supposed to be keeping Annie company.

85

HENRY   Annie understands, don't you? Sure she does. See you later, Annie, Felix. (*He goes out.*)

GINGER   See you later, Annie. (*She goes out.*) Wait a minute, Henry!

ANTHONY   This is important, Annie. We're with you. (*He goes out.*)

AVERY   (*follows him out.*)   Now, Anthony! Anthony, son! I've been wanting to discuss that merger with you . . .

ISOBEL   (*smiles at* ANNIE *and* FELIX *nervously.*)   It's very warm today.

ANNIE   Yes.

ISOBEL   Sticky.

ANNIE   Why don't you take a bath?

ISOBEL   I think I will. That's a splendid idea, Alma. (*Starts out.*)

ANNIE   Annie.

ISOBEL   What?

ANNIE   I'm Annie.

ISOBEL   Yes, dear, I know.

She goes out. The servants are left alone in the big room.

ANNIE   (*to* FELIX.)   Would you like a cherry pie? (*She gets up.*)

FELIX   Never touch the stuff. (*He gets up.*)

REMBRANDT   I would.

They walk into the kitchen.

ANNIE   Not the way good old Alma what's-her-name used to make them.

FELIX   Don't let them bug you, Honey. They're not poor enough to have good manners and too rich to care whether they do or not. It's very sad.

ANNIE   If being rich and having bad manners is sad, it's the kind of sadness I'll welcome.

FELIX   Not really. (*Taking his jacket off.*)

ANNIE   Beng poor with good manners is silly.

86

FELIX It's a luxury only the poor can afford. (*Takes out a beer.*)

ANNIE Like bed bugs.

REMBRANDT Can I take my funeral clothes off?

ANNIE They're not funeral clothes, darling. They're your Sunday clothes. You wore them today out of respect for your grandma, who loved you very much.

REMBRANDT And I loved Grandma.

ANNIE (*unbuttons his jacket.*) I know, darling, I know. We all did. Your grandma was a wonderful person. She gave forty years of her life to those nitwits in there!

FELIX Temper, temper. (*He picks up a canvas and looks at it.*)

REMBRANDT *goes up the back stairs.*

ANNIE Forty years, and what did she get to show for it— promises!

FELIX What promises?

ANNIE A great rich inheritance. She was in Mr. Avery's will.

FELIX Really? (*Sets the canvas on his easel.*)

ANNIE Trouble is, she died first. They worked her to death.

FELIX She didn't have it so bad. Nice surroundings, good food.

ANNIE You sound like an ad in the employment section of the paper. "Girl, young and healthy, to sleep in. Unlimited opportunities with sweet family. Must do everything and stay for forty years. Mentioned in will, if you live that long."

FELIX Sounds like a very attractive ad.

ANNIE Sometimes you disappoint me, Felix.

FELIX Why?

ANNIE You don't care about anything.

FELIX That's not so. I care about a lot of things.

ANNIE Doesn't it bother you that there's such injustice in the world?

FELIX Of course, I'm an artist!

ANNIE I'm not talking about humanity at large. I'm talking about specific individuals like the idiot Pane family.

FELIX They'll get theirs. Besides, I've got more important things on my mind.

ANNIE More important! What's more important than Rembrandt's education?

FELIX What's Rembrandt got to do with this?

ANNIE Just everything, that's all.

FELIX Well, what?

ANNIE Well, everything!

FELIX Oh, that's a beautiful answer.

ANNIE Twenty years ago Mr. Pane's father—the one who made the family fortune—promised Alma he would take care of my education.

FELIX Well?

ANNIE Well, he lied; that's what.

FELIX How?

ANNIE Felix, you amaze me. Sometimes you really amaze me. I finished high school, that's all. And he didn't have to pay for that.

FELIX So, what's the problem? (*He begins sketching.*)

ANNIE I'm beginning to think you are. He promised my mother he would send me to the University. He didn't.

FELIX He died, so how could he?

ANNIE That's no excuse! It was in his will, but they got around it.

FELIX You can't fight City Hall. Anyway, I went to college for two years and, Baby, let me tell you, I was never so bored in all my life. It's a false life.

ANNIE And being a chauffeur and handyman is real true life adventure.

FELIX (*indignant.*) I'm an artist! Whatever I do, I do for my family and my art. I don't apologize and I'm not ashamed.

ANNIE What about Rembrandt? Will he be a chauffeur, too?

FELIX He can be President, if he wants to.

ANNIE President of the poor house? Mr. Pane promised Alma he would take care of Rembrandt's education.

FELIX Oh?

ANNIE   He hasn't said anything about it in quite a while.

FELIX   I'll take care of my son's education.

ANNIE   All I want is what's been promised. That's the only reason I'm staying here. When you give a lifetime to someone, they have an obligation. I intend to see that he keeps it.

FELIX   Dear Annie-girl, I love you.

ANNIE   (*puts the coffee on the fire.*)   What do you mean by that?

FELIX   It means you're my naive girl, and I love you for it.

ANNIE   Felix, we just buried Momma today. And you shouldn't be drinking; you know how you begin seeing things when you drink.

FELIX   Haven't had a drop. Just that beer. And I don't see things that aren't there inside—even if they aren't there outside.

ANNIE   Then why are you calling me a nitwit?

FELIX   You're a trusting soul, not a nitwit.

ANNIE   I don't even trust myself.

FELIX   Oh, but you trusted Providence and *he done you wrong.*

ANNIE   You are drunk, Felix.

FELIX   Drunk with insight, perhaps. You must see, Baby, that Mr. Avery Pane has no intention of sending Rembrandt to college. Nor has he ever had.

ANNIE   He promised.

FELIX   To keep the help in good spirits.

ANNIE   You have to have more faith in people, Felix; it may help your painting.

FELIX   What's wrong with my painting?

ANNIE   They're not selling. (*Taking down a cup and saucer.*)

FELIX   Which reflects on the public taste, not my work.

ANNIE   Which is why I want Rembrandt' to go to college.

FELIX   And be what?

ANNIE   A gentleman, among other things. And if he drives a car, I want it to be his own.

FELIX   I have transportation of my own.

ANNIE   A scooter? You call that transportation?

FELIX   I own my scooter. If I had a car it would own me! That's what life is all about—freedom!

ANNIE   Well, I don't want to be free. I want a big house with lots of rooms. I want two cars, one just for shopping. I want to travel and see the great sights of the world! I want luxurious slavery!

FELIX   Are you sure *you* haven't been drinking?

ANNIE   And I want the world for Rembrandt, and a piece of it for you, too.

FELIX   I'll settle for a cup of coffee.

ANNIE   And we'll go to Brazil where coffee comes from.

FELIX   Why not Heaven where such dreams come from?

ANNIE   Not Heaven, Felix, this house. My dreams come from this house.

FELIX   Just don't be disappointed.

ANNIE   (*laughing.*)   Look on the good side, darling.

FELIX   Which is?

ANNIE   We have a home as long as the nitwits live. (*They laugh.*)

FELIX   You're crazy.

ANNIE   Of course, it's charity of a kind. (*She kisses the mouth of the cup as she gives him a cup of coffee.*)

REMBRANDT *comes back in.*

FELIX   Not at all.

ANNIE   There's a kiss on the cup. (*He kisses the cup.*)

REMBRANDT (*reaching for the cup.*)   Can I have the kiss, Dad?

ANNIE   That one's for your father. Come here my Little Tit. (*He rushes into her arms and she kisses him.*) There!

FELIX   Why do you call him that?

ANNIE   What?

FELIX   You know damn well what. Little Tit.

ANNIE   Because he *is* my little tit. Aren't you my little tit, Baby?

REMBRANDT   Yes. (*They hug.*)

FELIX   You're going to give him all kinds of complexes with
that kind of talk.

ANNIE   He's mother's little helper, aren't you?

REMBRANDT   Yes.

ANNIE   And you're no bigger than a little tit, are you, Hon?

REMBRANDT   No.

FELIX   With a nickname like that he'll never belong to a gang.

ANNIE   Then he'll be a one-man gang. He's going to be somebody. A man of substance; a man apart.

FELIX   Only part man if you don't stop kissing him.

ANNIE   He'll be okay. One in a million. I'll see to that, just
as soon as Mr. Pane keeps his promise.

REMBRANDT   Momma?

ANNIE   (*pours herself a cup of coffee.*)   Yes.

REMBRANDT   I threw a kiss to Grandma.

FELIX *frowns.*

ANNIE   That was nice, Baby.

REMBRANDT   Do you think she'll get it?

ANNIE   Yes, Baby, she'll get it.

AVERY *and* ANTHONY *return to the living room. The servants
can still be seen in the kitchen but not heard. The conversation shifts from area to area.*

AVERY   (*looking around.*)   Now look what we've done. We
let Annie down when she needed us.

ANTHONY   Oh, Dad, you don't really care about Annie.

AVERY   You think it's easy getting good help?

ANTHONY   I've got more important things to think about.

AVERY   Those silly experiments of yours?

ANTHONY   They work.

AVERY   So does Annie, and much more efficiently.

ANTHONY   How can you compare a domestic with *my* work?

AVERY   I'd much rather live without your work. Your work
may kill us all sooner or later.

ANTHONY   So might Annie's cooking.

91

AVERY   Nonsense! The girl's a born cook.

ANTHONY   And I'm a born scientist!

AVERY   You should be spending your time on company business.

ANTHONY   This will eventually add a new dimension to our business.

AVERY   Yes, oblivion!

ANTHONY   You're living in the past, Dad. You worry about trivial matters such as servants, tradition, conservatism . . .

AVERY   The things that built this nation.

ANTHONY   And now hold it back.

AVERY   And your transistor bombs are the answer?

ANTHONY   Just another link in the chain of progress.

AVERY   The only link I'm concerned about right now is keeping Annie happy.

ANTHONY   All right, I'll smile along with the rest of you.

AVERY   Good, good! You'll see that just a little smile goes a long way.

ANTHONY   And we'll all live happily ever after.

He goes out and AVERY *begins reading the paper as the scene shifts back to the kitchen.*

ANNIE   (*to* REMBRANDT.)   Go get some fresh air. Go on now, scoot. (*Sipping her coffee, she speaks to* FELIX.) Sometimes I think my mother was a nut.

FELIX   Why? (*Still painting as* REMBRANDT *goes up the back stairs.*)

ANNIE   A sweet nut, mind you. How can anyone spend forty years in somebody else's kitchen?

FELIX   Ask me in forty years.

ANNIE   Not me, Baby, not me. Not unless it was *my* kitchen.

FELIX   Now there's a happy thought. Wait until Christmas and ask Santa Claus.

ANNIE   Heaven helps those who help themselves.

FELIX   Not if you're an artist. It's not enough to know your work is good. You need someone well-thought-of to discover you.

ANNIE   Felix, I don't like to butt in, but . . .

FELIX   Go ahead! You might as well be an art critic, too!

ANNIE   All I know is what I like.

FELIX   And you don't like my work; is that it?

ANNIE   (*going behind him.*)   I don't understand it.

FELIX   You have to look at it with more than just your eyes. Look with your mind and your imagination.

ANNIE   (*looking at the painting.*)   All I see is a dead ant.

FELIX   That's all you see?

ANNIE   You keep telling me that I should see the history of the world through the insides of a dead ant, but all I see is a dead ant! That's all, Baby.

FELIX   The ant is not dead.

ANNIE   He looks dead to me.

FELIX   He's not dead!

ANNIE   With all those people and machinery coming out of his stomach?

FELIX   The ant is a symbol of eternity. Stronger and more durable than man and time itself!

ANNIE   You sure he's not just another dead ant?

FELIX   (*exasperated.*)   Didn't you hear what I said?

ANNIE   (*hugs him.*)   Darling, if the ants are going to take over the earth again, I won't have to worry about Mr. Pane.

FELIX   That's right. Everybody goes!

ANNIE   But all that may be years. (*She walks away.*)

FELIX   The ants are in no hurry.

ANNIE   But I am.

REMBRANDT *comes back carrying a skateboard.*

REMBRANDT   Can I go out and ride my skateboard a while?

ANNIE   (*holds out her arms.*)   Come here, Little Tit.

FELIX   (*shakes his head.*)   Don't be too long, Son, we may go to a movie later.

ANNIE (*hugging him.*) Here's a kiss for you and one for your skateboard. When you come back, you can help Momma fix lunch.

REMBRANDT See you. (*He runs out.*)

ANNIE There goes my little man.

FELIX Your little tit, huh?

ANNIE That's right, and no cracks.

FELIX I didn't say anything. Not a word.

ANNIE You really think your son is becoming a sissy?

FELIX No! Not yet, anyway.

ANNIE You're a big help.

FELIX Actually, it might be fun to be a woman.

ANNIE Oh?

FELIX Yeah. People should be able to have both experiences—male and female.

ANNIE You've got an artist's mind all right.

FELIX It would be the only way to get the total experience of life! It might even help with my painting.

ANNIE What would you do?

FELIX Hmmm . . . (*He laughs.*)

ANNIE No, seriously?

FELIX Well . . .

ANNIE Yes?

FELIX I'd probably be beautiful. (*He smiles knowingly.*)

ANNIE Naturally.

FELIX Sexy as hell!

ANNIE Of course.

FELIX You know my type—all fire.

ANNIE Yes.

FELIX (*holding his hands to his chest.*) I'd have two great big—you know the kind I mean—pointing straight up like the horns of a bull, and tearing my blouse away whenever I got excited.

ANNIE (*sarcastically.*) I ruin more blouses that way.

FELIX I'd have a round tail—not too big. Some women look

94

like they have basketballs in their back pockets. Not me!
I'd be volleyball size.

ANNIE   All right, so now you're a perfect creature.

FELIX   Yeah. (*He chuckles.*)

ANNIE   So what?

FELIX   What do you mean, so what?

ANNIE   What would you do with all that loveliness?

FELIX   Hmmm. (*He chuckles.*)

ANNIE   That supposed to mean something?

FELIX   You really want to know?

ANNIE   If you don't mind, *Miss.*

FELIX   Well, I'd stay in bed until twelve . . .

ANNIE   And?

FELIX   And get to know myself; being such a doll and all.

ANNIE   You have got a nasty mind!

FELIX   I'm an artist!

ANNIE   What has this to do with art?

FELIX   How can I paint female emotions unless I experience
them? All I want to do is basic research.

ANNIE   And I thought I had the only problem.

FELIX   Aw, it's silly talking about it.

ANNIE   Yes. (*She goes to the door leading to the living room.*)

FELIX   Too bad, though. I could have had fun.

ANNIE   You're having fun just thinking about it. (*She peeks
through.*)

FELIX   Yep! (*He smiles.*) It's a pleasant thought.

ANNIE   He's all alone now, Felix.

FELIX   Who?

ANNIE   Mr. Pane.

FELIX   So?

ANNIE   Now's my chance to talk to him.

FELIX   You're not really?

ANNIE   I've got to know. He promised and he's got to keep
his promise.

FELIX   He'll only lie to you if he answers you at all.

ANNIE What should I do?

FELIX Forget about it. We'll manage. (*He gets up.*)

ANNIE What's right is right, and he promised.

FELIX Go on, go on out there and get embarrassed. I'm going up to change clothes. (*He starts toward the back stairs.*)

ANNIE Just don't put on one of my dresses.

FELIX *frowns at her and goes out. She takes a deep breath and walks into the other room.*

AVERY (*looking up.*) There you are, Annie. How are you, girl?

ANNIE Fine, sir.

AVERY Good, good! Glad to see you taking things so well. Sign of good character. Not enough of that in the world these days. People not strong-willed like they used to be. Can't take a little jolt and bounce back. Go all to pieces over nothing. Not that your loss was a small one by any means. Believe me, girl, we all share in your loss, and that's the plain truth.

ANNIE Thank you, sir.

AVERY Oh, don't think I don't know about death. The last war was hell! Made forty-seven jumps. 17th Airborne. Paratroopers, you know. Yeah, saw my share of death. I was lucky. Not one scratch. Imagine that, not one scratch in forty-seven jumps!

ANNIE Amazing, sir.

AVERY After that I discovered mountain climbing. I was good. Sure-footed as a mountain goat. Balance and strength of purpose—an unbeatable combination! (*He rubs his chest.*) An imperfection of the body stopped me. Heart condition.

ANNIE Sorry to hear that.

AVERY Don't know what good the heart is anyway.

ANNIE May I speak to you, sir?

AVERY Why you just go ahead.

ANNIE (*hesitant.*) It's about Rembrandt.

AVERY Great little fella. Just great! You ought to be proud of him, Annie.

ANNIE I am, sir, very.

AVERY Good! Our future depends on our children.

ANNIE (*quickly.*) I'm glad you feel that way, sir. That's what I want to talk to you about—Rembrandt's future.

AVERY His future's assured.

ANNIE Sir?

AVERY Sure it is! Right here in this house with you, Felix, and the rest of us. He's got a roof as long as he wants it.

ANNIE I was thinking more of his education.

AVERY Now we won't worry about that just yet.

ANNIE But we should start early.

AVERY There's no rush, girl! Besides, didn't I promise I'd take care of him? Just as if he was a member of my own family. Why, he's in for a share of everything when we go.

ANNIE I want to do what's right for Rembrandt.

AVERY Sure you do.

ANNIE I want him to go to college.

AVERY We'll see when the time comes. Life can be awfully exciting without college. It can't compare with climbing a mountain. Believe me, I've had both. Now I can hardly climb the stairs. (*He goes to the alcove.*)

ANNIE I'm sorry about that, sir.

AVERY Huh?

ANNIE About your weak heart.

AVERY I'll live to be a hundred if I stay off mountains. (*He goes out.*)

ANNIE (*after a pause.*) Dear Annie-girl, what you need right now is a mountain! (*She sings as she walks into the kitchen.*) "Gonna build a mountain, gonna build it high. . . ."

Both scenes black out.

Scene 2

Later that night. As the light comes on ANNIE *enters the kitchen, wearing a robe. She goes to the table and takes up* REMBRANDT's *skateboard, holds it up and spins the wheels. She plants a kiss on the skateboard. She walks into the darkened living room. She can be heard climbing the stairs. She returns and hurries back into the kitchen. She opens the side door. As she busies herself she sings "Gonna build a mountain." Then she goes to the intercom house phone; she presses one of the buttons and waits. She presses it again and again until a voice comes over the speaker.*

AVERY What is it?

ANNIE (*answering excitedly.*) It's me, sir, there's something wrong in the kitchen.

AVERY Where's Felix?

ANNIE I can't wake him, sir! You'd better come quick!

AVERY (*mumbling.*) Middle of the night! Can't even sleep in this house any more.

ANNIE Please, sir!

AVERY I'm coming! Keep your pants on.

ANNIE *shuts the intercom off and smiles as she sings again. She goes to the door and waits. After a moment she hears a loud yell and the crash of a body falling down the stairs. She rushes across the living room. After a moment she returns carrying the skateboard, which she places back on the table. She closes the outside door. The intercom board begins to flash and buzz from all the rooms. She kisses the skateboard and hums as she goes up the back stairs. The lights black out, except for the flashing intercom board.*

Scene 3

Three days later. All are sitting in the living room, wearing black, exactly as they were in the former funeral scene. Except now AVERY *stands in the center picture frame;* ANTHONY *is in* AVERY'S *former place; and* ANNIE *is placing lemonade on a tray in the kitchen.*

ANTHONY (*pacing.*) Beautiful ceremony. Just beautiful!

ISOBEL Avery would have appreciated that eulogy.

ANTHONY People say such nice things about you when you're gone. Things they should say when you're around to hear them.

GINGER Poor old Avery.

HENRY I'm hungry.

They ignore him.

ANTHONY Seems like only yesterday Dad was heading out for one of the big mountains.

FELIX He sure could climb.

ANNIE *brings the tray in.*

HENRY Yeah.

ANTHONY (*walking over behind* HENRY'S *chair.*) He was more to us than a father. He was a pal.

HENRY A buddy.

ANNIE *passes the drinks around.*

ISOBEL He was sweet.

GINGER Like a father to me. Practically raised me from a pup.

ANTHONY All of us.

HENRY Yeah.

GINGER We'll miss him.

ISOBEL Yes.

ANNIE He was a dear.

FELIX Yes.

ISOBEL   He was sweet.

ANTHONY   We'll miss his strength.

ISOBEL   Did you know that in forty years of marriage, we never separated; not even for a day.

ANTHONY   Dad loved you very much.

GINGER   He was a dear.

ISOBEL   He was so sweet.

ANNIE   We'll miss his strength.

ANTHONY   Yes, we will.

HENRY   I'm hungry.

GINGER   Knock it off!

HENRY   What's with you?

ANTHONY   Dad wouldn't want us to be bickering among ourselves today.

HENRY   What did I say? All I said was that——

ANTHONY   All right! All right!

HENRY   Funerals make me hungry.

GINGER   I married a stomach.

ANTHONY   (*sadly.*) He must have climbed up and down those stairs more than a million times.

FELIX   Easily that, sir.

ANTHONY   Yeah, more than a million. Now the old mountain climber is gone. What was it they used to call him? . . . (*He thinks.*)

ANNIE   Sure-foot, sir. Old Sure-foot!

ISOBEL   Yes, I remember that name.

ANNIE   Balance and strength of purpose.

ANTHONY   That's what he used to say! Balance and strength of purpose!

ANNIE   Forty-seven jumps and not a scratch.

GINGER   He's climbed his last mountain.

HENRY   And made the big jump.

ISOBEL   After forty years of marriage. I'll miss him. (*She gets up.*)

ANTHONY   Where are you going, Mother?

ISOBEL   I think I'll take a warm bath. It's sticky today.

ANNIE   (*getting up.*) If I may?

ANTHONY   Yes, Annie.

ANNIE   I want the family to know that you have our deepest sympathy.

ANTHONY   Thank you, Annie.

GINGER   That's sweet.

ISOBEL   You're a dear. (*She goes out.*)

HENRY   You going to fix lunch, Annie?

ANNIE   Right away, sir.

HENRY   (*to* REMBRANDT.)   And you're going to help her, aren't you?

REMBRANDT   Yes.

HENRY   That's a good boy.

ANNIE   He's mother's little helper.

GINGER   That's sweet.

FELIX *goes into the kitchen.*

ANNIE   I'll get lunch started now. (*She and* REMBRANDT *start for the kitchen.*)

ANTHONY   Oh, Annie, ask Felix to get the car out again. I have to go to town.

ANNIE   Yes, sir.

She goes into the kitchen. REMBRANDT *goes up the back stairs.*

HENRY   I'm going to change clothes. After lunch I think I'll take my boat out for a while.

GINGER   I'll go with you.

HENRY   Can't I even brush my teeth without you holding the brush?

GINGER   Oh, come on, silly.

They go out.

ANTHONY *pulls a small gadget from his pocket. He sits down and begins examining it.*

FELIX *is pouring himself a glass of lemonade in the kitchen.*

Tom Harris · *Always with Love*

ANNIE Did you see the flowers he got?

FELIX He didn't have to pay for them.

ANNIE I've never seen so many flowers!

FELIX Neither did he.

ANNIE And did you read the cards?

FELIX I gave some of them a peek.

ANNIE There must be over five hundred telegrams in the hall-way. I saw one from that famous lady writer.

FELIX Who?

ANNIE You know, the one who writes dirty books, and knocks everybody in that gossip column.

FELIX Her? I always thought she hated him because he fired her from his magazine years ago.

ANNIE Her telegram said, "Get well quick."

FELIX Oh, that's better.

ANNIE Did you know that the President sent a wire? I didn't know they were friends.

FELIX He's called here many times.

ANNIE Yeah, but on official business. His telegram sounded very friendly.

FELIX He couldn't very well write him a poison-pen letter at a time like this.

ANNIE Can you imagine, all of his factories and office buildings all across the country are closed today in his honor!

FELIX They're probably happy to get the day off.

ANNIE To be able to do that; that's power—that's money! He's on the front page of every newspaper in the world. That's importance! Oh, Felix, I tell you, that man was well liked. They'll probably fly the flag at half-mast.

FELIX (*pours himself another glass of lemonade.*) I wish I had something to make me fly at half-mast.

ANNIE Don't drink too much of that.

FELIX Why, is it poisoned?

ANNIE (*looks shocked.*) What do you mean?

FELIX What are you looking so serious about? It was just a joke.

ANNIE   You shouldn't joke like that. I only meant it's hot today.

FELIX   So?

ANNIE   So you could get cramps. (*She begins preparing lunch.*)

FELIX   I've already got cramps. I've been bending over too many caskets lately. I feel like Boris Karloff.

ANNIE   Shame on you, Felix. You shouldn't joke about a thing like that.

FELIX   Funny about that accident.

ANNIE (*stopping.*)   What?

FELIX   That old man never got up in the middle of the night before. Not for anything.

ANNIE   Maybe he couldn't sleep. His conscience.

FELIX   It's true he had his share of sins, but he never lost any any sleep over them.

ANNIE   They just finally caught up with him. (*She goes back to preparing lunch.*)

FELIX   Well, something caught up with him.

ANNIE   Something?

FELIX   It just wasn't like him to dive down those stairs like that.

ANNIE   It's not like any of us to die. It's just not in character.

FELIX   He was a paratrooper—a mountain climber.

ANNIE   He was a liar.

FELIX   What do you mean, a liar?

ANNIE   He didn't keep his promise.

FELIX   Well, being a liar never killed anybody.

ANNIE   I guess not.

FELIX   'Course not, or else nine-tenths of the world would be dead. The whole Pane family for sure.

ANNIE   Whatever you say, Felix. Mr. Anthony wants the car again.

FELIX   I can't understand why that light wasn't working at the top of the stairs.

ANNIE   The bulb burned out.

FELIX   But I thought I'd changed it just a couple of days ago.

ANNIE   I wouldn't worry about it, Hon. The family seems satisfied.

FELIX   Overjoyed is more like it. It means millions for all of them. Well, we got our share.

ANNIE   Five thousand dollars! You call that a share!

FELIX   It's more than we had yesterday.

ANNIE   Not enough for forty years. It's not enough for Rembrandt's education. Yes, it's more than we had yesterday, but I'm thinking about tomorrow.

FELIX   Who knows, maybe somebody else around here will kick off and leave us a bundle.

ANNIE   *I wouldn't be surprised.* You'd better get the car now.

FELIX   Yeah. I'll get the hearse out. (*He gets up.*)

ANNIE (*softly.*)   Felix?

FELIX   Yes.

ANNIE   Nothing.

FELIX   Okay. (*He starts to go out.*)

ANNIE   Felix?

FELIX (*goes to her.*)   Yes, Baby.

ANNIE   Suppose . . .

FELIX   Yes.

ANNIE   Suppose you were to discover that I'm not really me at all?

FELIX   Who would you be?

ANNIE   Somebody else—anybody else! What would you do?

FELIX   I'd probably ask you who you were. Then I'd get to know you all over again. Remember, I turned into a sexy broad.

ANNIE   That's not what I mean.

FELIX   Well, clear the line. What do you mean? (*He hugs her.*)

ANNIE   It's not important.

FELIX   Are you sure?

ANNIE   Here's a kiss to drive on. (*She kisses him.*)

FELIX   That's only one way. I'll need something to get back on.

They kiss again.

ANNIE   Drive carefully. I wouldn't want anything to happen to you.

FELIX   See you later. (*He goes out.*)

ANTHONY *starts for the kitchen.*

ANNIE   Well, Annie-girl, one down.

ANTHONY (*coming into kitchen.*)   Oh, Annie, don't bother fixing lunch for me.

ANNIE   All right, sir.

ANTHONY   I'll get a bite downtown.

ANNIE   Felix is getting the car.

ANTHONY   Good. (*He starts out.*)

ANNIE (*motions to the gadget he carries.*)   Is that one of them, sir?

ANTHONY (*proudly.*)   Yes, it is. (*He holds it up.*)

ANNIE   Why, it's no bigger than a book of matches.

ANTHONY   That's the beauty of it. No bigger than a book of matches, but very deadly! No problem to conceal. Imagine the importance of these in time of war.

ANNIE   Or any emergency.

ANTHONY   Exactly.

ANNIE   You could plant those anywhere.

ANTHONY   Under a bridge, in a large gun, in factory machinery . . .

ANNIE   Under a pillow?

ANTHONY   Yes, even under an enemy's pillow. It's that sensitive.

ANNIE   Is it really?

ANTHONY (*showing her.*)   You see this button?

ANNIE (*very attentive.*)   Yes.

ANTHONY   Once you push this button down, it is activated.

ANNIE   I see.

ANTHONY   Then the slightest pressure on this disk on top and this room would be just a memory.

ANNIE   Oh, how wonderful!

ANTHONY (*takes a metal cap out of his pocket.*)   Of course, it won't function without this firing cap. It inserts in this little hole here. (*He shows her.*)

ANNIE   Then it's complete?

ANTHONY   Then it's complete.

ANNIE   You do have a fine mind, sir.

ANTHONY   Thank you.

ANNIE   That's the most amazing thing I've ever seen. Is this the only one you have?

ANTHONY   I've got several in my workshop. The Army is going to test this one today. I'm sorry it has to be on the day of Father's funeral.

ANNIE   Wherever he is, I'm sure he's very proud of you.

ANTHONY   It's a nice thought, anyway.

ANNIE   The whole family should be proud of you. You've discovered a sneaky way to kill millions of people.

ANTHONY   I wouldn't put it exactly that way.

ANNIE   I didn't mean that you were sneaky, sir. It's just that sneaky people always win the wars.

ANTHONY   Why do you say that?

ANNIE   Did David fight Goliath fair? He didn't! He used a sneaky slingshot. Goliath didn't have a chance. And those Greeks, with that sneaky Trojan-horse bit. After that the Trojans weren't in the race.

ANTHONY   That's not the same thing.

ANNIE   Perhaps not.

ANTHONY   You surprise me, Annie.

ANNIE   How, sir?

GINGER *comes into the living room. She has changed clothes.*

ANTHONY   I had no idea you thought about such things.

ANNIE   I try to keep up.

GINGER (*comes into kitchen.*)   Am I intruding?

ANTHONY   Don't you always?

GINGER   Of course.

ANTHONY   I'll be home for dinner, Annie.

ANNIE   Yes, sir.

ANTHONY (*touching* GINGER's *colorful dress.*)   Is this the color of your grief?

GINGER   Black doesn't become me.

ANTHONY   Green is more to your liking?

GINGER   At times.

ANTHONY   I was referring to money green.

GINGER   My favorite color.

ANTHONY *goes out.*

ANNIE   Was there something I could get for you?

GINGER (*absentmindedly.*)   Yeah, a new life.

ANNIE   Excuse me?

GINGER (*snapping out of it.*)   What I need is a new life—new skills. My husband is all stomach, so I have to cope with that stomach. He'll be the master of this family eventually, and I don't intend being left at the starting gate. Where he goes, I go.

ANNIE   He's a lucky man to be so loved.

GINGER (*coughing lightly.*)   He's a pig! But, he's a rich pig. And don't worry, he knows what I think of him. Now, I need a cookbook.

ANNIE   Yes, right here. (*She gets the book.*)

GINGER (*looking through it.*)   These scrawls are your additions to the recipes?

ANNIE   Yes.

GINGER   You have an awful handwriting. I'll try to make out. Now, listen carefully, girl——

ANNIE   Yes.

GINGER   ——I want to know all there is to know about my husband's favorite dishes. In the beginning, you'll prepare them. After a while, I'll take over. I'll take this book and study it.

ANNIE   All right.

GINGER   One thing more.

ANNIE   Yes?

GINGER   We're spending the day together on the boat Saturday. We'll need a complete lunch.

ANNIE   Very well.

GINGER   I promised him a cherry pie made with my own little hands. Of course you'll make it and say I did.

ANNIE Of course.

REMBRANDT *comes in carrying his skateboard.*

GINGER We understand each other then.

ANNIE Clearly.

GINGER You'll get right on with lunch. (*She points to* REMBRANDT.) And you, young man.

REMBRANDT Yes, ma'am.

GINGER You'll help your mother, won't you?

ANNIE He'll help me. He always does.

GINGER Can you skateboard?

REMBRANDT Not very well.

GINGER I wouldn't worry about it. Skating always seems a waste of time. What good are skateboards, anyway?

ANNIE *They have their uses.*

GINGER Well, don't disappoint me. (*She goes out.*)

ANNIE (*looking away.*) You won't be disappointed, I promise you that. (*She whirls and holding out her arms to* REMBRANDT.) Come here, my Little Tit! (*He runs into her arms.*) Ho! How's my Little Tit?

REMBRANDT I left a kiss for you upstairs.

ANNIE (*kneels down to him.*) Thank you, my big man! I promised you that I would take care of your future, and I will. Are you my Little Tit?

REMBRANDT Yes.

ANNIE Are you mother's little helper?

REMBRANDT Yes.

ANNIE Then we've got work to do. We'll fix lunch.

REMBRANDT (*pulling away.*) I'll help.

ANNIE Saturday we'll make a cherry pie for that sweet lady and the stomach she married. I guarantee you they'll get a great big bang out of this one! (*Jumping up.*) To work!

They dance around and sing as they gather up pots and pans. They sing: "Shall we bake a cherry pie, Billy Boy, Billy Boy, Shall we bake a cherry pie, Charming Annie?"

Lights fade.

Scene 4

The lights come up on the same set; it is Saturday morning. The Pane family is having breakfast in the dining area while ANNIE, FELIX, *and* REMBRANDT *are having their breakfast at the kitchen table.* ANNIE *serves both parties.*

HENRY I've been thinking.

GINGER Hmmm.

HENRY *frowns at her.*

ISOBEL What about, dear?

HENRY About a trip around the world.

ANTHONY What?

HENRY I've had my boat for eight years now.

ANTHONY So?

HENRY I'm a pretty good sailor.

ISOBEL It's rather small, dear.

HENRY Much bigger than the *Kon Tiki.*

GINGER That was a raft.

HENRY Raft, canoe—what difference? I'm getting bored hanging around here.

ANTHONY Forget it!

HENRY Just like that?

ANTHONY With Dad gone we're both needed here in the business.

ISOBEL Poor dear. Poor dead dear.

HENRY I don't care anything about the business. I'm a romantic. I'm a nature lover, a free soul searching for the meaning of life.

GINGER Pie in the sky?

ISOBEL Don't tease him, dear.

The women smile at each other.

ANTHONY I'll take my pie right here and so will you if it comes to that.

GINGER   Which reminds me.

ISOBEL   Yes, dear?

GINGER   I baked a pie for Henry this morning.

HENRY   Oh, no.

ISOBEL   Did you really?

GINGER   With my own little hands.

ANTHONY   Something new for you, isn't it?

GINGER   I've decided to take a greater interest in my Henry.

ISOBEL   Sweet.

HENRY   Clammy is the word.

GINGER   We're taking the boat out. It'll be our first picnic.

ISOBEL   At least out there on the boat you won't have to worry about the ants spoiling your lunch.

GINGER   Nothing will spoil my first lunch for Henry.

HENRY   Except the lunch itself.

In the kitchen.

ANNIE   How would you like a trip around the world?

FELIX   You know any more jokes?

ANNIE   I'm serious.

FELIX   Pass the cream.

REMBRANDT   (*passing cream.*)   Here, Dad.

ANNIE   I've been thinking, Felix. About your painting.

REMBRANDT   Are you going to paint us tickets for the movies today?

FELIX   Maybe later, Rem.

ANNIE   That's what I mean!

FELIX   What?

ANNIE   Prostituting your talent that way. Making counterfeit passes to the movies.

FELIX   That doesn't mean anything. I just did it as an experiment.

ANNIE   But that's dishonest. It's also embarrassing.

FELIX   We've only been caught once. I had the wrong day and the wrong color tickets.

REMBRANDT (*laughs.*)   I remember that time.

ANNIE   I'll never forget it.

REMBRANDT   They threw us out, huh? Remember?

FELIX *laughs.*

ANNIE   That's not funny!

HENRY *jingles the bell on the table.*

FELIX   It is now.

ANNIE (*taking the coffee into the next room.*)   More coffee, sir?

HENRY   You're a mind reader, Annie.

ANNIE (*pouring.*)   Not really, sir.

HENRY   You know what we want by instinct every time.

ANTHONY   With you that's not very difficult.

ISOBEL   May I have a cup, dear?

ANNIE *goes to her and pours.*

HENRY   I don't pretend to enjoy food, I do enjoy it. And Annie, your food is the best.

ANNIE   Thank you, sir.

GINGER   Wait until you taste my cherry pie.

HENRY   I can hardly wait.

ANNIE *goes back to the kitchen.*

FELIX   You said something about my painting.

ANNIE   It's different and . . .

FELIX   And?

ANNIE   And being different it may require a different setting. Perhaps Paris.

FELIX   Paris?

ANNIE   Why not? It's the home of . . . different art and artists. Who knows, you might find your style there.

FELIX (*thoughtful.*)   I've always wanted to go to Paris.

ANNIE   You'd have a whole new audience and probably a more appreciative one.

FELIX That makes sense.

ANNIE And I could have my own chateau and give elegant parties.

FELIX I wouldn't have to drive a car any more.

ANNIE We'd have our own chauffeur.

FELIX Oh, what the hell are we talking about?

ANNIE About going around the world.

FELIX We can't even afford to go around the block!

ANNIE I have a feeling we can.

FELIX What kind of a feeling?

ANNIE Oh, just a feeling of pennies from Heaven.

FELIX Can you also predict the weather by the pain in your feet?

ANNIE No, but I can look into the near future.

FELIX And what do you see?

ANNIE I see us all in Paris. We're dancing on top of the world.

REMBRANDT Do I have a bicycle?

ANNIE (*shouting.*) Yes, my Little Tit, you have seven. One for each day in the week! And trains, and every toy ever made! And a pony! Would you like a pony?

REMBRANDT A real pony?

ANNIE If he doesn't eat hay, we won't keep him.

REMBRANDT And skateboards?

ANNIE Skateboards? (*She calms down.*) Why not? Skateboards can be very useful. (*She bucks up again.*) Yes, and lots and lots of skateboards. A skateboard for me! A skateboard for Felix! Skateboards for everybody! We'll put all of Paris on skateboards.

FELIX I had a dream about skates once.

ANNIE Yes?

FELIX It was weird.

ANNIE Well?

FELIX In this dream I was stark naked.

ANNIE Naturally.

FELIX   There I was on this big empty highway without a stitch of clothes on.

ANNIE   Really?

FELIX   I was just cruising along as free as a bird in a breeze. (*He demonstrates.*) Just out for my early morning skate.

ANNIE   Naked?

FELIX   The better to skate, my dear. Anyway, it was a beautiful day. The sky had just gotten up, the sun was peeking over the mountains, and the moon had slipped into the ocean for another day. It was some kind of beautiful! And I was sailing along wrapped in all this beautiful glow.

ANNIE   Naked?

FELIX   As the day I was born, but twice as innocent. (*His mood changes.*) Then, all of a sudden a puff of cold air ran over my shoulders! The sky got dark and the road began to rumble.

REMBRANDT (*excited.*)   Yeah!

FELIX   Quickly, I looked over my shoulder, and what did I see?

REMBRANDT   What, what?

FELIX   A great black shadow had blotted out the sun!

REMBRANDT   Really?

FELIX   Then it began moving toward me. Closer and closer it came until I could see it clearly. It was ugly! It was huge! It was mean!

REMBRANDT   What was it?

FELIX   It was a great big, mean, ugly, black grizzly bear!

ANNIE   Did he have his clothes on?

FELIX   He was all covered with hair. Not fur—hair. All of a sudden I knew I was skating for my life! Sparks started leaping from my skates and fire jumped from the bear's mouth as we flew down the highway! (*He lunges.*) He grabbed for me and I jumped out of the way!

REMBRANDT   Did he hit you?

FELIX   Not that time! Then I really started turning on the speed, because the bear was just about to catch me.

113

REMBRANDT How fast?

FELIX So fast my skates got red hot!

REMBRANDT Wow!

FELIX Then the road began to melt, and melt, and melt until it was as soft as jelly. I looked over my shoulder and that old bear was stuck and sinking down, down, down in that tar. Me—I just cruised along on my merry way.

REMBRANDT Then he didn't catch you?

FELIX He tried, but I was a skating fool that morning. (*He shakes his head and starts up the back stairs.*) Well, I've got to do some work in the garden.

ANNIE Hooray! We'll give all the bears skates!

REMBRANDT (*laughing.*) Bear's don't skate, Momma.

ANNIE Then we'll teach them. Oh, my Little Tit, I have a good feeling in my soul! (*She hugs him and they dance around the kitchen.*)

In the other room.

ISOBEL (*jumping up.*) Oh!

ANTHONY What is it?

ISOBEL I don't know.

GINGER Daydreaming again, Mother?

ISOBEL I just had the funniest feeling. (*She begins waltzing in unison with* ANNIE *and* REMBRANDT.)

HENRY How?

ISOBEL (*still waltzing around.*) As if someone was dancing on my grave. Strange feeling.

HENRY Weird. (*He gets up.*)

ISOBEL Maybe Avery is trying to tell me something.

HENRY Well, you listen, old girl, I'm going sailing. (*He goes out.*)

GINGER I'll get the lunch. (*She gets up.*)

ISOBEL I think I'll go out into the garden. It's warm out there.

ANTHONY I'll be in my workshop if you need me.

ISOBEL I'll be all right. (*She goes out through the French doors.*)

ANTHONY *and* GINGER *look around, then they embrace lovingly.*
The scene is played for corn, like a passionate silent movie.

GINGER   Darling!
ANTHONY   Dearest!

They kiss.

GINGER   It's torture pretending to be nasty to you.
ANTHONY   It's horrible not being able to love you openly.
GINGER   He's my husband.
ANTHONY   He's my brother.
GINGER   If only I'd met you first.
ANTHONY   If only you had!
GINGER   Things would be different now.
ANTHONY   Yes, different.
GINGER   I want to be close to you always.
ANTHONY   I couldn't live without you.
GINGER   Please, don't try.
ANTHONY   I won't. I can't!
GINGER   We must be careful.
ANTHONY   Lest they suspect!
GINGER   Darling!
ANTHONY   Dearest!
GINGER   I must go!
ANTHONY   Must you?
GINGER   I must.
ANTHONY   Yes.
GINGER   Reluctantly!
ANTHONY   Yes.
GINGER   Darling!
ANTHONY   Dearest!

They embrace with a flourish.

GINGER   Farewell for now!
ANTHONY   Adieu, my darling!

They back away throwing kisses. He goes off to his shop, she into the kitchen.

ANNIE *is hugging* REMBRANDT.

GINGER   Well, mother and son. A very touching scene.

ANNIE   We're very close, my big man and I.

GINGER   I've come for the lunch basket. Is it ready?

ANNIE   It's ready.

GINGER   Good!

ANNIE *(taking the basket down from the shelf; handling it very carefully.)*   Here it is.

GINGER *(looking inside.)*   Looks good.

ANNIE   Thank you.

GINGER   The pie looks a little lumpy.

ANNIE   Extra large cherries.

GINGER   Oh?

ANNIE   Very special cherries!

GINGER   Wonderful!

ANNIE   Since it is your first pie, I wanted it to be special.

GINGER   Do we need this plastic on it? *(Starts to remove the pie cover.)*

ANNIE *(excited.)*   Yes! It's to keep anything from getting on it until you're ready to eat it.

GINGER   Well, all right. I just hope he likes it.

ANNIE   I can promise you, he'll get a great big bang out of it.

GINGER   If it's that good, I may just eat a piece myself.

ANNIE   Believe me, you won't complain.

GINGER *goes out with the basket.*

REMBRANDT   Why couldn't I have a piece of that cherry pie?

ANNIE   Not that one, darling. It's a little too spicy.

REMBRANDT   Oh.

ANNIE *(coming alive.)*   But I made one especially for my Little Tit! Anyone for cherry pie?

REMBRANDT (*jumps up and down.*) Me, me, me!

ANNIE Then come on, and give me a big wet kiss!

He runs to her as the lights go out.

Scene 5

When the lights come on it is two hours later. ANNIE *is alone, sitting at the kitchen table staring off into space.* FELIX *comes in carrying two small bottles which he places on the table.*

FELIX Penny for your thoughts.

ANNIE What time is it?

FELIX Almost twelve. Why?

ANNIE It's almost lunch time everywhere.

FELIX You don't say.

ANNIE It's lunch time in big houses, little houses, in offices, on trains, on big ships, and even on little boats.

FELIX I believe you.

ANNIE Isn't it a beautiful day?

FELIX I thought so. Now, I'm not so sure.

ANNIE I've been thinking.

FELIX So I gather.

ANNIE I've been thinking about selfishness. Why is everybody so against it?

FELIX Isn't it obvious?

ANNIE I've just discovered how obvious.

FELIX Is anything wrong, Baby?

ANNIE It's lunch time and it's a beautiful day!

FELIX Where does selfishness come in?

ANNIE Because, my darling, being selfish can be wonderful. Who do we accuse of being selfish, and why? I'll tell you.

FELIX Please.

ANNIE We accuse those people who seem to have everything, and why? I'll tell you that, too. It's because we want what they have! I think it might be fun to have everything I want and keep it all for myself. Except for my family, of course.

FELIX   You see, you're not selfish at all.

ANNIE   It takes time to build character.

FELIX   It's just not your nature to be selfish.

ANNIE   "I see," said the blind man. (*She gets up.*)

FELIX   "A little softer," said the deaf man. (*He covers his ears.*)

ANNIE   "Care to dance?" said the momma bear. (*Holds open her arms.*)

FELIX   "My pleasure," said the poppa bear.

They waltz around the room.

ANNIE   Oh, Felix, it is a beautiful day!

FELIX   I feel a little silly.

ANNIE   On such a day? No one should feel silly.

FELIX   Dancing with no music?

ANNIE   But there *is* music! Music all around. Music on the bay and music in the air.

FELIX   "A little loud," said the deaf man.

ANNIE   "I see," said the blind man.

FELIX   Here I am bouncing around when I should be out working in the garden.

They hug as they stop dancing.

ANNIE   All right, Poppa Bear, I'll let you get back to it.

FELIX   On a day like this I should be painting, not digging in a garden.

ANNIE   There'll be other days. (*She looks at the two bottles on the table.*)

FELIX   I won't be young enough to enjoy them.

ANNIE   What's in the bottles? (*She lifts one up.*)

FELIX   Don't touch those!

ANNIE   Why?

FELIX   That's a very deadly acid.

ANNIE   Oh?

FELIX   Nitric mixed with something else Mr. Pane gave me from his shop. It's for the weeds between the cracks in the sidewalk.

118

ANNIE   It looks just like bath salts. Is it really deadly?

FELIX   It can take the flesh right off you in a matter of seconds.

ANNIE   Really?

FELIX   (*takes the bottles.*)   More deadly than a flame thrower.

ANNIE   How odd. It looks just like bath salts.

FELIX   Well, I'm sorry I can't demonstrate its power.

ANNIE   I'll take your word for it, darling.

FELIX   I'll put these away where Rem can't stumble over them.
(*He places them in a bottom cabinet.*) I'll get them out of here
as soon as possible. Where is he, anyway?

ANNIE   He's in the back, reading his storybook. (*She presses
the intercom button.*)

FELIX   It's a lazy day. She's sitting out in the garden watching
those two sail up and down the bay, while I work my tail
off. I'd sure like to change places with them today.

ANNIE   Oh, darling, be thankful for what we have.

FELIX   What happened to Miss Selfish?

REMBRANDT *comes in carrying his book.*

ANNIE   I'll get lunch together.

FELIX   (*looking at his watch.*)   Good, it's two minutes to twelve.

He goes out.

ANNIE   I hope that pie didn't spoil your appetite.

REMBRANDT   (*sits at the table with his book open.*)   Oh, I'm still
hungry.

ANNIE   Any good stories in that book?

REMBRANDT   (*shaking his head.*)   Nope, not really.

ANNIE   I'll tell you one then.

REMBRANDT   An animal story?

ANNIE   A human animal, kinda. It's about a glutton.

REMBRANDT   Is that an animal?

ANNIE   Kinda. There once was this glutton who lived in a
great big house with his own servants. All he did was eat, eat,
and eat. He'd eat anything.

REMBRANDT   Like a goat?

ANNIE Yes, like a goat. He wasn't a very nice goat. He wasn't bad really, but he was just kind of a nuisance and he was in the way. In fact, he was from a family of goats. Not bad goats under normal circumstances, but they had a very rich milk which someone needed to feed her family and her ego.

REMBRANDT The evil witch?

ANNIE No.

REMBRANDT The big bad wolf?

ANNIE A very hungry, but deserving, person. So one day this person, who meant no harm, decided the only way to get the rich milk for her hungry family was to get rid of the selfish goats. (*She pauses.*)

REMBRANDT Go on.

ANNIE She knew the young glutton goat would eat anything, anywhere, and any time. So she made him a special lunch. Then she waited.

REMBRANDT Did he come?

ANNIE Yes, he came.

REMBRANDT Did he eat it?

ANNIE I'm not sure. I figured about noon he would have finished the sandwiches, the salad, the juice, and the celery. Then he would take three sips of his lemonade. He would put the glass down and take out the pie. He would look at it, smile, and lick his lips. He would take up the knife to cut it, but she would insist on doing it herself. She would have the pleasure, as usual.

REMBRANDT Another goat?

ANNIE (*not hearing.*) She would tease him a little by holding the pie up to his nose. Then she would slide the pie around and around, looking for a place to insert the knife. Smiling, she would cut. She would cut lightly at first, to measure it into slices. Then she would cut—deep!

At that instant there is a resounding explosion offstage. The deafening noise startles REMBRANDT. *He jumps.* ANNIE *does not move.*

REMBRANDT   Wow! What was that? (*Turning around.*)
ANNIE (*lightly.*)   The sound of goats giving rich milk.

Lights black out.

Act Two

Scene 1

Morning. Three days later. When the lights come on FELIX,
ISOBEL, *and* ANTHONY *are in the living room. They are again
in their black funeral clothes.* HENRY *and* GINGER *now appear
in their respective picture frames.*

ISOBEL   Poor, poor dears.

ANTHONY   I still can't believe it.

FELIX   Beautiful ceremony. Just beautiful.

ISOBEL   We'll miss them.

ANTHONY   Yes. (*He seems dazed.*)

FELIX   Terrible accident.

ANTHONY   Yes.

ISOBEL'   It happened right before my eyes.

ANTHONY   Yes.

ISOBEL   They came sailing along like a big cloud, sails billow-
ing . . .

ANTHONY   Yes.

ISOBEL   I waved to them, and as I brought my hand down . . .
they went up . . .

ANTHONY   Horrible.

ISOBEL   Poor dears.

ANTHONY   What could have gone wrong?

ISOBEL   All I did was bring my hand down . . .

FELIX   I was pulling out a weed and . . . wham!

ANTHONY   Why? Why *her?*

ISOBEL   Now now, Son, you must try and forget.

ANTHONY   I'll never forget.

ISOBEL   Please excuse us, Felix.

FELIX (*gets up.*)   On behalf of my family——

ISOBEL   We understand.

FELIX   I'll put the hearse up. (*He starts out.*)

ANTHONY (*startled.*)   What?

FELIX (*quickly.*)   The car! I'll put the car up. (*He goes out.*)

ISOBEL   Uncanny.

ANTHONY   What?

ISOBEL   The marvelous loyalty of our help.

ANTHONY (*answers blankly from here on.*)   Yes.

ISOBEL   I don't know what we would do without them.

ANTHONY   Yes.

ISOBEL   Annie taking care of us—one by one . . . as if we were her own family. And Felix demonstrating over and over again the joy of serving us.

ANTHONY   Yes.

ISOBEL   I tell you, dear, we are blessed to have them.

ANTHONY   Yes, Mother.

ISOBEL   Especially this year. This hasn't been a very good year for us.

ANTHONY   No.

ISOBEL   We seem to be disappearing somehow. It's all very strange, and not very encouraging.

ANTHONY   No, Mother.

ISOBEL   Yet, in spite of our shortcomings, our servants have not deserted us.

ANTHONY   No, Mother.

ISOBEL   Now that should prove something.

ANTHONY   Yes, Mother.

ISOBEL   It proves that they love us.

ANTHONY   Yes, Mother.

ISOBEL   Dead or alive, they love us.

ANTHONY   Yes, Mother.

ISOBEL   No matter what happens to us, you must think about that.

ANTHONY   Yes, Mother.

ISOBEL   And take comfort in it.

ANTHONY   Yes, Mother.

ISOBEL   Now you must try and forget. (*As he gets up.*) Where are you going?

ANTHONY   To my room. There is something I must do.

ISOBEL   I'll have Annie bring you some soup.

ANTHONY   Thank you, Mother. Soup will do just fine. (*He starts out.*)

ISOBEL   Just keep this in mind. Somebody out there loves us.

He goes out. ANNIE *comes into the kitchen from the rear as* ISOBEL *comes in.* ANNIE *is wearing her black outfit.*

ANNIE   May I help you?

ISOBEL   Would you take some soup to my son. He's not feeling well.

ANNIE   Oh, I am sorry. I'll take care of it right away.

ISOBEL   Thank you, dear.

ANNIE   You're welcome.

ISOBEL   You can't realize what a comfort your loyalty and thoughtfulness have been.

ANNIE   I'll do whatever I can.

ISOBEL   Your kindness will not go unrewarded.

ANNIE   I'm rewarded more and more every day. Just being here is reward enough.

ISOBEL   Bless you, dear.

ANNIE   Is there anything else I can do for the family?

ISOBEL   Just keep doing what you're doing, dear. . . . It means so much to us.

ANNIE   You can count on it.

ISOBEL   Thank you, Alma. (*She starts out.*)

ANNIE   Annie, it's Annie.

ISOBEL   Yes, dear, I know, I know. (*She goes out, crosses the living room and to the stairs.*)

FELIX *comes in from the outside and finds* ANNIE *busy preparing soup.*

FELIX Anything wrong?

ANNIE Mr. Anthony is ill. (*She opens a package and pours it into a pot.*)

FELIX He did seem a little subdued.

ANNIE I'm making some soup for him. (*She puts the pot on the stove.*)

FELIX What he needs is a rabbit's foot.

ANNIE Why? (*She takes down a bowl, plate, and tray.*)

FELIX He needs all the luck he can get.

ANNIE Don't worry, *nothing* will happen to *him.*

FELIX Oh, you know that, do you?

ANNIE I think *he's quite safe.*

FELIX Well, I think he ought to sleep in a casket. That way he'll be ready for anything! Talk about bad luck! That family should live in a graveyard.

ANNIE Oh, Felix!

FELIX I tell you, I've been to more funerals than the Holy Bible. I've spent more time in the graveyard than I have in the bathroom.

ANNIE I know, Baby, but it just couldn't be helped.

FELIX What couldn't be helped?

ANNIE Why the family misfortune.

FELIX And you thought they were very lucky because they were rich.

ANNIE (*takes down crackers.*) I still do.

FELIX After everything that has happened to them?

ANNIE Especially after everything.

FELIX I don't understand you.

ANNIE I *hope* not. (*She pours the soup into the bowl.*)

FELIX Ask a silly question.

ANNIE Anyway, I feel a certain friendship for *this* Mr. Pane. He's the only one who ever treated us very friendly. (*She picks up the tray.*)

FELIX   I wonder if he's next off to the happy hunting grounds.
ANNIE   I have a feeling he'll survive. He's nice.

As ANNIE *walks through the living room carrying the tray she hums "Poor People of Paris." Lights dim out as* ANNIE *goes out.*

Blackout.

Scene 2

When the lights come on it is one week later. We find ANNIE, FELIX, *and* ISOBEL *in the living room. There is a man standing in the living room talking to them. He is a police lieutenant.* ANTHONY *is now in his picture frame.*

OFFICER CLARK   And you say, Mrs. Jones, you were the only one to handle the soup from the time it was taken out of the package until the time Mr. Pane took it?
ANNIE   Yes.
OFFICER CLARK   Was the soup the only food he'd had that day?
ANNIE   Except for a few crackers.
ISOBEL   It wasn't a good day for eating.
OFFICER CLARK   Yet Mr. Pane did, in fact, eat. The coroner's report showed he ate soup, crackers, and a rather large unappetizing dose of arsenic.

They all seem shocked.

ANNIE   Arsenic?
ISOBEL   Oh, dear—dear!
OFFICER CLARK (*sternly.*)   Mrs. Annie Jones!
ANNIE   Yes.
OFFICER CLARK   I'm placing you under arrest and charging you with the murder of Mr. Anthony Pane.
ISOBEL   Oh, dear! (*She seems crestfallen.*)

Lights black out.

Scene 3

Two days later. The lights come up on a suggested jail cell. The scene is played with lights pinpointing the actors' faces; the background is blocked out. ANNIE *and* FELIX *are talking.*

FELIX Is everything all right, Baby?

ANNIE Oh, yes, they're pretty nice, considering.

FELIX Do you need anything?

ANNIE Not a thing. I have someone to wait on me hand and foot. Oh, it's a little confining, but so is the kitchen at times.

FELIX I can imagine.

ANNIE But I have lots of company.

FELIX That's nice.

ANNIE People coming and going all the time.

FELIX If there was only something I could do.

ANNIE Oh, I don't really mind. It's just that it's kind of unfair, my being here for the reason I am.

FELIX I know, Baby.

ANNIE You know I wouldn't hurt Mr. Pane. He was nice to us. He was the only one that was.

FELIX You don't have to convince me.

ANNIE I hate to keep saying I'm innocent. The people in here all seem to say that. It's sort of traditional. It's a little embarrassing at times.

FELIX How?

ANNIE I'm here under false pretenses. Most people have earned the right to be here in one way or another. Last night there was a group of student demonstrators in here. They had tied themselves to the pillars at City Hall. I felt so proud of them. I was too ashamed to tell them I was in here only for murder.

FELIX Don't you worry, I've got Mrs. Pane working hard to arrange bail. She should have you out any time now.

ANNIE Last night I had a lot of time to think.

FELIX About what?

ANNIE About Paris.

FELIX Yes?

ANNIE If the fates are so unkind as to play this kind of a trick on me, I want you to go to Paris, no matter what.

FELIX We'll all go.

ANNIE I'm quite serious. You'll have money now. Mr. Pane provided for that in his will. And who knows . . . there's still one will to be counted yet.

FELIX Don't talk like that!

ANNIE I've had my share of fun and I've no regrets, except——

FELIX Rembrandt?

ANNIE (*smiling.*) My Little Tit—Mother's little helper.

FELIX You'll see him soon.

ANNIE Yes. (*She begins laughing.*)

FELIX What is it?

ANNIE I was just thinking about the fickle finger of fate.

FELIX Oh? (*He seems a bit puzzled.*)

ANNIE The rewards of good works; and the comparison between homemade cherry pie and a package of unseasoned store-bought soup.

She laughs as the lights black out.

Scene 4

A month later. As the lights come up we find ANNIE *and* FELIX *in the kitchen.* ANNIE *is icing a cake.*

FELIX You're a wonder, Annie.

ANNIE Why do you say that?

FELIX The trial starts today and you're not even upset.

ANNIE Not upset, but a little disappointed in Mrs. Pane.

FELIX I know.

ANNIE Why wouldn't she put up my bail?

FELIX I don't know. She seemed so anxious to help.

ANNIE I thought she liked me.

FELIX I can't understand it.

128

ANNIE   She seemed pleased with my work.

FELIX   All of a sudden she changed her mind. Said it wouldn't look right if she put up the bond.

ANNIE   It's a good thing we had the Paris money.

FELIX   Yeah.

ANNIE   You see, darling, it pays to be prepared. You just can't depend on other people.

FELIX   Maybe we ought to just head for the hills.

ANNIE   And lose all of that money?

FELIX   Your life is at stake!

ANNIE   No one ever got anything by running away. Besides, there are two officers outside the house waiting for me.

FELIX   Yeah.

ANNIE   Anyway, I'm innocent.

ISOBEL *crosses the living room.*

FELIX   If we only had some proof! I only hope justice triumphs.

ANNIE   *That's what I'm afraid of.*

ISOBEL   *(comes into the kitchen.)*   There you are, dear.

ANNIE   *(smiles at her.)*   Mrs. Pane.

ISOBEL   Oh, Felix, did you pick up my bottle of bath salts?

FELIX   It's on the counter. *(He takes it out of its bag.)*

ISOBEL   Thank you, dear. I don't know what I would do without you two. Especially now.

FELIX   *(reading the label.)*   "Invitation to Paradise." *(He puts it down.)*

ISOBEL   It's new. Supposed to do wonders for the skin.

ANNIE   Will you be at the trial, Mrs. Pane?

ISOBEL   Why, of course, dear. As soon as I've had my bath.

ANNIE   I'll have Rembrandt run your bath.

FELIX   I think he's out in the yard. I'll send him in. *(He goes out.)*

ISOBEL   There is something I wanted to say to you. You see, I know you didn't kill Anthony.

ANNIE   How do you know?

ISOBEL You couldn't kill a fly. Besides, that would be a breach of loyalty and *that* you would never do. To say nothing of etiquette and professional ethics.

ANNIE You know me better than I know myself.

ISOBEL I pride myself on knowing human nature, dear. However, there is something else to be considered.

ANNIE Yes?

ISOBEL The family. The family must be kept together at all costs.

ANNIE I was working on just that.

ISOBEL That's sweet, but I speak more of the family name, and it is a good name. There must be no hint of scandal attached to it. This is in my hands . . . and yours.

ANNIE Mine?

ISOBEL Precisely! It is in your capable hands, dear.

ANNIE How do you mean?

ISOBEL We both know you didn't poison Anthony. In fact, I have every reason to believe he committed suicide.

ANNIE You know this?

ISOBEL I'm sure of it.

ANNIE Then you must tell them! You must!

ISOBEL And the newspapers would make such an ugly mess of it. Oh, no. No, I couldn't have that.

ANNIE It's the only thing to do.

ISOBEL There's a better way. Yes, a better way. I was sitting in the tub last night when it came to me. Why not leave things just as they are?

ANNIE You can't mean that.

ISOBEL But I do, dear.

ANNIE You're talking about my life!

ISOBEL I know, and that bothers me. But all in all, it is the best way.

ANNIE Why that's unfair!

ISOBEL Think of it this way. You have your little boy. And you want the best for him, I know that.

ANNIE Yes.

ISOBEL   Last night I had him included in my will for a very substantial sum. He'll never want for anything. Plus a hefty cash settlement—immediately. Also, I would have to deny knowing anything about Anthony's death in court.

ANNIE   You want me to plead guilty?

ISOBEL   That's a little too much to ask. All I want is your silence. Let justice take its course. It can't mean very much to you, but it can help your darling little boy.

ANNIE   You've already taken care of this?

ISOBEL   My lawyer was here last night. You let him in. This morning I wrote the check. It's on my table.

ANNIE   After I keep my part of the bargain, you could change your mind.

ISOBEL   I wouldn't let you down, dear, any more than you would let me down if the situation was reversed.

They smile at each other.

ANNIE   I see.

ISOBEL   Do we have an understanding?

ANNIE   We always have, Mrs. Pane.

ISOBEL   Your mother would be proud of you, dear.

ANNIE   I'm sure of it.

FELIX *comes back.*

ISOBEL   I'll be there to cheer you on . . . in a manner of speaking. (*She goes out, leaving the bath salts.*)

FELIX   Did she say why she didn't put up the bail?

ANNIE   The golden rule. Do unto others as you would have them do unto you—but do it first!

FELIX   What the hell does that mean?

ANNIE (*laughs and shouts.*)   It means the sky will explode and rain money, money, money, money, money! Lots and lots of beautiful money!

FELIX (*sadly.*)   I'll get the car. (*He goes out.*)

ANNIE (*shouting after him.*)   Make it a golden chariot! (*She picks up the bottle of bath salts and looks at it. She opens the bottom cabinet and removes a bottle of acid. The bottles are the same size. She places the bath salts in her purse and the acid on the counter. Then she goes to the back door and calls.)* Rembrandt! Rem! *(She walks back into the room. In a moment he comes dashing in and crashes into her arms.)* Hey!

REMBRANDT   Was that fast? Was that fast?

ANNIE   The fastest man on two feet.

REMBRANDT   As fast as anything?

ANNIE   Faster. I know my big man can do anything, can't you?

REMBRANDT   Yes.

ANNIE   Give me a kiss! *(They kiss.)* Give me a hug! *(They hug.)* Now another kiss! *(They kiss.)* A bigger kiss! *(They kiss.)* You're my Little Tit, aren't you?

REMBRANDT   Yes.

ANNIE   You're my little helper, aren't you?

REMBRANDT   Yes.

ANNIE   I have a job for you.

REMBRANDT   We gonna bake a cherry pie?

ANNIE   In a way. *(She looks at the acid.)* But, in another way you might say we are going to *cook a goose*. Now there's a bottle of bath salts on the counter. I want you to take it upstairs, run the tub full for Mrs. Pane's bath, and pour the soap in. Don't spill any of it. Don't get *any* of it on you; you don't want to smell like a sissy. Can you do that?

REMBRANDT   I've done that lots of times. *(He grabs the acid.)*

ANNIE   Don't run!

REMBRANDT   All right.

ANNIE   I left a kiss for you on your pillow. *(He goes out, skips across the living room singing "Gonna bake a cherry pie." She takes the bottle of bath salts out of her purse and holds it up.)* "Invitation to Paradise"? Invitation accepted!

She puts the bottle back on the counter and pulls on her gloves as the scene blacks out.

Scene 5

Courtroom. One day later. Only ANNIE's *face is lighted; background black.*

JUDGE'S VOICE *(speaks with authority.)* Mrs. Annie Mason Jones, you have been found guilty of murder in the first degree, in what must be the shortest murder trial on record. I can only commend the jury for returning a fair and impartial verdict stemming from the evidence as presented. Have you anything to say before sentence is pronounced?

ANNIE Do unto others as you would have them do unto you.

JUDGE'S VOICE Thank you for reminding us, Mrs. Jones, but you should have thought of that before.

ANNIE Better late than never, your Honor.

JUDGE'S VOICE The sentence of this court is that the prisoner be taken from this court to the State Prison where on the morning of July fifteenth she be put to death in the manner prescribed by law——.

SECOND VOICE *(shouting.)* Your Honor, your Honor!

Pause during which inaudible whispering is heard.

JUDGE'S VOICE I have just been informed that Mrs. Isobel Pane, the mother of the late Anthony Pane, has just been found dead. The victim of a horrible accident in her bath.

ANNIE *(sadly.)* Poor, poor goose.

Lights black out.

Scene 6

When the lights come up we find ANNIE *and* FELIX *talking to each other through the suggested jail cell. Everything else is blacked out.*

FELIX I've tried everything, but it seems hopeless.

ANNIE In twenty-four hours I join the Pane family. Hey,

133

wouldn't it be funny if they hired me for a cook, wherever they are? (*She laughs.*)

FELIX How can you joke at a time like this?

ANNIE I won't be very good at it tomorrow.

FELIX There must be something I can do!

ANNIE There is.

FELIX Anything!

ANNIE Go to Paris and become a great artist. Then you won't have to paint counterfeit movie tickets.

FELIX Oh, Baby.

ANNIE And don't you ever let me catch you painting the insides of dead ants again.

FELIX It's symbolic!

ANNIE A dead ant is a dead ant! Listen, I know dead ants when I see them. I've stepped on enough of them.

FELIX Baby, you just don't have the artist's mind.

ANNIE I'm an artist in my own way. As a matter of fact, I'll give my final performance tomorrow morning.

FELIX You wanted me to fight with you to make me forget tomorrow, didn't you?

ANNIE Tell me about Mrs. Pane.

FELIX Rembrandt put the wrong bottle into her bath. The inquest cleared him. He still doesn't know what he did. We told him it was sweet soap. We couldn't let him have a thing like that on his conscience.

ANNIE And her will?

FELIX Rembrandt gets a very large cash settlement. Did you know she also made out a large check to him that very day she died?

ANNIE Now wasn't that sweet. Bless her little heart.

FELIX We both receive money and so do several charities. And the house goes to you.

ANNIE (*excited.*) Really!

FELIX Yes.

ANNIE Oh, I love that house! There are so many things I can do with it. I . . . aw . . . what a shame!

FELIX Baby, my time is up. I have to go.

ANNIE Felix?

FELIX Yes.

ANNIE Take home a couple of kisses for Rembrandt.

They kiss.

THIRD VOICE Mrs. Annie Jones.

ANNIE Yes.

THIRD VOICE You are free to go, Mrs. Jones.

FELIX Free? What is it? What happened?

THIRD VOICE A letter was found in Mrs. Pane's safety-deposit box.

ANNIE Yes?

THIRD VOICE It contained Mr. Anthony Pane's suicide note. It seems he was in love with his brother's wife. The letter also contained Mrs. Pane's reason for hiding it. It was to be opened only upon her death. If she hadn't died, you would have! You are a very fortunate woman, Mrs. Jones.

ANNIE (*she begins chuckling.*) Yes, I am.

FELIX Darling, you're free! We're free!

ANNIE Well, I'll be damned!

Blackout.

Scene 7

The lights come up on the living room of the Pane house. ISOBEL *is now in the last of the picture frames.* ANNIE *and* FELIX *are sitting on the sofa drinking champagne. A couple of empty bottles sit on the table. They are having a high time.*

ANNIE More champagne? (*She takes up the bottle.*)

FELIX If you please, madam.

ANNIE (*fills his glass.*) Dee-lighted, sir! (*They raise their glasses.*)

FELIX Here's to freedom! (*They drink.*)

ANNIE Here's to Paris! (*They drink.*)

FELIX   Here's to good times from now on! (*They drink.*)

ANNIE   Here's to—hey, mine's empty!

FELIX   A minor, minor problem. Easily, easily fixed. (*He fills both glasses.*)

ANNIE   Back in business! (*They are getting high quickly.*)

FELIX   And business is just fine.

ANNIE (*pats his knee.*)   A toast!

FELIX   Yes, yes . . . yes?

ANNIE   Here's to suicide notes! (*She raises her glass.*)

FELIX (*raising his glass.*)   Here's to suici—what kind of a toast is that?

ANNIE   If it wasn't for suicide notes I'd be burnt toast.

FELIX   True—true, but on the other hand, it was *fate* that took a hand—on the other hand.

ANNIE   Your point, your point.

FELIX   But back to the first hand, fate had no other choice but to take both hands and smash open those iron bars that were unjustly holding you.

ANNIE (*nods agreement.*)   That's pretty.

FELIX (*nods.*)   Fate *always* protects the *innocent!* From the biggest man to the smallest ant.

ANNIE (*raises her glass.*)   A toast to the ants!

FELIX (*holds up his hand.*)   Wait! This toast is *not* for the ants. It is not *even* for fate.

ANNIE   No?

FELIX (*becomes serious.*)   This toast should be to innocence! (*He raises his glass.*) That divine condition you shall always remain in. (*They drink.*)

ANNIE (*hugs him quickly.*)   You're so wonderful, Felix.

FELIX (*bows.*)   A condition I shall always remain in.

ANNIE (*leans over.*)   A kiss to seal the bargain. (*They kiss.*)

FELIX   How about the best two out of three? (*They kiss again.*)

ANNIE   Felix, Honey? (*She pecks him about the mouth.*)

FELIX   "Yes," he said.

ANNIE   "You have educated lips," she said.

FELIX   "The better to teach you," he said.

ANNIE (*giggles.*) I'm not too bright. Please teach me again. (*They kiss again. When they part she begins chuckling softly.*)

FELIX What . . . what, what, what . . . what?

ANNIE I was just thinking. What would old-man Pane and old-lady Isobel think if they could see us now—right here in their own living room, having a ball?

FELIX (*chuckles lightly.*) I don't suppose they'd like it very much.

ANNIE No, I don't suppose. Now, I wonder what made me think of them all of a sudden? (*She asks a rhetorical question.*)

FELIX It's their booze! (*He holds the bottle up.*) Nineteen fifty-five.

ANNIE (*becomes sad for a moment.*) Why is there so much sadness in the world, Felix?

FELIX Idle hands, idle minds. You know something, Honey, *that* is the secret. Man must have a purpose—a burning desire—ambition! It could be anything! No matter what! As long as he has a goal. He should reach out and keep reaching, letting nothing stand in his way until he gets it. Even if he's a *crook* or a *murderer* . . . he should be the *best murderer* the law will allow. Practice, practice, practice! (*He pounds his thigh.*)

ANNIE (*innocently.*) I agree completely! Do the *best* job you can!

FELIX Exactly! It's his constitutional right! (*He is very tipsy now.*) Now, it's true some people have all the best to begin with, like the Pane family—but they had no goals and were quite unhappy.

ANNIE Do you think they're happy now?

FELIX Honey, I don't think dead people have very much fun. I guess it all depends on if hell is anything like New York. (*He giggles.*)

ANNIE Still, I wonder about them. (*She empties her glass.*)

FELIX (*after a pause.*) You know, I still can't get over how quickly they all went bye-bye. It's all so unnatural. Don't you agree?

ANNIE   I certainly do agree. But they were kind of kooky, anyway. They always did things with a flair.

FELIX   It gives me the creeps thinking about it, though. They were so alive. (*He drinks.*)

ANNIE   In a dead sort of way. (*She giggles.*)

FELIX   (*seems not to hear her as he becomes involved in his thoughts.*)   It seems like only yesterday. They'd be sitting around here fighting with each other.

ANNIE   Now they're at peace. That's a *good thought* to hold, Felix. Now they're all together and at peace. It's right that a family should stay together. It's almost bibli—*biblicable!*

FELIX   (*looks at her, searching her face.*)   Annie?

ANNIE   (*puts her glass up to her eye and looks through it.*)   Yes!

FELIX   Is there something you haven't told me?

ANNIE   Like what, Felix?

FELIX   I don't know. I thought you might have something to tell me.

ANNIE   Like what?

FELIX   Maybe like . . . current events! I don't know like what.

ANNIE   Nothing much happened in prison that you don't know about.

FELIX   I mean before that. Anything about the Panes you want to . . . (*He shrugs as she giggles.*)

ANNIE   (*shaking her finger.*)   They shouldn't have lied to me, Felix. That wasn't very nice. They *promised*—they *promised*.

FELIX   Please, Honey, say what I'm thinking isn't true! (*He pleads.*)

ANNIE   People should keep their promises, Felix, or take the consequences.

FELIX   Consequences! What consequences?

ANNIE   Whatever they are.

FELIX   What about the Panes?

ANNIE   I'm sure they're not sore losers.

FELIX   (*to himself.*)   I just don't believe this!

ANNIE   Let's not talk about dead people, Felix.

FELIX   I'm beginning to *wonder*. I mean *really* wonder! Now there's some question in my mind if they got *dead* all by themselves! I mean, I'm really beginning to wonder! I mean you need help to die in such—beautiful ways! Why they literally exploded off the scene like a rocket! No, no dying in bed for them. No old age! No cancer! They were beautifully strange people who were *flushed down magnificently!* But I want to know if someone else pulled the chain?

ANNIE   Let's drink to that! (*She reaches for the bottle.*)

FELIX   You're changing the subject. I still believe that . . . that . . .

ANNIE   What is it?

FELIX   (*staring off blankly.*)   I think I've had too much to drink. I—I keep hearing those people talking.

ANNIE   (*humoring him.*)   Well, don't you worry about it, Honey. They'll go back where they came from after I give you some coffee.

FELIX   I can hear them talking. I swear I can. (*He grabs his ears.*)

ANNIE   Well, don't you talk to them. They'll only lie to you. I'll bet they still haven't gotten out of the habit.

As she goes into the kitchen AVERY, ISOBEL, ANTHONY, HENRY, *and* GINGER *begin talking.* FELIX *stares in disbelief. The Panes are all in the picture frames now.*

ISOBEL   The weather has gotten very sticky these days.

AVERY   Mmmm. . . .

ISOBEL   Oh, if only I could take a warm bath, Avery.

AVERY   I would think you'd had one bath too many.

ISOBEL   Don't scold, dear.

AVERY   Surely you must be waterlogged by now. What's-her-name really cooked your goose.

ISOBEL   Yes, I was forgetting about that. She really took care of us. By the way, Anthony, I was wrong.

ANTHONY   About what, Mother?

ISOBEL   Nobody out there loves us.

ANTHONY   I know, Mother, I was just trying to bring some peace to the world.

ISOBEL   Yes, dear, and I'm sure your bombs would have solved everything.

FELIX   I don't believe it!

GINGER   We're going to be so happy, Henry.

The doorbell rings, but FELIX *is spellbound.*

HENRY   You mean you're going away, somewhere?

GINGER   Of course not, silly. I'm going to be with you wherever you go.

HENRY (*sarcastically.*)   Happy, happy.

GINGER   I'm going to cook all of your favorite dishes.

HENRY   Why don't you just leave the cooking to Annie?

GINGER   Annie doesn't live here any more.

The doorbell rings again. FELIX *doesn't stir.*

HENRY   Nonsense! What would she do without us! She cooks our goose so well.

GINGER   What's wrong with the way I cook? Didn't you like the pie I baked?

HENRY   I was lucky. I didn't get to taste it. Still it gave me the world's most god-awful headache!

ANNIE (*coming back into room.*)   That was the door, Felix. Didn't you hear it?

FELIX (*in a daze.*)   No. (*Looking at picture frames.*) Didn't you hear *them?*

ANNIE   Oh, Felix! (*She goes to the front door as* FELIX *gets up very unsteadily and walks about staring at the picture frames in disbelief.*)

FELIX (*to himself.*)   I'm not crazy!

ANNIE *comes in with the detective who arrested her.*

ANNIE   Felix, you remember Detective Clark from the police?

FELIX   Unhappily I do . . . but come in, anyway.

OFFICER CLARK (*walking into room.*) Thank you. (*He looks around.*) You folks been celebrating, I see.

ANNIE   We had a drink together.

FELIX   We had a *ball!* A real *ball!*

ANNIE   Please sit down, Mr. Clark. The place is kind of a mess.

OFFICER CLARK (*sits next to* FELIX.) New tenants always face that problem. Out with the old and all.

ANNIE   Oh, you're so right! I just can't believe our good fortune. I must be one of God's children.

OFFICER CLARK   I wouldn't doubt it.

FELIX   Amen!

ANNIE   Why they left this all to me is anybody's guess.

OFFICER CLARK   Maybe *you* can guess?

FELIX   What do you mean?

OFFICER CLARK   Just that it's traditional for rich families to remember their loyal help in their wills, and Mrs. Jones must have been very, very loyal.

ANNIE   I did my best and showed no favoritism whatsoever.

FELIX   That you can believe, Clark.

OFFICER CLARK   Oh, I do. I do! Knowing the Pane family I'm sure she took care of them all with equal pleasure. They were not bad people, really.

ANNIE   They were sweet.

FELIX   They were dears.

OFFICER CLARK   Not bad, really.

ANNIE   We'll miss them.

FELIX   We'll miss their strength.

ANNIE (*nodding.*) Yes.

OFFICER CLARK   Avery used to come down to the station and play checkers or chess with me for hours at a time.

ANNIE   That was just like him.

FELIX   Yes.

OFFICER CLARK   I'll miss him.

ANNIE   He was sweet.

FELIX (*breaking the monotony.*) Is this a business call, Clark?

OFFICER CLARK   I wouldn't say that exactly. Not that I'm satisfied with the record, mind you. I'm what they call a "bone man" at headquarters. Whenever there's a tough one—I get it. Every criminal makes a boner somewhere along the line, and like a dog I just go sniffing around until I find that hidden bone. But this call is more like a one-man welcoming committee, calling on new neighbors.

FELIX   Oh?

ANNIE   In that case (*She gets up.*) refreshments are in order.

OFFICER CLARK   Champagne's a little rich for my blood. Besides, I'm still on duty.

FELIX   Sorry you have to leave so soon, then. (FELIX *gets up.*)

ANNIE   Not until he's had his pie and coffee, Felix. (FELIX *sits down.*) Can't have him sniffing around on an empty stomach.

OFFICER CLARK   You're very thoughtful, Mrs. Jones.

ANNIE *goes into the kitchen.*

FELIX (FELIX *and* CLARK *smile at each other.*)   Well.

OFFICER CLARK (*nods.*)   Uh-huh.

FELIX (*uneasily.*)   So, you're a bone man?

OFFICER CLARK (*pats his nose with his finger.*)   The best nose on the force.

FELIX   You smell anything?

OFFICER CLARK   Perhaps. Is there anything to smell?

FELIX   Not even incense.

OFFICER CLARK   Fine, fine.

OFFICER CLARK *nods as the Panes from their picture frames begin to speak again.*

ISOBEL   Poor Officer Clark. He's in for it now.

AVERY   Oh, let them alone. You are the nosiest woman!

ISOBEL   But Clark is a friend of yours, dear.

AVERY   He's no friend of mine. The man is crude. Besides, he cheats at checkers. Whatever Annie does to him is all right with me.

FELIX (*jumping up.*)   No! It's not true.

OFFICER CLARK What is it, Jones? (*He gets up, too, as* ANNIE *comes in with the tray.*)

ANNIE Here we are, gentlemen. The cure for what ails you.

ISOBEL It just may cure him of everything. Oh, it is sticky today.

OFFICER CLARK There's something wrong with Mr. Jones.

ANNIE (*puts the tray down.*) He's just not used to champagne. He'll be all right.

OFFICER CLARK He's acting mighty strange.

FELIX *is still staring at the pictures.*

ANNIE (*pouring the coffee.*) I'll bet you can't get coffee like this at headquarters.

GINGER That's for damn sure!

HENRY You're always sticking your two cents in. I suppose you could do better?

GINGER My coffee has less punch than hers, I'm sure.

ANNIE (*offering* CLARK *the coffee.*) Here you are.

OFFICER CLARK Thank you. (*He starts to take the cup, but* FELIX *grabs it.*) Hey!

FELIX I *always* get the first cup! It's a game we play.

OFFICER CLARK Oh?

ISOBEL Just a short reprieve, but it won't be long now, dear.

ANTHONY All is lost anyway, without my love and my bombs.

AVERY Splendid! The man cheats! No character, anyway.

GINGER Saved by the bell.

ANNIE Just a game we play. Here, this one's for you. (*She offers it, but* FELIX *grabs it too.*)

OFFICER CLARK Hey!

ANNIE Felix!

FELIX Two cups! I always drink *two* cups!

OFFICER CLARK At the same time?

FELIX It's a quirk! (*He holds up both cups but does not drink.*)

OFFICER CLARK You should see a doctor (ANNIE *begins to pour again.*) —Never mind, Mrs. Jones. I drink too much coffee, anyway.

GINGER   She'll get him with the pie. I'll stake my life on that!

ANTHONY *(sniffling.)* You already have and lost. Oh, what a waste of my beautiful bombs!

AVERY   What's wrong with Annie's pie? It's the best there is.

ISOBEL   It's changed dear.

AVERY   Changed? What do you mean, changed? We always got a big bang out of her pies.

ISOBEL   Too rich for the blood.

HENRY   Or any other part of the body.

GINGER   A little lumpy, as I recall.

ANNIE *(begins to pass the pie.)* Your pie, Mr. Clark (FELIX, *juggling the cups in one hand, grabs the pie tray with the other.)* —stop, Felix!

FELIX *(as he grabs the pie.)* And I always eat the first pie!

OFFICER CLARK   The whole pie?

FELIX   Yes, yes, I eat the whole pie. All of it. All of it! It's this thing I have.

OFFICER CLARK   I know, I know—the quirk again.

FELIX   Yeah, the quirk. *(He stands balancing the pie tray on one hand and the two cups of coffee in the other.)*

ANNIE   Oh, Felix!

OFFICER CLARK   Well, I really must be going, anyway. Duty, you know. *(He gets up.)*

AVERY   Duty, my foot! He's got a hot checker game going. Him and his nasty nose.

ISOBEL   I'm happy for old Clark. At least it wasn't his last supper.

ANNIE   You will come again, Lieutenant? *(They walk toward the door.)*

FELIX   Any time.

OFFICER CLARK   I'll be sniffing around now and then.

FELIX   If I find any bones I'll send them to you.

OFFICER CLARK   You do that. *(He goes out with ANNIE.)*

FELIX *(waving.)* Ta-ta.

HENRY   I'm bored hanging up here.

GINGER   Me, too.

HENRY (*mocking her.*)   Me, too! Me, too! Me, too!

ISOBEL   Be nice to each other, children.

HENRY   I'm hungry. I wish I could take a walk down by the lake.

GINGER   Not without me, Piggy.

HENRY   I wish you'd fall in the lake and drown all over again!

ISOBEL   Aren't they sweet? (*She smiles at them.*)

AVERY   Sticky.

ISOBEL   Oh, Avery . . .

AVERY   What's the matter now?

ISOBEL   Oh, if only I could take a quick bath—and you could wash my back, dear.

AVERY   Oh, deliver me!

ANTHONY   Dear God, what will happen to the world without the secret of my transistor bombs?

HENRY   I wouldn't worry too much. Perhaps they'll discover the secret recipe for Annie's explosive cherry pie!

FELIX   I don't believe any of you! You're all liars!

ANNIE   He's gone now, Felix.

FELIX *looks up. He turns quickly around the room. He raises his arms.*

FELIX   Ha! (*He claps his hands.*) Poof! Just like that! Everybody's gone! Darling, everybody's gone!

ANNIE   Wonderful! (*She begins laughing.*) Wonderful!

They begin waltzing around the room laughing as they go.

FELIX   Around and around we go!

ANNIE   In our own little house on top of the world!

FELIX   And where we stop, nobody knows!

They fall on the sofa, laughing.

ANNIE   Oh, I can't quite get over it. My own little castle! (*She jumps up.*) I've got so many changes to make. This room is too drab! It should swing with gay colors and bright sunlight!

FELIX   Hooray for sunlight!

ANNIE (*bouncing around.*)   And these silly looking chairs! They've got to go!

FELIX Silly looking chairs are out!

ANNIE Everything is going to be new and bright! And if there are any ghosts left over, they've got to go as well!

FELIX Shh! They may hear you! (*He looks about anxiously.*)

ANNIE Let everybody hear, dead or alive! I'm going to start my own collection of ghosts! (*She jumps on* FELIX *who falls back on the sofa.*)

FELIX Hey! (*They laugh for a few seconds.*)

ANNIE We've built a mountain, Baby, and climbed right to the top! From here we can see the whole world at our feet.

FELIX That's beautiful as long as we don't fall off.

ANNIE (*jumps up.*) Fall? Not a chance! The foundation was built too well. The character is well made. Like you said, Baby, practice . . . practice . . . practice! You were *so* right, Honey! That's the secret. Give it your very best, and with love. Whether it's building a company, painting dead ants, or cooking a goose. Always with love! Always with love!

FELIX Amen!

ANNIE (*spins around.*) Wow!

FELIX (*laughs.*) Wow!

ANNIE (*rubbing her clothes.*) I've got a closet full of clothes upstairs. I'm going to go change again.

FELIX Get beautiful, Baby.

ANNIE I'll do my very best, because tonight, my darling, tonight I'm going to make you the world's most fabulous dinner. (*She starts upstairs and then suddenly stops and turns back.*) Tonight would have been my last dinner, but I must live right, because here I am, and from now on, I'm invincible!

FELIX Like a rock!

ANNIE Life is good, Baby, and it all begins right now! So have a kiss, my darling. (*She throws him a kiss which he returns. She goes out.*)

The telephone rings and FELIX *moves slowly to answer it.*

FELIX Top of the world! Oh, hello, Captain Harris. Say, you know you're a good old skate—cutting all that red tape and getting us out of there. I'm gonna do something great for you. One of these days I'm gonna send you a couple of my special passes to the movies. (*Pause while he listens.*) No, no she's not bitter at all . . . she's sitting on top of the world! (*Pause.*) Well, there is one thing, Captain. That Lieutenant Clark. He's some kind of weirdo. Doesn't he know the case is closed? He'd follow a guy into the grave. (*He listens.*) What's that? (*Pause.*) Yeah, from now on it's smooth sailing—and Paris is the next stop. So like the Germans say—Adiós, Baby! (*He slams down the phone.*)

FELIX *salutes* AVERY's *picture, picks up the tray of pie and coffee and goes into the kitchen as* REMBRANDT *comes skipping down the stairs.*

REMBRANDT   Can I go out and ride my skateboard a while?

FELIX   What?

REMBRANDT   It's still early. Can I go out for a while?

FELIX   Your mother's just come home. She wants to spend some time with you. (*Smiling, he picks* REMBRANDT *up.*) She wants to pick you up . . . and hug you like nobody's ever been hugged before, even by a grizzly bear (*They laugh.*) . . . but with love!

REMBRANDT   I just saw her and I gave her a kiss.

FELIX   Dee-lightful! Where is she now?

REMBRANDT   She's upstairs.

FELIX (*goes to the intercom and presses it.*)   Annie—hey, Annie Baby, I've got a message for you! (*He listens but gets no answer.*) She's not in the bedroom, is she?

REMBRANDT   She's in the bathroom.

FELIX   Oh. (*He pushes another button and calls.*) Annie? Annie, it's me, Baby. Hey, are you there? Annie? (*To* REMBRANDT.) She must be sleeping.

REMBRANDT   No, she's taking a bath.

FELIX   Taking a bath? Are you sure?

REMBRANDT   Yes, 'cause I ran the tub and put another bottle of that bath salts in the water.

FELIX   What bath salts?

REMBRANDT   That was under the counter. You know, the kind Mrs. Pane liked so much. I found another bottle under the counter.

FELIX   (*stares at him in horror.*)   Annie! (*Softly at first and then progressively more intense.*) Annie! Annie! Annie! (*He runs out of the kitchen, across the living room, and up the stairs as he shouts her name.*)

REMBRANDT   (*picks up his skateboard, goes into the living room, and skates around as he sings.*)   "Gonna bake a cherry pie, Annie-girl, Annie-girl. Gonna bake a cherry pie, charming Annie."

Slow fade.

Thank You, Miss Victoria

A Play in One Act

WILLIAM M. HOFFMAN

For Neil Flanagan

Edin Hoffman

WILLIAM M. HOFFMAN: "Born in New York City. Studied Latin at CCNY. Besides Cino, La Mama, and Off-Broadway presentations of *Victoria,* productions include *Spring Play* and a narration for *Three Mask Dances* at La Mama, *Good Night, I Love You* and *Saturday Night at the Movies* at the Cino, *Up-*

X   X

tight! (a musical revue) and X   X at Old Reliable Theatre

X

Tavern. New Works: *Red/Orange–Orange/Red, or The Judges' Play* and *Amsterdam* (a musical). Has directed and acted with great pleasure. Poetry published in *31 New American Poets* and many journals. *The Cloisters* (song cycle) published by G. Schirmer. Also: movie scripts, reviews and other journalism. Editor of New American Plays series and former Drama Editor of Hill and Wang."

Thank You, Miss Victoria was first performed at the Caffe Cino on August 17, 1965, by Neil Flanagan, under the direction of Bernard Gersten. On April 12, 1966, the play was produced at the Martinique Theatre by Theodore Mann and Paul Libin as one of *6 from La Mama*. Ellen Stewart's La Mama Repertory Company, starring Michael Warren Powell, with Jacque Lynn Colton, Kevin O'Connor, and Victor LiPari performed under the direction of Tom O'Horgan.

Thank You, Miss Victoria

Scene: An executive office, Wall Street. It is handsomely furnished with a large, expensive desk and swivel chair. There is a suggestion of wood paneling. There are pictures of the founders of the firm on the wall and, perhaps, some contemporary paintings. There is a door (nonfunctioning). On the desk is a telephone with buttons, one of which is for the intercom. An elegantly dressed young man is seated at the desk thumbing through the East Village Other.

Intercom buzzes. He picks up receiver and presses one button after another.

Yes? . . . Yes? . . . Yes? Sorry. Yes. Yes. Yes. Yes? Yes! . . . Yes? . . . Uh-huh.

Three what?

Ah, button three. Most helpful, Miss—what is your name?

Genovese. From Genova.

Nothing, Miss Genovese.

He presses button.

Stewart. How good to hear from you.

Today. Father threatened to cut me off.

I give myself a week, allowance or no allowance.

Marie-Louise? With the long, lithe legs?

How sad. How?

Is this just hearsay, or were you there? I'd hate to pass this on if it's mere rumor. I have my reputation as an informed source.

Definitely a down. What was she on?

Intercom buzzes.

Hold on. Something's buzzing.

Be right back.

He finds "hold" button and presses it. Presses intercom button.

Call me Harry. I detest formalities, Miss Genovese.

Thank you. (*Presses button.*) Judson, Judson, and Lester. Harry Judson speaking. You may call me Harry. I detest formalities. What can I do for you?

You know my father, you say.

Ropes? I'm sorry, but I haven't the foggiest about ropes. I just started to work here today and I am totally disoriented. What say we talk about it over drinks at Twenty-One, six o'clock, on me?

Stocks, bonds, whatever. What is your name again? I shall make a note of it.

Spell it.

L-E-V-E-R. As in Brothers.

Are you as rich as we are? Don't tell me. I'm holding another party on the phone. Will you hold on?

Thank you.

Presses hold. Presses button.

Hello, Stewart.

Lever as in Brothers. He's holding.

Son, I imagine. I'm having drinks with him later.

That is *your* perversion. I have twelve of my own. Sweetheart. Is that what you call each other?

Lies. I must hang. Lever awaits.

Good-by, sweetheart.

Presses button.

Please forgive the interruption, Mr. Lever. Stewart Streeter was on three. He's richer than either of us. And queer as they come. He thinks you're cute—Lever, are you there? (*Hangs up.*) Uptight, isn't he? (*Dials intercom.*) Miss Genovese, call Lever —you'll find him in the Yellow Pages under soap—and tell him that I cannot make it to cocktails this evening, after all. Prior commitments.

Four? Thank you. Come in later and I'll chase you around the desk, or whatever is customary.

Presses button.

Hello, Dorothy.

Bored, Dorothy. How are you?

Yes, I heard about Marie-Louise. I was about to call you.

How final. And I thought she was indecisive.

(*Annoyed.*) Oh, why anything? She was bored and beautiful and rich and spoiled and on whatever it was she was on and her wop gigolo jilted her.

No!

Go to a hotel.

I'll send you a check. You cannot stay with me. You keep chasing me around my apartment and you know I'm impotent with girls of your class.

I'd rather starve than live with you, although you know I adore you otherwise.

You leave your fat plastic curlers about. You get hair in my sink.

Be that as it may, you're disorderly, you're a dope fiend, and you have this masochistic attachment to me.

It's my Scorpio.

Well, let her in. See you at Andy's.

Of course you're invited. If you're worried, I'll pick you up and take you there.

Answer your door, Dorothy. (*Hangs up.*) Dorothy, Dorothy. (*Dials intercom.*) Miss Genovese, where do they keep the liquor around here?

I quite understand: my father asked you to remove the liquor. (*Takes out a joint and smokes it.*)

I'll bet he told you I'm somewhat temperamental, too.

How much is he paying you? Anything under four hundred a week is ridiculous. I'm impossible. By the way, what am I supposed to be doing here? Somewhere along the line Father forgot to tell me what my position entails besides arriving at the office at ten and leaving at four.

Convertible debentures? Convertible to what?

Well, then I'd better call him, shouldn't I?

Oh, Miss Genovese, I'm harmless, if you're worried about that. I'm impotent with girls of your class. But I wouldn't enter my office without knocking, if I were you. I'm a compulsive masturbator. What time is it?

156

Noon. What a camp.

Camp.

Don't you find noon a camp, Genovese, old girl?

I guess you wouldn't. Go to lunch, why dontcha? Don't tell me; you brought it along. Saving for your dowry? With the money Dad's paying you, you could eat at Schrafft's. *Bon appétit. (Hangs up.)*

Arranges writing materials on top of desk. Neatly rearranges them. Toys with telephone. He glances at the Other. *Suddenly and resignedly he dials the intercom for another part of the building.*

Albertson, this is Harry. May I speak to my father?

Thank you, Miss Albertson. . . . Father? This is Harry, your son.

Oh, I'm sorry. I'll start all over again. (*Very Ivy League.*) Hi, Dad, old man.

How are stocks, Mother, and what *is* her name?

I'm sorry.

I said I'm sorry.

I *have* responsibilities: to Brooks Brothers, the Diners' Club . . . my connection.

It would cause a minor recession if I were to stop spending your money.

We've been through this, Dad. You earn it; I spend it. Division of labor.

Look, I'm here. I arrived at the office at ten, flirted with your spy, and chatted with my friends. Now what am I supposed to be doing as work, *sir?*

As in Brothers? Some joker named Lever did call but I'm afraid, well, I'm afraid I offended him in some way, so you'll have to get someone else down here to show me the ropes.

Oh I don't know. Some people take offense easily. *Chacun à son goût.* A lively little French girl named Marie-Louise taught me that expression——

In person? I'd be honored. When should I expect you? I don't want you walking in on me and Miss Genovese—you wouldn't believe how she's been selling it, sweet thing.

One hour? Groovy. (*Hangs up. Looks through* East Village Other. *Intercom buzzes.*) Yes?

(*Southern accent.*) Line five. Why, thank you, Genevieve.

(*Presses button.*) Stewart, help, I'm smoking my last joint.

No, never mind. My father's coming down in an hour.

Yes, I'm bored. I'm sitting here reading *EVO.*

Naked acid-crazed revolutionaries. Oh, you wouldn't understand such things. How depressing. (*Thumbing through newspaper.*) Here's one that looks like Dorothy. Can't stand aggressive women.

Or aggressive men. Stewart Streeter, you maintain a most lopsided view of the universe. . . . Get this. Oh, you're not going to believe it.

Personal section. "Modern young couple, Scarsdale area, wants to exchange French and Greek lessons with swinging singles. Box 110."

Mais oui!

"Mature Wall Street executive wishes to study all cultures with ambitious young lady. Race no bar." I bet my father wrote that one. Ah, here's one for you, sweetheart: "Male would like to correspond with white male gay. Must be handicapped. Please send photo."

412.

You are Box 412. Love it. . . . Oh, Jesus Christ, listen to this. "Aggressive New York business woman will employ male secretary. Experience and accuracy required. Telephone Miss Victoria, *Rector* 5-1296." Is that to be believed?

Strictly from Krafft-Ebing.

You have no imagination.

Of course.

Would you like to make a little wager?

You should be so lucky. I'd rather sleep with Dorothy again.

Whoever loses has to sleep with Dorothy. I'll call Victoria right now.

I'll get back to you, 412. (*Hangs up.*) Victoria, Victoria sweet Victoria. (*Starts to dial. Intercom buzzes.*) Yes?

Tell her I'll call her back.

I'm in conference.

I'm schizophrenic, or haven't you noticed?

Miss Genovese, tell her I'll call her later. I have an important call to make. Oh, and don't listen in or I'll maim you. I don't really like spies. (*Hangs up and dials. He realizes that he has misdialed.*) Yes, yes, yes. (*Dials Miss Genovese. Sexy, heavy breathing. Hangs up quickly. Dials.*) Hello, may I speak to Victoria?

Is this Rector 5-1296?

Victoria. *Miss* Victoria.

Ah, this is *Miss* Victoria.

I'm calling in response to your advertisement in *EVO,* mam. I hope the position hasn't been filled. The job you outlined looks like just the work I've been——

Please don't let me interrupt you. I'm terribly sorry. When may I call back?

Yes, mam, fifteen seconds. (*Hangs up. Counts on his fingers, laughing.*) Thirteen chimpanzee, fourteen chimpanzee, fifteen chimpanzee. Dialing is definitely a down. (*Dials.*) Hello, Miss Victoria?

Harry.

Streeter. Harry Streeter.

Pardon me, mam, I think we have a bad connection. I could hear you better if you would speak more *sharply.*

(*His ear has been blasted.*) Thank you. I appreciate your letting me call you like this. I hope the position isn't filled. It's just the kind of *job* I've always wanted. More than I can say.

None. I'm sorry to admit I've had no experience as a secretary. But I'm a quick *learner.* I feel secure enough to say that I can promise full *satisfaction.*

My previous experience, unfortunately . . . teaching.

Correctional institutions.

Seven years.

French, mam.

Well, enough, considering that my heart isn't in my present occupation. But I'm a *dutiful* person and I always try to fulfill my *obligations.*

Somewhat, Miss Victoria.

You're quite right. I'll remove it immediately. (*Makes sounds as if removing suit jacket but does not actually remove it. He is amused.*) I have taken off my jacket, Miss Victoria.

It was kind of you to concern yourself about me. I trust you are perfectly comfortable.

I'm sorry, mam. It was stupid of me to imply that you'd be otherwise. *Mille pardons.*

That's *French*—a thousand pardons. . . .

What would you like to know?

I'm twenty-eight, five feet *ten* inches, and I weigh one hundred and seventy-five pounds.

You're right. I hope that doesn't bother you.

I mean if you would like me to lose weight, I certainly would try to *comply* with your wishes.

(*Annoyed.*) I have all my hair, mam.

Weak blue-gray.

No, I have twenty-twenty vision.

Most definitely eager, mam. You couldn't find a more eager employee. I'd work very hard. My time is your time.

May I suggest that you give me a trial period of employment and I'll prove to you my worth. I realize that there must be *stiff* competition for the position—for any position with a lady of such importance and distinction as yourself—but if you let me I can show you that an ardent beginner can be better than an old *hand* of no matter how much experience. I know that this is a great presumption on my part, but I think that an interview, an *inter-view*, would be to our mutual advantage.

I know, Miss Victoria, I know. Please forgive the impertinence.

Thank you.

No.

I don't know. (*Serious.*) That's a good question.

I don't know. I guess I never met the right girl.

No, I live alone, Miss Victoria.

Three rooms.

Pardon me?

Yes. The bedroom.

Yes, neat. How did—? Never mind. I'm very neat. I don't like a maid around doing a sloppy job. I'm sure I'd have to clean up after her. I like things just so. Everything in its proper place.

I couldn't stand one. They're messy. They leave hair all around.

I didn't mean to imply that I don't like animals. I just wouldn't want one for myself, that's all.

I'd take very good care of them, I'm sure. Just as you wish.

Pardon me?

My tie. I'll take off my tie. (*Takes off tie.*) I have taken off my tie, Miss Victoria. . . . Miss Victoria, are you there?

I'm sorry. Of course you're not accountable to me. You have the perfect right to hang up at any time. *I* called *you.* . . . I called you. . . . It's I who am applying to you for a position and it's your right as an employer to treat me as you will. I should be grateful for the privilege of speaking to you.

That's most generous of you. . . . Miss Victoria? . . . Miss Victoria? Hello, hello? (*Jiggles phone. Hangs up. Intercom buzzes.*) Okay, Genovese, so you saw the little light go off. Who's calling? (*Presses button.*) What's so urgent, Dorothy?

That's none of your damn business. In conference means do not disturb.

I cannot rap right now. Take a down. (*Hangs up and dials.*) Hello, Miss Victoria? We were cut off.

Is this Miss Victoria?

This is Harry Jud—Streeter.

I was calling you for an interview—— (*Amused.*) Oh, thank you for hanging up on me, mam. That sure put me in my place. Thank you.

For taking the time to speak to me.

Is there anything I can do to prove my intentions are real? Yes.

(*Looks down at rug.*) Persian.

Yes, mam. (*He pretends to spit on rug.*)

I did it.

Mam?

I spat on the rug.

I swear I did, Miss Victoria.

Please don't hang up!

Yes, mam. (*He spits on rug and rubs it in with his shoe.*) I *did* it, Miss Victoria. . . . When may I see you?

I realize you're very busy. What do you do? Mam?

Clothing buyer. That sounds like a very important job. I'm sure that a lady with your *aggressive* spirit would do it justice. I'd be proud and honored——

I'm sorry I talk too much. I'll try to correct that deficiency— one among many, I'm sorry to say.

I—drink too much.

(*Uncomfortable.*) Yes, mam, I do have difficulties in that direction.

Shoes?

Shoes. I've never thought about shoes. (*To himself almost.*) That's a lie. Shoes. I think about shoes. (*Intercom buzzes.*)

(*Panicked.*) The doorbell.

I don't know who it could be. I'd better answer it. I'll call you right back. (*Intercom buzzes.*) I'll call you right back. (*Hangs up and presses button.*) Genovese, I'm busy! There is no one I wish to speak to.

Tell her I'll call her in fifteen minutes. (*Hangs up and starts to dial. Intercom buzzes.*) I know; it's urgent. (*Presses button.*) What, Dorothy!

No, darling, you're not in the slightest like Marie-Louise.

I'm positive, my sweet.

If you're that worried, call your astrologer.

Dorothy, I'm *not* your astrologer. That's your bag. I'm busy right this second and I haven't the time to discuss your entire mode of living.

That *is* the way I feel about it.

Honey, you *love* it.

Dorothy, I'm hanging up. And, oh, by the way, I don't think I'll be able to take you to Andy's. But Stewart is dying to. Do you mind?

That's just a vicious rumor. I'll call you later. (*Hangs up and dials quickly.*) High-heeled shoes, Miss Victoria!

I beg your pardon, sir. (*Hangs up. Dials.*) Hello, Miss Victoria?

It was nothing important. We were talking about shoes. . . .

I like shoes, mam, . . . especially high-heeled ones with stiletto points, and black mesh stockings?

Yes, it's sweltering in here. May I open my shirt? (*Starts to open shirt. Closes shirt to top.*) Thank you for not allowing me to do what I would like to do.

I was hoping, since you asked me—I'd never have dared express my desires otherwise. Desires. Someone such as I should not have desires, but should remain silent. Thank you for allowing me to express them. Otherwise I would have remained silent. Silent as a sponge. The instrument of a lady with high heels.
As you wish.

Servant. Yes. Let me—let me be your servant, Miss Victoria, your all-round servant. On call twenty-four hours a day, seven days a week. Constantly waiting for your commands, constantly anticipating your least desires. Fulfilling your wishes, no matter what they may be. Having no will of my own. Having mere *reflexes* to fulfill your desires. I'm talking too much. I'm tiring your ears. Your ears, which are used for important communications, for your *business*. For hearing praise from other men, none of whom are worthy to kneel before you, to kiss the tread-marks of your high-heeled shoes on the plush carpets of your bedroom. The footprints of your feet on the wet bathmat. To clean——

I didn't hear anything.

(*Panicked.*) No. It must be the connection.

I'm alone in the apartment.

There's an extension in the kitchen. Hold on, Miss Victoria, and I'll check the *kitchen*. (*Presses hold. Dials intercom.*) Genovese, get off the line.

I'll give you some cheap thrills later, bitch, but stay off the line.

(*Holding phone away from ear.*) Thatta girl! (*Presses button.*) There's no one. If I could only see you, Miss Victoria, glance at you from a distance and then lower my eyes. If I could only come to your door, be allowed to set foot on your doormat, and press the button, and glance but once at your face to see your anger at my intrusion——

I know I'm not worthy.

Forgive me for using words that you have used. I have plagiarized, trespassed, befouled. I'd like to hand you a handkerchief to wipe your lips, which I have touched so inadvertently.

My excuses nauseate me. Forgive one who is never to be forgiven.

Yes, Miss Victoria. (*Slaps himself lightly on the face.*)

Thank you.

Yes, Miss Victoria. (*Slaps himself harder.*) Thank you.

I'm on my knees. (*Goes to his knees.*) I'm in the correct posture to address you, as you desire.

It tires me, but does that matter?

I should be stripped for you, madam, as before God. May my body not offend your eyes. May I strip, Miss Victoria? (*Slowly strips as he talks.*)

Thank you, Miss Victoria, for permitting me to do what I would like to do. I would like to strip naked for your examination, for your use. I would like to have my disgusting slave's body naked for your use. It's trembling to be at the disposal of a superior woman.

I'd love to come crawling to you like a dog, with a dog collar on my neck, by which you lead me where you will, guide me, mount me, and drive me like a horse, not a proud horse, but a pack mule, stubborn, to be led with a riding crop.

I am in your house for your use—to be your secretary, to be your maid. Yes, your maid. I wear an apron when you tire of seeing my disgusting body. But I still wear the dog collar. Thank you, mam, for the collar which puts me in my place, and for the *whip* which corrects the slightest errors a menial makes. (*He has stripped naked.*)

Yes, mam, the floor. Naked on the floor. (*Lies on the floor.*) I am on the floor.

He kisses the floor. He binds himself to a leg of the desk with his necktie.

I am chained to the foot of the bed when I am not in use. You control all my motions. I never leave your house except on maid's errands. To buy cleaning materials and soap to scrub the floors. Or the lipstick which covers your commanding lips. The blood-red lipstick. Or your imperious *stockings*. You permit me these privileges. But I have to earn them by being completely obedient for days.

When you're indulgent you treat me like a pet dog and I lie at your feet. I scratch at the door when I need to relieve myself. At night you lead me like a dog into your garden, and naked like a dog, a mongrel dog, I am permitted to relieve myself to your disgust. You train me until my every motion is due to your command and breathing is the only independent action allowed me. And I thank you for that.

HARRY *barks like a dog.*

(*He howls.*) I'm a good dog, Miss Victoria.

Yes. Thank you.

Yes, thank you.

Yes. Yes.

Yes.

Yes.

Yes.

Yes, madam, yes, madam, thank you, thank you, oh, oh, OH, THANK YOU! (*Intercom buzzes.*)

(*Long pause. Heavy breathing.*) Slave, slave. . . . *When may I see you?* (*Intercom buzzes.*) It's the doorbell. May I call you tomorrow?

Three, yes, three o'clock, Miss Victoria. I'll call you again. (*Hangs up. Intercom buzzes twice.*) Yes, Miss Genovese. Now what can I do for you? (*Beat.*)

He is?

(*Beat.*) Well, tell the old boy I'll see him in a minute. And, oh, thank you, Miss Genovese.

Slow fade. HARRY *dresses.*

Black.

The Golden Circle

A Fantastic Farce

ROBERT PATRICK

For Bubbles and Melody

"ROBERT PATRICK was born September 27, 1937, in Kilgore, Texas. He grew up in Oz, Hollywood, and Off-Off-Broadway. He has had 66 productions of 41 plays as of October 3, 1969. He directed most of them and acted in many. He was the first doorman of the Caffe Cino. His Off-Off-Broadway career spans the Cino, La Mama, Playwrights Workshop, Theatre Gallery, and, above all, his 30 productions in 18 months at Norman Hartman's Old Reliable Theatre Tavern. He received *Showbusiness'* award for best OOB playwright in 1969. His Off-Broadway productions include *Camera Obscura* in *Collision Course* (published by Random House) and *The Haunted Host*. *The Golden Circle* is based on the Rosicrucian-astrological doctrine of the Great Epochs and the recession of the sun. Production is planned for La Mama in the fall of 1969. His hobby is writing, directing, composing, choreographing, lighting, stage-managing, and acting in plays."

There are twelve figures on the stage, holding hands in a great circle. They move in a circle, carefully keeping up a rather complex step and rhythm, as if playing an intricate variation on "Crack the Whip." They are

CORNY *A rather cynical-looking, somewhat hard man, gross physically but thoughtful and experienced-looking. To his left—*

SAGE *Lean, dignified, and wise, with great clear eyes. To his left—*

SNAKE *A dark, brooding person with heavy lids and huge sensual lips. To his left—*

JUSTINE *Slender, pretty, coy, gracefully calculating the pulls and pressures between* SNAKE *to his right and to his left—*

ERGO *A small, perfectly-formed person whose contribution to the rhythm of the circle is so precise as to amount to jitters. To his left—*

LEO *Tall, perfect, golden, muscular, proud. The staid center of the line and the pivot of the vibrations. To his left—*

CANNY *Long, large-chested, always slightly unshaven, nervous, sad-eyed, doglike, smiling to* LEO *on his right and to his left—*

172

JIMINY *Curly-headed, charming, cherubic, whistles under his breath, hums, speeds up the vibration when it is let go slack by* CANNY *to his right, or to his left—*

BULL *Looks like his name, but with considerable dignity. Highly annoyed by* JIMINY *to his right, and to his left—*

EGO *The originator of the rhythms, clearly "cracking the whip." Lean, concentrated, and wolflike as compared to* CANNY's *doggish aspect. To his left—*

FISHY *Tiny, round-eyed, sniffling, terribly shaken by* EGO. *To his left—*

MEDIA *Coolly beautiful, brunette, with a rather banal smile of benevolence*

The actors may be dressed in accordance with the classical attributes of their signs, or in any other fashion. They may be played by any combination of male and female players. I suggest, however, that LEO be male.

The Golden Circle

CORNY   C'mon, c'mon, keep it regular or we'll never get anywhere.

LEO   The idea is not to get anywhere, but to keep going.

MEDIA   I'm sorry if I didn't keep the rhythm going right.

FISHY   Did I break it? It's so complex. It's hard to know. I
mean it's just coming and coming.

MEDIA   No, you didn't do anything, really. Could you let me
have it again?

EGO   Get it right. If I can start it, you can keep it regular.

BULL   I do exactly what you do. If it breaks, it's your fault.

ERGO   All this quarreling and interruption merely overac-
centuates certain rhythms, that's all. I'm terribly sorry, Leo.
I try to straighten them out before they reach you.

JUSTINE   *I'm* sorry, Ergo, I probably added an extra fillip
before it got to you.

SNAKE   Shut up and shake, Justine.

LEO   It doesn't really matter. As long as we hold together, I
can keep the cycle going.

EGO   *You* can keep it going? Who starts it?

JIMINY   Well, who can say? I mean, it's always been going.

EGO   Like to see what would happen if I stopped for a while?

FISHY   Don't! Don't!

MEDIA   It's all right, Fishy, sweet. You rest. I'll carry it for a while.

CORNY   The whole thing's getting lopsided.

MEDIA   I'm sorry. I was talking to Fishy.

BULL   Okay, Ego, I'll keep it going.

JIMINY   You're rather mechanical about it. One-two-three, one-two-three . . .

SAGE   You all know what's going to happen if we don't keep it up.

JUSTINE   Well, good morning, Sage.

CANNY   Hey. Hey. Hey, Corny, it's getting awfully—I don't know—unsteady.

SNAKE   (*to all.*) If you don't quit all this rocking and rolling, I'll scream.

JUSTINE   Sage, you've scared Snake.

SNAKE   I am not scared.

LEO   It *is* getting a little unsteady. I suppose this had to happen someday.

FISHY   It's going to be all right, though.

EGO   I guess you're all going to blame me.

LEO   Not at all, Ego.

CORNY   Keep it going.

ERGO   There's no blame to be placed.

EGO   Oh, yeah?

LEO   Everyone leave Ego alone.

EGO   I can take care of myself.

EGO *shakes violently. The line reacts.*

FISHY   Oh, don't.

CANNY   Oh, wow!

SAGE   There he goes.

JUSTINE   All right, smart-ass.

ERGO   It was no one's fault to start with, but if we don't stop this bickering——

MEDIA   Yes, now cut it out, kids.

The rhythm is restored.

ERGO   The basic problem is that Ego is too touchy.
EGO   I am not. Who said that?
JUSTINE   . . . and distracted.
FISHY   No, it was partly my fault.
SAGE   I'd say so.
MEDIA   I shouldn't have started talking.
ERGO   And in addition, Canny and Fishy are always so nervous
  —we should all take care of them.
CANNY   I'm sorry.
FISHY   I just get so upset when everything isn't going right——
SNAKE   Everything's going right. Be still.
JIMINY   You don't mean literally . . .
CORNY   If you'd all keep shaking like you're supposed to . . .
LEO   Please. Please. Steady.

Quiet for a moment.

FISHY   This is how I like it.
LEO   There. It's all right again.
ERGO   I'd just like to finish what I was saying if I——
SAGE   We all know what you were saying . . .
JUSTINE   Let Ergo finish—darling.
JIMINY   We're all interested, Ergo.
SNAKE   Not all of us.
JIMINY   Well, some of us.
CORNY   Not me.
ERGO   I just wanted to say——
LEO   Take turns, take turns . . .
ERGO   I just wanted to say that we all owe a debt to Ego and
  we should try not to upset him.
JIMINY   Three cheers. Rah. . . . Well . . .
SAGE   I knew that was what you were going to say.
EGO   I don't need taking care of.
SNAKE   Well, someone could take over for him for a while . . .

EGO   Just try.

BULL   I do the best I can.

CORNY   We all do. That's not fair to give Ego all the credit . . .

JIMINY   Well, of course he starts it, but it wouldn't be anything without the rest of us.

EGO   It'd be quieter!

FISHY   Oh, what is this all for?

JIMINY, ERGO, and SAGE   In what sense?

SNAKE   (*of* FISHY.)   Make that whining idiot shut up!

SAGE   It does originate with Ego, in a way, but it ends with Leo.

CANNY   Yeah, I mean Leo knows more about it than the others.

SAGE   Consciously, perhaps.

EGO   What do you mean, conscious? I know *all* about it. I *start* it!

JIMINY   Well, both are true. Ego starts it, but Leo receives it . . .

EGO   Well, let him try to start it then.

FISHY   It's getting very strange—Snake——

SNAKE   Let it!

EGO   Let him try if I start something different.

LEO   Ego, you'll destroy it.

EGO   Well, who said it had to be this way?

CORNY   Stop him!

BULL   How?

FISHY   You can't stop anything . . .

EGO   Maybe you'll see who started it, then!

MEDIA   I can't keep controlling this forever.

SNAKE   Oh, let it go!

CORNY   *You* can't keep controlling it forever?

JIMINY   It's hard when you have to think about it.

CORNY   What if you had this creep to keep on his toes? (*Meaning* SNAKE.)

SAGE   Well, that's what *I'm* here for.

FISHY   Please, don't fight.

MEDIA   Will somebody watch the rhythm?

FISHY   Leo, don't let 'em fight.

LEO   They know better.

ERGO   This is getting all unbalanced.

JUSTINE   You're telling me?

MEDIA   I can watch everything but the rhythm!

SNAKE   You want to try it without me?

JUSTINE   Snake, you're getting just a little bit off, darling.

ERGO   (*to* LEO.)   I'm doing my best.

MEDIA   Fishy, you're leading.

FISHY   I don't mean to. I'm confused. Everybody fighting.

BULL   Ego, what in hell are you doing? You've started a whole new rhythm.

EGO   See how they handle it over there. Leo, Leo, Leo . . .

ERGO   The whole trouble started when Corny and Ego——

SNAKE   It's all over.

SAGE   Don't, Snake, it is *Ego*.

CORNY   I don't want ever ever ever to hear that again . . .

EGO   Take that! and that!

LEO   I'm going to have to take over!

MEDIA   Do, for God's sake. I can't control Fishy.

CORNY   I hate you all. I hate you all.

SNAKE   Not as much as I hate you.

CORNY   Me? Hate *me?*

ERGO   I told you this would happen.

SAGE   Anyone could have told us that.

JIMINY   Corny started it.

MEDIA   Nobody started it.

EGO   I started it!

LEO   I have to stop this!

JUSTINE   (*they are coming apart.*)   Oh, well, it's a change. Everybody grab somebody.

FISHY   We're coming apart.

MEDIA   Everyone be careful.

BULL   You hadda go and change things, Ego!

EGO   Leo did it.

CORNY   Leo didn't do anything.

EGO Well . . . he should have!

They are by now whirling apart in the darkness. From the darkness we hear their parting cries, quickly overlapping.

EGO I did it, I did it, and I can do it again, so there. . . . I was the cause, I was, I will be and I am. . . .

BULL I did what I was supposed to do and everybody else messed up. I had it right. I had it right. I had it right.

JIMINY I thought this would happen. I figured it out just before it happened. I wonder what will happen now? I wonder. I wonder.

CANNY Help me. I'm scared. What's out there? Oh, help me. Help. Help. Help.

LEO It must have been my fault. There must have been more that I could do. I take the blame. I will. I will.

ERGO I told you how it happened. I told you all. I saw it coming. I saw. I saw.

JUSTINE Well, I tried, darlings. We all tried. Don't worry. Everything will come out for the best. We all did our best.

SNAKE I wanted it to happen. I wanted it to. Now you know. Now you all know.

SAGE I tried to warn you all. I told you it was inevitable. I told you. And I was right. I was right, wasn't I? I was right.

CORNY All right, all right, this is it, now we know, okay, don't blame me, I didn't do it, don't try to pin it on me. . . .

MEDIA I knew it would happen. I should have found some way to stop you all. Forgive me for failing.

FISHY I can't believe it. I can still feel you all. We'll get back together again. I know we will. I believe we will. I can see it. I can feel it. . . .

They fall into the darkness in couples, clutching one another, yet struggling. Suddenly the light flares up to reveal a clearing in a semitropical climate. Completely shielded by trees, the clearing fills the stage. Many varieties of trees, stones, plants, plus driftwood, vines—everything necessary to manufacture the various artifacts mentioned in the script. This scene is empty for a moment, then CORNY *and* CANNY *roll on together, crashing into the center of the stage as if dropped from above.*

CORNY   Mmmmf. What are you doing here?

CANNY   Where are we? Where are the others?

CORNY   Untangle from me and shuddup about the others. I wanna forget the others.

CANNY   Where's Ergo? He'll tell us how all this——

CORNY   I especially don't want to see *that* one again. Let's find out where we are.

CANNY   But don't you want the others? Where are you going?

CORNY   I'm going to find out where we are.

CANNY   (*marking a great X center stage.*) We're here. If we stay here we know where we are. So stay here. Where we know.

CORNY   You notice anything to eat around here? Anything to cover us from the rain?

CANNY   What rain?

CORNY   There'll be rain.

CANNY   Don't say that.

CORNY   That won't stop it.

CANNY   But don't say it.

CORNY   It won't start it.

CANNY   Stop it.

CORNY   (*starting off.*) Stick it.

CANNY   You're going away again.

CORNY   To get things.

CANNY   What things?

CORNY   Whatever things.

CANNY   No, you'll get lost.

CORNY   I am lost. We're both lost.

CANNY   Then there's no sense in one of us getting lost.

CORNY   What?

CANNY   Look, you stay here. I'll go. I'll go out and get things. And I'll bring 'em back. And you'll be here so I know when I'm back.

CORNY Look, I'd just as soon be alone.

CANNY You will be. You will be. I'll bring things back and you stay here. And we'll make it nice, huh?

CORNY Just stay out of my way.

CANNY I will. You won't know I'm here.

CORNY What are you doing?

CANNY Gathering up things. Sticks, stones.

CORNY Go gather things further.

CANNY I will. . . .

CORNY (*starts off.*) Or I will. . . .

CANNY No, I will.

CORNY When will you?

CANNY I will now.

CORNY I don't believe it.

CANNY Oh, I will.

CORNY Go.

CANNY If you'll stay.

CORNY I promise.

CANNY If you go away you might get lost.

CORNY M-hm.

CANNY And you couldn't find your way back.

CORNY Go, go.

CANNY And you'd be all terrified and—and you wouldn't have anyplace to come back to.

CORNY Why not?

CANNY 'Cause I would have gone to look for you and got lost myself.

CORNY Canny. If you promise to go and get lost—I promise not to come look for you.

CANNY Promise me.

CORNY I promise.

CANNY Good.

CORNY Now, get lost!

CANNY I am. (*He exits.* CORNY *sags.* CANNY *reappears.*) Don't go.

CORNY (*throws rock.*) GET OUT OF HERE!

CANNY (*exits, re-enters with rock.*)   We might need this. (*Exits.*)

CORNY   Oooooooooh. Now wait. Now wait. It may rain anyway. Need something over my head. (*Begins to put up rude
shelter.*) I wisht I was an animal. Then I wouldn't have
to put up this. Aw, make do. Make do.

JIMINY *and* SAGE *enter.* JIMINY *carries several snares,* SAGE *a
string of birds. They peek in carefully.*

SAGE   Here. I told you we were near them. I could hear.

JIMINY   Yes, and here we are. Where are they? Oh, it's fairly
nice. Hi, Corny. What's this?

CORNY   It was a shelter against the rain. (JIMINY *has knocked
it down with one gesture.*)

JIMINY   What rain?

CORNY (*erecting it again.*)   Never mind.

SAGE   It wasn't very strong, was it?

CORNY (*menacingly.*)   What do you want?

SAGE   Uh-oh.

JIMINY   Corny, it's us. We've found you. And look, we figured
out a way to catch things. It's a snare, see.

SAGE   We didn't figure it out. You did.

JIMINY   Well, yes, I did—but you figured out where the animals would be and when, and all that.

SAGE   Well, one can see.

JIMINY   He underrates himself. He's really wonderful. Look,
isn't it great we're all together? Where are the others?

CORNY   Shut up about the others. What have you got there?

JIMINY   Little birds.

SAGE   He can see.

CORNY   What are you going to do with them?

JIMINY   Well, eat them.

CORNY   Where? Out in the woods?

JIMINY   Well, no. . . . Here.

CORNY   Then you'll have to give me some.

JIMINY   Sure, of course, well, my gosh, yes. Wow, what a nice
place you've got set up.

SAGE   Who else is here?

CORNY   Canny. Why?

SAGE   I saw you looking for him.

JIMINY   Wonderful. Gosh, we'll need a bigger place. And lots more things. You'll see, Corny, it'll be great.

SAGE   Quit that. We can make our own clearing. Who do you think he is—Leo?

CANNY   (*re-entering with armload of roots.*)   I got roots. Oh, hi. Oh, you're here. Wonderful. You're gonna stay, aren't you?

CORNY   That depends. Canny and me set this place up. You fellas'll have to build your own place. And give us one of them—what do you call them? Snares?

JIMINY   Why, sure. And I'll show you how to make them.

SAGE   No, don't. We'll supply the birds if you supply the shelter.

CANNY   You can stay with us. We can all curl up together. Oh, look, it's a home.

SAGE   That won't keep rain out. Leaves would do it better.

JIMINY   Crossed over each other—big ones.

CANNY   Oh, I'll go get them. That's great. I'll get a lot. Y'all don't go 'way, though, huh? (*He exits.*)

JIMINY   This is great. Isn't this, Sage?

SAGE   Just gimme the snares. I'd rather be out in the woods.

JIMINY   (*hopping to work on snares.*)   Oh, wonderful, and I'll make some more. (SAGE *exits.*) See, Corny, everything's okay. I know you're upset and nervous. I could tell. Because sometimes I get nervous myself, and——

CORNY   Just—keep quiet, will you?

JIMINY   Sure, I'll make more snares. It's easy. You see, you put a stick in it to hold it apart, and (*The stick shoots into the woods—he has invented the bow and arrow.*) —say, that's something. (*Shoots another.*)

There is a loud cry of agony from the woods.

CORNY   There's something out there.

JIMINY (*nervously playing with stick and snare.*)   Gee, I hope that Sage is all right. And Canny, too, of course. We'd probably better stay here, though, don't you think?

CORNY   You leave me alone and I'll break you.

JIMINY   Well, gee, I wouldn't do that, go off and leave you all nervous. (*He has made fire with the bow and a stick.*) Oh, looky!

CORNY   Oh, my God, get that out of here.

CANNY (*re-entering.*)   What's that? I heard something and I saw something and I got scared. Where's Sage? What's that?

JIMINY   I don't know. Do you like it?

CORNY   It's dangerous.

CANNY   It's warm. I like it. Where's Sage?

JIMINY   Out there.

CANNY   Who's with him?

CANNY *has seen, entering leaning on one another,* SNAKE *and* BULL. SNAKE *has an arrow in his shoulder.*

CORNY   You.

CANNY   Snake. Bull.

SNAKE (*extracting arrow.*)   Who did this to me?

BULL   What are you all doing here?

JIMINY   Oh, gosh, Snake, I'm sorry. It's something I made.

SNAKE (*reaching for bow.*)   Give it to me.

BULL   Give it to *me*. (*Takes bow.*) I'll keep this so nothing will happen.

JIMINY   Okay. I have more.

CORNY (*to* JIMINY.)   Sssshhhh.

BULL   More? Where are they?

JIMINY   There.

BULL (*appropriating them.*)   I'll take them.

SNAKE (*as* BULL *moves away, letting him fall, to* CANNY.)   Hold me.

CANNY   Sure. Gee, it's good to see you all. I guess we'll need a lot more of everything, huh? I'll go get some.

SNAKE   No.

JIMINY Gee, Bull, I can make all the snares you need.

SNAKE NO.

JIMINY No?

CANNY No?

SNAKE No. Not till we get to the bottom of this.

CORNY Look, this is my place. What are you——

JIMINY Bottom of what?

CANNY It's *our* place.

CORNY (*to* CANNY.) Yeah?

JIMINY (*to* SNAKE.) Why can't I make more snares?

CANNY (*to* CORNY.) Isn't it?

CORNY (*to* CANNY.) Then just try to leave it.

SNAKE (*to* CORNY.) No.

CANNY (*to* SNAKE.) Why?

BULL (*to* SNAKE.) Yeah, why?

SNAKE Not till we——

JIMINY Till we what?

SNAKE (*indicating wound.*) ——find out who did this to me!

JIMINY It was an accident.

BULL (*indicating* JIMINY *and bow.*) *He* did it with *this,* Snake.

SNAKE (*re fire.*) And what's that?

JIMINY Oooo—fire?

SNAKE What does it do?

JIMINY (*whipping out bow and stick.*) Oh, I don't know, you just rub two sticks together, and——

BULL (*ducking.*) He's got another one.

SNAKE Get it!

BULL (*grabbing bow.*) Gimme.

JIMINY No!

CORNY (*to* JIMINY.) Yes.

JIMINY (*to* CORNY.) Why?

SNAKE Because you hurt me with it. And you might hurt me again.

BULL Yeah, you can hurt people with these things. But it *was* an accident.

SNAKE (*to* JIMINY.) You might have hurt Bull.

BULL   Wow, yes. You got more?

JIMINY   No.

SNAKE   And what does this stuff do? (*Touches fire.*) Agh!

BULL   Get back.

SNAKE   Get rid of it. It's hot.

CANNY   No, it's warm.

CORNY   Look, it's getting awfully crowded here.

BULL   So leave.

CORNY   This is my——

CANNY   Our——

CORNY   ——place. We built it, and——

SNAKE   You did a sorry job of it. (*To* CANNY.) What's that *you* got?

CANNY   Stuff. For the roof. Corny?

BULL   (*grabbing leaves.*)   I'll take that.

SNAKE   Guard those things.

BULL   I am. (*He drops them at his feet.*)

CANNY   Where ya goin', Corny?

CORNY   (*starting off.*)   Away.

CANNY   (*letting go of* SNAKE, *who falls on leaves.*)   I'll come with you.

CORNY   No.

CANNY   You can use me.

BULL   (*to both.*)   Where do you think you're goin'?

CORNY   I wanted to be alone to start with.

SNAKE   No!

BULL   (*to* CANNY *and* CORNY.)   Yeah, you stay here.

JIMINY   Look, why don't we sit down and talk this over?

SNAKE   *You* just watch that—fire or whatever you call it. Bull, keep an eye on these two.

CANNY   (*puzzled.*)   What for?

BULL   (*considering.*)   Yeah, what for?

SNAKE   They're trying to get away.

BULL   So let 'em.

SNAKE   They'll set up another place. God knows what they'll do *there.*

BULL   What can they do?

SNAKE   What can they do? What have they done? Obviously they're out to get us.

BULL   For what?

SNAKE   Who knows how their minds work?

CANNY   This is our——

CORNY   Your——

JIMINY   Their——

CANNY   What? Oh. This is our place and we don't like you——

SNAKE   (*to* BULL.)   You see?

BULL   (*to* SNAKE.)   You're right.

JIMINY   What?

CORNY   Oh, my.

SNAKE   You don't like us?

BULL   You don't like us!

CANNY   (*trying to explain.*)   We don't like you *coming in here* like this.

SNAKE   (*playing his wound.*)   I know.

BULL   Why shouldn't we come in?

CORNY   (*in exasperation.*)   No, no, no.

CANNY   No, I didn't mean——

BULL   You want us to stay out there in the woods?

JIMINY   No—we mean——

CORNY   *He* means.

SNAKE   We know what you mean.

CANNY   Look, *Sage* is out in the woods——

CORNY   (*to* CANNY.)   Shhh.

BULL   Hey, is he?

SNAKE   (*as if onto a scheme.*)   M-hmmm.

BULL   (*to* CANNY.)   What's he up to out there?

CANNY   What do you mean?

BULL   You know.

CANNY   NO.

BULL   (*grabbing* CANNY.)   Yes, you do!

JIMINY and CORNY   Hey, no.

THE GOLDEN CIRCLE

BULL (*to* JIMINY *and* CORNY.) BACK UP! (*To* CANNY.) What's Sage doing?

CANNY (*terrified.*) I won't tell you.

BULL (*letting go of* CANNY, *grabbing bow and arrow.*) Yes, you will. I bet he's got one of these things!

SAGE (*entering, armed.*) Indeed, he has.

CANNY Sage, they came and took everything.

SAGE It had to happen.

He and BULL *stand aiming at one another.*

BULL Give me that.

SAGE Where?

CORNY Look, I don't want any part of this.

SNAKE You, get to work on that roof.

CORNY Who, me?

JIMINY (*trying to keep peace.*) Corny, we'll need that, whatever happens.

SNAKE (*to* CANNY.) You, help him.

CORNY Why should I? . . .

SAGE Don't do it, Corny.

BULL (*to* SAGE.) You want us to start in using these things?

SAGE No . . .

BULL Then put yours down.

SAGE No . . .

BULL Listen——

JIMINY Corny, c'mon—I'll show you how.

CANNY I'll help you, too.

JIMINY Corny—to keep peace.

SAGE I'll be seeing you—I'll be watching you. Here. (*Throws a string of birds.*) There's some more food. I'll be back. (*Exits.*)

BULL (*flourishing bow.*) Hey, you come back.

JIMINY (*grabbing* BULL's *arm.*) Don't. Don't do that. He said he'd be back.

CANNY Don't hurt anybody.

189

JIMINY   I—I won't put up the roof if you do. I mean, why should I? If you're just gonna hurt me?

SNAKE   Bull, let Sage go. He'll be back when it's dark.

BULL   How do you know?

CANNY   'Cause this is his place, too.

SNAKE   Right. And that fire stuff makes a light. He'll be back. But the rest of you get to work. Bull, you keep an eye on them.

BULL   Them? They won't try to get away.

SNAKE   They tried before.

CORNY   What makes you think we'll do this, huh?

BULL   You want to get stuck?

SNAKE   Bull—no. (*To* CORNY.) You want to get wet when it rains?

JIMINY   He's right, Corny. Canny. C'mon. I'll teach you how and Canny can help you. Okay?

They go to work on the roof.

SNAKE   There. They'll behave. We got here just in time. This place was coming apart.

CANNY   Not before you——

JIMINY and CORNY (*to* CANNY.)   Sssssh.

CORNY (*to* JIMINY.)   What are *you* shushing him for?

JIMINY   Why were you?

CORNY   Oh, shut up.

BULL (*overhearing.*)   What?

CANNY, CORNY, and JIMINY (*to each other.*)   Sssssh.

JIMINY   Nothing.

BULL (*ominously.*)   Keep it up.

SNAKE   That's right, Bull. You keep an eye on them while I rest.

BULL   While you rest. Why should you rest?

SNAKE   I'm hurt. I'm weak.

BULL   Yeah . . .

SNAKE   Or do you want to rest and give me the thing?

BULL   All right, I'll watch. I'll watch *everybody*.

SNAKE (*settling himself.*) That's right. And don't let them suspect any kind of disagreement between us. Play them off against each other.

BULL Yeah, that's the way.

SNAKE That's the way. Just call me if there's any trouble. You watch the stuff, and the guys working—keep an eye out for Sage. You (*To* JIMINY.) —fix up some of that stuff to eat.

JIMINY Sure. (*To* CANNY *and* CORNY.) I'll be right back. (*Prepares food at fire.*)

CANNY This is awful, Corny. This is our place.

CORNY Well, learn to like it.

CANNY I wish Leo was here. He'd show them.

CORNY Well, he ain't, so shut up.

CANNY (*whimpering.*) Leo . . . Leo . . .

JIMINY Canny, hush, they'll get mad.

CANNY (*goes over to fire.*) I wish Leo was here.

JIMINY I do, too, Canny, I do, too. But hush up.

BULL (*to* SNAKE.) I wish Leo was here. I'd like to see him now.

SNAKE Hush about Leo. I was thinking about Leo. He'd mess the whole place up. We've got it working fine.

BULL Yeah, but what if Sage sneaks back? Or what if Ego comes?

SNAKE I don't know . . . (*Falls to thinking.*)

CANNY When will Leo be here, Jiminy? When will Leo come?

JIMINY I don't know, Canny. You just think about him and be good.

CANNY That doesn't do any good.

JIMINY Crying doesn't do any good either.

CANNY Maybe he'll never come.

JIMINY Oh, Canny, he'll come. He'll see the fire.

CANNY Yeah . . .

JIMINY See? It's bright. He'll see it. He'll come. You just watch the fire and remember. Now go on up and work and remember that Leo's coming.

CANNY I don't feel like he is, though.

JIMINY (*nervously glancing at* SNAKE *and* BULL.) Leo is coming,

Canny. Soon we'll see his golden head. Leo is coming. There's nothing to fear. If we can just hold on. Leo is coming.

CANNY   Leo is coming.

JIMINY   Right.

BULL (*to* SNAKE.)   What are they up to?

SNAKE   Leave them alone.

CANNY   Fix Leo something to eat.

JIMINY *makes a bow for* LEO *and sets it before the fire.*

JIMINY   See the fire. Leo will come. Watch the fire. Leo will come.

CANNY (*becomes entranced with the fire.*)   Leo, Leo, Leo, Leo. (*Suddenly sings.*)

> Leo, Leo,
> Leo, Leo's comin' soon.
> Leo, Leo,
> Leo,
> underneath the waxing moon.
> Leo, Leo,
> he'll be shining from afar.
> Leo, Leo,
> Leo,
> bet he's wondering where we are.
> So we gotta keep the fire going,
> make sure it's showing
> out into the darkest night.
> Gotta feed the fire,
> gotta keep it higher,
> till Leo comes to set things right.
> Oh my, oh me-o
> Leo,
> Leo, Leo's comin' home.

JIMINY *joins in, and even* CORNY *picks up the chorus of "Leo, Leo"—contemptuously, as a bass.*

BULL You gonna let them do that? You gonna let them sing that he's coming?

SNAKE Why not? He probably is.

BULL But what if he does?

SNAKE We can handle it.

BULL Handle Leo? How?

SNAKE We can handle all of them. Look, if anyone else comes——

BULL Yeah?

SNAKE ——we tell them it's Leo's fire.

BULL It's Jiminy's fire.

SNAKE Jiminy won't say that. And if Sage comes——

BULL I can handle Sage.

SNAKE You don't have to—we'll tell whoever else comes that Sage is trying to take over like Leo.

BULL Huh?

SNAKE Never mind. If Ego comes, we'll tell him Leo's coming. That'll keep *him* in line. (*He sings, slyly.*) "Leo, Leo, Leo, Leo's coming soon. . . ."

The scene becomes one of savage tranquility, all singing softly while JIMINY *cooks and serves,* CANNY *plays at the fire, perhaps strumming on one of the bows, and* CORNY *works on the roof. Then we slowly become aware that* JUSTINE *and* EGO *are peeking from around a downstage bush.*

EGO Hey, look, they're all here. Mmmmm. Smell that food.

JUSTINE Great. Do you think they'll give us any? Let me get my veils straight.

EGO Oh, hey, listen to what they're singing. Leo—they're singing to Leo.

JUSTINE He's not here, though. I don't see him.

SAGE (*popping out of the woods.*) No, he's not here. But he might be coming.

EGO Sage. Good to see you. What's going on? What's that thing you have? Bull has one, too. Can we get some of that food? Who all's here? We came a long way.

193

SAGE (*since* EGO *is impossible*.)   Justine, listen. Snake and Bull have taken over everything. They're making everyone work for them. And they're *doing* it.

JUSTINE   Well, Snake and Bull should be good at that. Of course there's no reason why they should be too much over everybody. But God knows the others couldn't hold anything together. Media might, but I don't see him. Or Fishy or Ergo.

SAGE   No, there's only us against the ones you see.

JUSTINE   Against?

EGO   Hey, Sage, why are they singing to Leo? And how come you're out here?

SAGE   They're hoping Leo will come and take control.

EGO   Oh, foot. Let's get out of here.

JUSTINE   Well, look, maybe we can work some sort of deal with them for something to eat first. Also, that light is nice, and I see they've got a place to stay.

EGO   Hey, let's take it from them.

JUSTINE   Ego, come on. We can't do that. (*To* SAGE.) Can we?

SAGE   I don't know. They have some hold over Jiminy and Canny and Corny.

EGO   Well, look, we've got to think of something. Justine?

JUSTINE   Oh, I'm sure Jiminy would much rather be with us. And the others seem manageable.

EGO   I wish they'd shut up about Leo. I can't hear myself think.

JUSTINE   Snake and Bull don't seem to be stopping them from calling Leo. Why don't we say that Leo sent us?

SAGE   That is a very good idea. But will they believe it?

EGO   I don't know if I want to say that . . .

JUSTINE   Ego—it would work. It would also make sure that Canny and Corny were on our side.

SAGE   It's not a bad idea.

EGO   It's a bad idea.

SAGE   We'd have to act like Leo, of course—and talk like him.

EGO   I don't want to do that.

JUSTINE   We have to, darling, it's all a matter of presence and personality.

EGO   Listen, I've got just as much presence and personality as Leo.

JUSTINE   Of course you have, darling. We could say you're Leo's emissary.

EGO (*shocked.*)   What?

SAGE (*shocked.*)   What?

EGO (*offended that* SAGE *is shocked.*)   *What* what?

SAGE (*falling in with* JUSTINE's *scheme.*)   What an idea!

EGO   I could do it. I won't, but I could.

JUSTINE   What a shame. I'll bet you could do it so well, too.

EGO   Well, sure I can do it!

JUSTINE   Wonderful. (*To* SAGE.) Thanks.

SAGE   That's all right. (*They laugh.*)

EGO   What are you two laughing at?

SNAKE (*to* BULL.)   Do you hear something?

BULL   Yes, I hear something.

SNAKE   I wonder if it's Leo.

JIMINY   If it is, you'd better do some of this work. Leo won't like our having to do it all.

BULL   You just——

SNAKE   Bull. Look, Jiminy, Leo always liked everyone to do his part, right? Well, each of us is doing what he's best at, and that's what Leo likes. You're all working, and Bull is watching over us.

CANNY   What did he say? Did he say Leo? Is Leo coming?

CORNY   We can do without *him*. Shut up and get back to work. I don't trust Snake.

JIMINY   Hush. Be still, Canny, everything will be all right. Here, you tend the fire and sing. Uh, look, Snake . . .

EGO (*to* JUSTINE.)   Jiminy gives me a headache. Look, he's taking food to Snake.

JUSTINE   He's trying to—you don't understand Jiminy.

SAGE   I don't understand him either—any more.

BULL (*to* CANNY.)   Hey, you, shut up all that singing about Leo and get to work.

SNAKE   Bull, let them.

CORNY   Look, this is all done enough. I'm hungry.

BULL   You stay where you are. You come down when I tell you.

CORNY   Then tell me quick, for I'm comin' down.

BULL (*sticks him with arrow as he descends.*)   No, you're not.

CORNY   Ouch. Who are you, anyway?

BULL   I'm the guy with the stick.

CORNY   Yeah, well, who's gonna do your work if you use it?

BULL   My work? Your work, you mean.

JIMINY   Hey, fellas——

SNAKE   I'll handle this.

BULL (*whacks* CORNY.)   I'll handle it. Get back up there.

CANNY   Hey, don't hit us.

CORNY   Us?

CANNY   Run, Corny.

JIMINY (*as* BULL *goes for* CORNY.)   Bull, don't.

SAGE (*to* EGO.)   Now!

EGO   Now what?

SAGE   Now charge. Remember we come from Leo.

JUSTINE   LEO! LEO!

SAGE *and* EGO *charge in.* SAGE *subdues* BULL *and stands on his neck.* EGO *more or less terrifies everyone.* JUSTINE *remains behind in the bushes.*

SNAKE (*standing weakly.*)   What's happening here?

CORNY (*to* SAGE.)   Kill him. Kill him.

CANNY (*to* CORNY.)   Are you hurt?

CORNY   Leave me alone.

EGO (*broadcast.*)   Leo sent us. Leo sent me. Leo sent me and Sage and—hey, Justine.

JUSTINE (*entering the clearing.*)   That's right. Hello, darlings. Leo sent us. Leo sent Ego to handle things until he gets here, Snake.

EGO (*to* JUSTINE.)   Where were you?

JUSTINE (*sotto voce.*)   I'm here now. Shut up.

CANNY   Ego. Justine. Hi. Are y'all here to help us?

CORNY   We don't need them.

CANNY (*offended by* CORNY's *refusal of sympathy.*) *You* don't need them.

BULL (*still under* SAGE's *foot.*) Snake, help me.

SNAKE You overdid it, Bull.

SAGE Now be still everyone and listen. Ego has something to tell you.

EGO What? Oh. Listen. Leo heard all of you singing his name and he sent me—and Sage and Justine—to take care of you till he gets here. So just gimme that thing, Bull.

BULL I won't.

SAGE (*taking bow.*) I'll take it.

JUSTINE (*taking it from* SAGE.) And I'll hold it. So nobody gets mad. Sing, Canny.

CANNY *happily sings "Leo, Leo."*

JIMINY (*bringing food for three newcomers.*) Gosh I'm glad to see you. (SAGE *turns away, angry.*) We've got everything set up.

EGO Right. So just—uh, who's singing? (JUSTINE *taps* CANNY, *who shuts up.*) Everybody just (*Bright idea.*) listen to Justine. He'll tell us what Leo wants us to do.

CORNY Why should we do what Leo wants us to do, anyway?

EGO Because I said so.

SAGE Because we mean to hold the place as Leo would want it until he gets here and we all get back together.

SNAKE And what are we supposed to *do?*

JUSTINE Excuse me? Everybody should just live together quietly until Leo gets here.

BULL (*still under* SAGE's *foot.*) And how do you mean to manage that?

SAGE The three of us (*Looks at* JIMINY.)—the four of us will see to it. Remember, we know what Leo wants and you don't.

SNAKE All right. Fine. They're right, Bull. Let them tell us what to do.

BULL What? These—fire and arrow boys?

SNAKE Yes, yes. Just relax. (SAGE *lets* BULL *up. To* EGO.) Now— tell us our places.

EGO Uh . . .

JIMINY (*to* JUSTINE, *referring to* EGO.) Is he in charge? I'm confused.

JUSTINE Uh—yes. Ego's in charge. Sage and I are here to help him remember what Leo wants, that's all. Go ahead, Ego. We'll help you. If you wish.

EGO Well . . . uh . . . Leo wants everybody to do what they're best at.

JIMINY Right, Ego.

CANNY Well, this is our place.

JUSTINE Uh—right. So you know more about it. Canny can take care of the place. Right, Ego?

EGO Uh—right, right. And (*He looks at* JUSTINE, *miffed*.)—and Sage can like figure out where everything can go. And Corny can build——

CORNY It figures.

EGO ——and Bull can take care of all the stuff, and Snake can . . . uh . . . take care of the fire. Canny, you get stuff from wherever Sage finds it to where Bull wants to keep it——

BULL And I'll make sure it all stays where it's supposed to.

EGO Uh . . .

JUSTINE That's a very good idea, Ego. Bull, you take charge of making sure no one breaks in unannounced and all.

BULL You bet I will.

EGO Yeah, you do that. And Jiminy can solve all the problems of . . . uh . . .

JIMINY A technical nature?

EGO Right. And Justine can . . . settle arguments. All right, Justine?

JUSTINE Whatever Leo says.

EGO And I'll—I'll—I'll . . .

JUSTINE You're the head of it all, Ego.

SAGE Yes, that's best.

CANNY   Well, I'd rather have him——

CORNY   Them.

CANNY   HIM—than Snake.

CORNY   It's all the same to us.

CANNY   To you.

CORNY   To me, anyway.

SNAKE   And whom——

JUSTINE and EGO   What?

SNAKE   Whom—if I may ask. May I ask?

EGO   You may.

SNAKE   Who is going to call Leo?

CANNY   Oh, yes, where is Leo?

JIMINY   Yes, where is he?

CORNY   Don't ask.

JIMINY (*to* CORNY.)   Why not?

CORNY   Don't ask why.

CANNY (*to* CORNY, *then* JIMINY.)   Why? Why?

JIMINY   Don't ask me.

EGO   Uh . . .

JUSTINE   Leo had some business of his own. (*Inspiration.*) He's out hunting for Fishy and Ergo. He was especially worried about them, wasn't he, Ego?

EGO   Uh, yeah, he was worried about everybody.

SAGE   He'll come in his own good time. Snake can keep calling for him.

SNAKE   That'll be quite a job. It will take all my time.

JUSTINE   Yes, Snake, you take all the time you need.

EGO   Yeah.

JUSTINE   And if there are any problems about it you just bring them to me and I'll consult with Ego.

EGO   Yeah.

SAGE   Ego, wouldn't you be happier here inside? And we'll bring our problems to you.

JUSTINE   Yes, then we'll know where you are—when we have a problem.

EGO (*exiting.*) Uh—yeah, sure. I think I will. You all keep doing like Leo wants, now.

JUSTINE (*to* SAGE, *aside.*) He did very well, considering.

SAGE He did very well. No one else could have drawn them together.

JUSTINE Well, we did our bit too, dear.

SAGE Yes, but—you know, he even looks a little bit like Leo.

JUSTINE So he does, rather. But let's us not mistake him for him, hm?

SAGE (*laughs.*) You're right. I almost did. Well, to work. I'll scout for things. Canny, you come with me. Everyone else has plenty to do, I'm sure.

BULL You're going out?

SAGE We are.

BULL Well, let me know when you want back in.

SAGE Oh, very well.

BULL Nobody's takin' me by surprise again.

SAGE That's wonderful, Bull. I'm proud if I've helped you see your former mistakes. . . .

JUSTINE Bull, you must be hungry. Jiminy, can you make sure that Bull and Snake are well taken care of?

JIMINY Sure, you can count on me, Justine.

BULL I don't know what Snake has to do.

SAGE Snake has to call for Leo to come soon.

JUSTINE A very important function.

BULL Humph!

SAGE Come, Canny. Justine, I leave it in your hands.

JUSTINE (*smiles.*) And those of Leo's emissary, of course.

SAGE (*smiles.*) Of course. (*Exits with* CANNY.)

SNAKE (*at fire.*) Oh, Leo, come, Leo. You of perfect judgment and golden light, your humble servant calls you. Come to save us from the cunning of the ambitious, Leo, come. Come to save us from the pride of those full of self-sufficiency, Leo, come. Save us from the anger of the greedy, the slavery of the servile, Leo, come. . . . Oh, Leo, you know the injustices we have suffered under——

JUSTINE (*calling into the woods.*) Canny! (CANNY *can be heard singing "Leo, Leo, Leo, Leo's comin' home. . . ." This stops* SNAKE*'s prayer.*)

Suddenly BULL *gives a shout, interrupting the now slightly more civilized working and worshiping scene.*

BULL (*running off.*) Hey, that's mine.

CORNY (*automatically.*) Ours.

BULL (*off.*) Bring it back.

SNAKE What is it?

JUSTINE Bull, what is it? Bull is after somebody.

EGO (*entering, miffed.*) Hey, what *is* up?

JUSTINE The opposite of down.

EGO Huh?

JUSTINE Oh, Emissary of Leo, Bull is after a marauder.

EGO How's that?

JUSTINE Somebody was in the food, apparently.

EGO Well, stop them. Leo wouldn't like that.

SNAKE (*slithering to* EGO.) I've been thinking about Leo, lord, thinking what he might want.

JIMINY That wouldn't have been Leo in the food, though.

SNAKE No, but I'm sure Leo sent them.

JUSTINE Them?

SNAKE I'm sure.

JIMINY Ergo and Fishy and Media?

SNAKE Only Leo knows.

JUSTINE (*who has been watching* SNAKE. *To* SNAKE.) What are you up to?

JIMINY Here he comes.

BULL *re-enters, carrying* FISHY *and* ERGO *under his arms.*

BULL Look who was snatching my——

CORNY (*who has, incidentally, continued building throughout all this.*) My?—my, my.

BULL *Our* food.

JIMINY Ergo. Fishy. Hello.

CORNY Two more of them. Oh, Leo.

ERGO Oh, hello. It's all of you.

FISHY I knew we'd get in trouble. I could feel it. But the food was right there. We didn't take much.

ERGO Will you please let go of me Bull! Justine, I presume you're in charge. Please tell him to let go of me.

EGO *I'll* tell him. Bull, let go.

BULL Who says so?

EGO I say so.

JUSTINE (*sotto voce.*) Leo.

SNAKE Leo says so.

EGO Uh—yeah, Leo says so. Hey, what is this, Justine? I thought you were supposed to settle arguments for me.

SNAKE For Leo.

EGO Leo.

CORNY (*satirically.*) Leo, Leo, Leo . . .

JUSTINE And so I shall. Here are two of our lost brothers returned to us. Everyone rejoice.

JIMINY Yea.

JUSTINE Bull, let go of them.

SNAKE Two lost brothers of Leo. Children of Leo. Come back to his fireside.

ERGO His fireside? Is Leo here? Are we all here? Where are Sage and Canny? And Corny?

CORNY Humph.

ERGO Ah, there's Corny.

FISHY It just feels terrible here. Everybody's mad. You're all mad at me and Ergo. We didn't mean to make you mad. We've been looking and looking for you and we didn't think you'd mind us taking a little something to eat.

JUSTINE Ergo just wanted to look the place over before coming in, I'm sure.

SNAKE Perhaps Leo told them to.

CORNY Me, oh my, oh-me-o.

ERGO Well, I'm sure Leo wouldn't want us to rush into anything. Is he here?

SNAKE   It was Leo's fire that brought you here, my children.

EGO   (*who has been ignored.*) Hey, listen, everybody.

FISHY   Oh, it's Ego. He's always mad at me.

JUSTINE   Ego is ruling in Leo's place till Leo gets here, Fishy.

FISHY   Oh, dear.

SNAKE   When is Leo coming, children?

ERGO   Then he isn't here?

JIMINY   No, but he sent Justine and Ego to rule over us.

EGO   He sent me to rule. Justine is just supposed to settle arguments.

JUSTINE   Of course, Ego. For you.

SNAKE and CORNY   For Leo.

JUSTINE and EGO   For heaven's sake.

ERGO   What *is* happening?

SNAKE   Yes, what is happening with Leo, children? He did send you, didn't he? Justine and Ego said he was especially worried about finding you—you must have some message from him for us.

BULL   I don't know what's happening here, but——

SNAKE   Bull, these are Leo's children. The food they took was Leo's food. They must come and rest by Leo's fire until they feel well enough to tell us of him.

JUSTINE   Let those people go, Bull. (BULL *finally releases them, reluctantly.*)

EGO   Let them go, Bull. (*To* JUSTINE.) And *you* just wait until there's an argument to settle. Now, Jiminy, get them something to eat and *I'll* explain to them.

SNAKE   (*leading* ERGO *and* FISHY *to fire.*) Come, children. Leo's emissary will come into Leo's home and tell you Leo's will. Rest by Leo's fire.

FISHY   It is a little bit like Leo was here. Leo is quiet and calm. I always feel better when I look at Leo. I wish he was here.

SNAKE   Ah, he is here, children. You can't see him, but he is here. He is here in the fire Justine and Ego have finally let you come to, and in the food Jiminy will bring you if Bull lets him, and in the houses Corny is building for us all. . . .

ERGO   Snake, where are Sage and Canny and what *is* going on?

SNAKE   Sage and Canny are out looking—with Leo's guidance—for you. And Justine is supposed to be settling some argument or other, are you not, Justine?

EGO   There's no argument. Snake can take care of Fishy and Ergo. Now everybody else just keep acting like Leo would want you to. I want to sleep. I'm tired. (*He exits.*)

JUSTINE   Ego has spoken.

BULL   Everybody back to work.

CORNY   I never stopped.

BULL   Well, don't.

SNAKE   (*taking food from* JIMINY.)   Thank you, Jiminy. (*Waits for* JIMINY *to retire.*) Now, you see, we are all waiting here for Leo to rejoin us. It's been rather hard and there have been some disagreements, but they'll all be over soon. There seems to be some question as to just where Leo is, but I'm sure that if you two will take turns tending the fire, I can think of where to find him. Wouldn't that be nice?

FISHY   Yes, I'd like that. When I look into the fire I feel I'm near him.

ERGO   Yes, I suppose tending the fire is essential. But what will you be doing while we tend it?

SNAKE   (*who has been plumping his bed.*)   Oh, I'll be . . . writing down everything I remember about Leo, to help settle any problems that arise.

ERGO   Very good, very good. I remember a great deal about him. As you may or may not recall, I stood beside him. I'll be glad, and, I think, qualified to help. Of course, I know what you're going to say—Canny also stood next to him. But I don't suppose Canny's recollections can really be trusted—he's so emotional, Canny. Now, let's us all get organized. I suppose Jiminy is the one to ask for things, eh? Jiminy, could we have something to write with? And to write on, of course. Thank you, Jiminy. Now, let's see . . . Leo. . . .

FISHY   (*staring into fire.*)   Yes, I almost feel that I can see him—golden and tall.

JIMINY   Do you, Fishy? Canny thought he did, too.

FISHY   Yes, I do, I do. Leo! Right there in the fire. (*Reaches into fire and recoils, fainting.*)

JUSTINE   What is it?

JIMINY   Fishy. He fainted.

SNAKE   He fell into the fire.

ERGO   Jiminy, put something around the fire. (*To* SNAKE.)   I'm *sure* Leo would want something around the fire.

EGO (*entering, piqued.*)   What is going on out here? Justine. Jiminy. Bull.

BULL   I'm doing my job. I'm making my rounds.

CORNY   So am I. Don't bother me. I'm better off alone.

SAGE (*entering with* CANNY.)   We followed the fire back. We have news.

EGO   Well, it's about time. Did you find Leo?

CANNY   Fishy. And Ergo. Hi. Aw, is something wrong with Fishy?

EGO   I don't know. My God, I can't get any sleep, and it's cold in there, and I want a fire, and—

SNAKE   Please—listen.

FISHY   I saw him. I saw Leo. He was calling to us. He stepped out of the fire and he said: "Everybody be good to each other. Everybody be kind."

ERGO   Well, that makes sense.

FISHY   He said: "Everybody be happy. I want everybody to be happy and quiet."

EGO   Well, so do I. So do I. Listen to me, everybody.

SNAKE   He isn't finished.

FISHY   I—I can't see it anymore.

SNAKE   Listen to me, all of you. Fishy had a message from Leo and Ego made him forget it.

ERGO   Ah, well, back to work.

EGO   Hey, I'm supposed to be leading—aren't I, Sage?

SAGE   It's the only way.

SNAKE   But Leo sent us messages through Fishy.

JIMINY   Who *is* ruling, will somebody tell me?

EGO   I am.

SNAKE   Leo is!

CORNY   Snake is.

JUSTINE   Am I or am I not supposed to settle arguments?

BULL   You get no arguments from me.

SAGE   Let's listen to Justine.

CORNY   I'll listen, I'll listen.

JUSTINE   Okay. Now, all this argument is unnecessary. I can't imagine why we're doing it. What is there to dispute about? We have, after all, a common goal, haven't we?

EGO   Sure. What?

JUSTINE   What?

CANNY   (*slapped by* SAGE.)   Leo, Leo, Leo's comin' home. . . .

JUSTINE   Leo, of course. (SAGE *slaps* CANNY *to be silent.*) Fishy is right—that Leo would want us to live in peace and perfect accord with one another.

EGO   I was going to say that.

JUSTINE   Of course you were.

CANNY   He'd want us all to stay together, too.

ERGO   Well, of course he would.

JUSTINE   Please. Ego, he'd want us all to listen, wouldn't he?

EGO   You settle the arguments, that's your job. Jiminy, I'm hungry.

JUSTINE   Feed the king, Jiminy.

JIMINY   Then, Ego is definitely the boss?

JUSTINE   Yes, yes. (JIMINY *turns a smile of unadulterated adoration on* EGO.) Now Fishy can wait for more messages from Leo.

SNAKE   As keeper of the fire——

JUSTINE   As keeper of the fire, I'm sure you should keep the fire. And Ergo can write down all anyone remembers of Leo. And everybody else can keep doing what they've been doing. Okay? Okay.

All return to tasks.

JIMINY (*to* EGO.)   You know, I have lots of ideas, but nobody ever seems to want to hear them, though.

EGO   Like what?

JIMINY   I mean, maybe they come from Leo or whatever. But they're good ideas. You know how hard it is to get people to listen to your ideas?

EGO   Yeah, sure. Look, I'm busy. What is it?

JIMINY   Well, I was just thinking that if we were to take arrows and set fire to them it would make good messages for Leo. Signals for Leo.

EGO   Leo. I don't know why we need Leo. I can keep everything in order as well as he could.

SAGE (*approaching them.*)   What were you saying?

JIMINY   I was just talking with the king.

SAGE   I have a message for him myself.

EGO   Well, what? I never have a minute for myself.

SAGE   We discovered a lot of land to the south. Only it's full of animals.

EGO   Yeah. And?

SAGE   If we had more space—if there were more room—perhaps there wouldn't be all of this fighting. Where's Bull?

EGO   Bull is minding everybody's business. Why?

SAGE   These bows that Bull and I have—they could take care of the animals.

JIMINY   Especially if we had flaming arrows.

SAGE   I hardly think we need flaming arrows.

JIMINY   Sure. Listen. I bet they'd run faster and faster if we had those.

EGO (*getting excited.*)   Hey, yes. Where is this place?

SAGE   To the south. But we'd need all of us.

EGO   Well, come on.

SAGE   But——

EGO   Hey, everybody. Listen. There's lots of land to the south. We're gonna take it over from the animals. Follow me. Hey, Bull.

207

BULL   I'm doing my job.

EGO   But, hey, let's go down and take over, huh?

SNAKE   For Leo?

EGO   Well, yes, sure, of course for Leo.

SAGE   Do you mean that? For Leo?

EGO   Sure. That's what it's all for, isn't it? For Leo? Come on. Jiminy. Bring bows and arrows.

JIMINY   And fire?

EGO   Sure, fire.

SNAKE   The fire is Leo's.

FISHY   I don't think Leo wants us to fight.

EGO   We're not fighting.

FISHY   You're going to fight.

EGO   We are not going to fight. Shut up! Justine, get a bow and come with us. Bull.

BULL   I'm here. I've got it. Let's go.

EGO   Corny.

CORNY   Not for the world. I have work to do and I have nothing against the animals.

EGO   But it's for Leo.

CORNY   Leo, Shme-o.

EGO   Justine, you're coming?

JUSTINE   I don't want to. Go ahead if you want.

EGO   Aw. Jiminy . . .

JIMINY   I've got them. And the fire.

EGO   Well, come on. Sage.

SAGE   Yes, I'll come.

JUSTINE   Sage, you're not?

SAGE   I must. There has to be a leader, you've seen that, and he is the chosen one.

JUSTINE   (*aghast.*)   My dear!

EGO   Snake. Ergo. Fishy. You comin' to fight for Leo and all?

SNAKE   We are staying here. We have work to do.

EGO   Oh, honestly. Leo'll come if he wants to. Who needs him, anyway?

FISHY and SAGE   Ego!

EGO   I mean, he's with us, isn't he? Fishy says he's in the fire.

JIMINY   And we have the fire.

EGO   And anyway we——

SAGE   We go forth to conquer in his name.

EGO   Yeah. Yeah. We go forth to conquer in his name. Come on. For Leo. For Leo.

EGO, SAGE, BULL, *and* JIMINY *start off, yelling "For Leo!"*

CANNY   Hey, I'll go, too.

JUSTINE   Canny. Why?

CANNY   It's for a bigger and better home. (*The adventurers exit.*)

SNAKE   Well.

ERGO   What a relief to have them gone. I have a lot to show you.

SNAKE   Now, now. Enough time for that later.

ERGO   THE WAY THINGS ARE GOING. I think the first moment we get Leo here the better it will be. Now, Leo liked us to stay together. He disliked for us to quarrel.

SNAKE   Really, this hardly seems the time——

ERGO   *He disliked for us to quarrel.* He liked us to listen to one another. He liked everyone to be equally considered. He didn't like people to try to dominate other people. (JUSTINE *laughs.*) Why are you laughing?

JUSTINE   With happiness, what else?

ERGO   Wisdom is the only real happiness.

JUSTINE   I know, and I'm getting so wise.

FISHY   He liked happy laughter, but not too much.

ERGO   Yes, dear. He liked laughter and happiness, but he knew that work was more important.

FISHY   He was always watchful for us, sad when we were happy and happy when we were sad. He balanced all vibrations.

ERGO   He liked everyone to do their own job.

FISHY   What is my job?

ERGO   He liked everyone to take turns.

FISHY   At what? What was his purpose?

ERGO   Well, that's something only he could know, darling.

FISHY   Perhaps he'll tell me.

ERGO   Watch out.

SNAKE   These are things we all know.

JUSTINE *has wandered over to where* CORNY *works on the roof.*

JUSTINE   Corny . . .

CORNY   Leave me alone. I'm working.

JUSTINE (*starting up ladder.*)   I'm very lonely. Things got out of hand down here.

CORNY   Well, don't come up here.

JUSTINE   I'll give you some help. I'll lend you a hand.

CORNY   The hand that things got out of?

JUSTINE (*on roof.*)   I just want to help.

CORNY   You'd be better off listening to them. They're up to something.

JUSTINE   Fishy and Ergo? Aw.

CORNY   Never you mind. I've been up here watching you all, and I know the signs. None of you ever think of me except to do your work, but I see, and I know. I know what Leo would want if he was here, but nobody asks *me*.

JUSTINE   What would he want?

CORNY   Well, first off he'd want me to stop for a while and have a drink.

JUSTINE (*looking at dipper.*)   What's that?

CORNY   Just a little combination of some root juices and a little rotted grain. Tastes great, though.

ERGO (*reading list.*)   Yes, that's about what Leo would have wanted. He wants us all to share one another's work.

FISHY   So we can share one another's vibrations and be one again.

ERGO   Hm? Well, yes, perhaps, but my way of putting it is so much clearer.

FISHY   Not to me. I feel him more in the fire than I do with all your words.

ERGO Well, yes, but we can't all feel your feelings and we can all hear my words.

FISHY But your words don't call him back. My feelings do. Can't you feel him when you look into the fire? Or when you see the sunset light? The peace, the strength.

ERGO It doesn't matter if I do or not. Oh, where's Justine? He always makes people understand each other.

SNAKE (*somewhat apart.*) He's up on the rooftop with Corny, ingesting something that makes them quite disorganized. Now maybe I can help you both. Didn't you say that Leo wants us to work together?

ERGO Certainly. I said that.

FISHY Is that what he wants? Is that what he wants?

SNAKE Now I'm sure he doesn't want this Ego running around following his whims or Sage acting as if Ego were Leo, or Justine and Corny misbehaving so, or Jiminy wasting all his possessions.

ERGO What *does* he want, Snake?

FISHY What does he want? What does he want?

SNAKE I believe he wants us to keep his fire going to call him here so that he himself can tell us what he wants. I believe that till then, in order to keep things sensible, he wants someone to rule his people kindly but firmly so that they won't come to harm. . . .

ERGO Well, certainly that's necessary until they learn what I've written here. . . .

FISHY Till all of their vibrations get back together. . . .

SNAKE Sweet child. (*To* ERGO.) Now, you're very busy with your intellectual efforts, and obviously no one else but you here is fit to rule. Why don't you let me take over for you? I'll see that they stick to your writings.

ERGO Well, thank you, Snake, I misjudged you, but that shouldn't be necessary. I'm sure they'll all listen to sense.

FISHY First they must vibrate together.

ERGO What are you expecting? An earthquake?

JUSTINE (*drunk.*)   Wheeeeeeeee.

CORNY (*drunk.*)   See, life's no good, is it?

JUSTINE   No, it's marvelous. Just to watch them all squabbling down there. What a joke.

SNAKE   Justice and industry seem to be upset.

JUSTINE (*dancing on the roof.*)   My, look at the sky spin. Or is it me that spins?

FISHY   Yes, spins and spins, chases itself, life all one, broken into pieces and chasing itself . . .

SNAKE   You see, that's what we'll get from the rest of them unless we servants of Leo stick together.

FISHY   Forces pulling at one another forever . . .

ERGO   But they're all servants of Leo, too.

SNAKE   Well, look what their ideas have brought them to.

FISHY   It is as if every action created an equal and opposite reaction . . .

ERGO   Well, I can't understand it.

SNAKE   Why try?

CORNY   Why try? Why not just do as we're told?

JUSTINE   But, darling, I've been in the habit of telling . . .

CORNY   Well, somebody else will.

FISHY   Nature abhors a vacuum. . . .

SNAKE   Let me take this burden off you and share your labor.

CORNY   Ah, life is no good and death is no rest.

JUSTINE   You think not?

CORNY   No, I think this whippin' back and forth and droppin' in and droppin' out never stops.

JUSTINE   But—why?

FISHY   Why? Why ask why? We don't know why. We are spared knowing why. The fragments drift, crashing against each other—no matter or energy is ever created or ever destroyed . . .

SNAKE   Do you see? Do you see why someone with the ability to administer a little discipline must be in control?

ERGO   I see that you are eager to administer discipline and will take any excuse to do it.

SNAKE   Is that bad? If it's needed?

ERGO   I—I don't know. Get them down and let's talk.

SNAKE   Are you giving orders to me?

ERGO   They're Leo's orders.

FISHY   All things move together . . .

SNAKE   How do you know Leo's orders?

FISHY   . . . from some one point . . .

ERGO   Why, we all do.

FISHY   . . . to another.

SNAKE   I'll do what I decide.

ERGO   And how will you feel when Leo comes?

SNAKE   Leo isn't coming.

FISHY   Leo will come. Eventually. In a flash of fire and a trembling of the earth.

JUSTINE   What are they all gabbling about? It's just rasping sounds, harsh music.

CORNY   Well, let's make some straight music.

JUSTINE and CORNY (*sing.*)

Oh, life is a mystery nobody understands,
to keep the blood out of our brains we walk on our back hands;
and where we came from or where we are going nobody really knows,
but everyone feels it's drawing to a close;
so drink, drink, don't think, let's be brave and true—
I won't ask nothing of me if you won't ask nothing of you!

FISHY   Oh, the fragments are spinning uncontrolled . . . they crash and crash against one another. . . .

SNAKE   Will Leo come to this?

ERGO   And if you are wrong? If he does come? What then? What will you say to him when he sees how you are splitting us all apart?

SNAKE   And aren't you splitting us all apart? Isn't he? Isn't every one of us keeping the others apart from him just by being? What are you afraid of? He'll rejoin us if he comes, don't you know that? In the meantime I will not be crushed by any other's desires!

ERGO Oh, my God. You're right. You're right. We are all to blame. We are all guilty.

FISHY I can feel him coming now. Leo comes.

There has been a sound of hoofbeats for some time, unnoticed. Now a tremendous roaring sound is heard and the glow of a tremendous but still faraway fire suddenly bathes the stage. We hear insane whooping and hollering and the adventurers— EGO, JIMINY, BULL, SAGE, *and* CANNY—*run on in various states of excitement and panic.*

JIMINY Our arrows worked.

EGO We've set the world on fire.

JIMINY They worked, though, our arrows.

CANNY *Your* arrows.

BULL It'll be here in about an hour—the fire.

CANNY Here, in our home!

SAGE Where's Justine?

ERGO Oh, we deserve this!

CORNY We don't deserve anything!

JUSTINE Here I am, drunk, drunk as you all are!

CORNY Did it, did you, darlings? Well, good luck to you!

ERGO Oh, Leo. Oh, someone. Help us!

EGO (*to* JUSTINE.) Help us put out the fire.

SNAKE You fools, you've destroyed us.

FISHY Nothing is ever created or ever destroyed.

ERGO We've all destroyed ourselves—and each other. We created ourselves. We created each other.

BULL What are they all blathering about? The fire——

SAGE The fire is coming.

CANNY What are we going to do?

JUSTINE Burn, baby, burn!

EGO Jiminy, you started it, you stop it.

JIMINY I started it, *you* stop it.

SNAKE (*to* FISHY.) How can we fight it?

ERGO   He doesn't want us to fight.

FISHY   Why fight it?

SAGE   We must flee.

CANNY   And leave everything we've built here?

CORNY   WE?

BULL   How did we get into this?

JUSTINE   WE?

ERGO   Wee, weee, wee, weee.

CANNY   Corny, Corny, our home will burn. Why don't you help?

CORNY   It's your home, not mine.

EGO   Justine, we need you now.

SNAKE   Justine is drunk.

BULL   You let this happen.

SNAKE   You got out of line.

SAGE (*to* JIMINY.)   You did it.

JIMINY   You led us to it!

EGO (*to* JUSTINE.) How could you let this happen? Where were you when the fire began?

JUSTINE   Well, where were you?

FISHY   The vibrations grow toward Leo.

ERGO   They grow toward chaos.

FISHY   There is no chaos.

ERGO   There is no Leo.

FISHY   All things are one.

ERGO   Everything is meaningless.

FISHY   It is as if every particle of matter in the universe attracted and was attracted by every other particle with a force directly proportionate to their mass and inversely proportionate to the distance between them. . . . (*Faints for real. This stuns everyone.*)

BULL   What does that mean? Does that mean anything? What did he say?

ERGO   It means that we are all brothers, all part of one another.

JUSTINE   Oh, my God, yes, darlings. What's happening? We should all join together, not fight. (JUSTINE *rushes to* ERGO.)

EGO (*running to* FISHY.)   We should all leave each other alone, you mean.

SNAKE   We should all join with the strongest. We should all join with the strongest. (*Rushes to* ERGO.)

BULL   We should *be* strong. (*Rushes to* FISHY.)

JIMINY   I understand what Fishy means, I really do. (*To* FISHY.)

SAGE   Ergo is right. We are. We are all brothers. (*To* ERGO.)

CORNY   We gotta help each other. (*To* ERGO.)

CANNY   He saw what I saw. Really. In the fire. (*To* FISHY.)

They are now suddenly two distinct camps. They are ministering to FISHY *and* ERGO *and then look up and see the division, with the fire between. They are silent, each group around their helpless center.*

ERGO'S GROUP   Come to us. This is silly. Join us. We're all brothers, darlings. Stop this separation. Let's get together.

FISHY'S GROUP   You come to us. Vibrate with us. Stop arguing all the time. We are all one. Love us. We love you.

Pause.

ERGO'S GROUP   Come on. This is foolish. What is this all about? Are you forgetting the fire? What do you mean, love? Make sense.

FISHY'S GROUP   You come on. We need you. You need us. Then don't be foolish. Well, let's get together. What do *we* mean by love? *You* make sense.

SNAKE   Love you? When you pull us apart this way?

CANNY   *You're* pulling us apart. Stop quarreling and come over.

ALL   Come over, come over. . . . (*Several do change sides, others start to and are dragged back or change their minds. One might run to the other side only to be swooped up by someone from* that *side changing sides and brought back with him. At any rate, the groups wind up again of equal size.*) Come on, come over. We've got to get together.

SAGE   Stop! We're doing something terribly wrong.

JIMINY   What?

SAGE   I don't know, but something.

EGO   You admit it, you're wrong.

JUSTINE   He said *we're* wrong, all of us.

BULL   You sure are.

CORNY   I swear I've seen the light. I should never have given in.

EGO   I should never have tried to run things.

SNAKE   (*running between groups.*)   No. No. This has to stop. Leo. Great golden Leo. Forgive me. Forgive us. Great ruddy golden god, wherever you may roam. Red Rover, red rover, let the others come over.

ALL   Red Rover, red rover, let the others come over. Come over. Come over.

SNAKE   No, no, everything I do, everything I say only compounds the separation. I do not want to exist. (*He flings himself into the fire, is dragged out, practically roasted over the fire by being pulled both ways. Screams.*) No, no, let me die, let me be the one, let me be sacrificed.

EGO   Look what kind of craziness you've brought us to!

CORNY   (*to* EGO.)   You were supposed to lead us.

CANNY   (*to* CORNY.)   You were supposed to follow.

CORNY   (*of* SNAKE.)   It's all his fault.

JUSTINE   Does that make everyone feel better? We've got to get together before we can do anything.

ALL   (*advancing in whatever combinations they happen to be in now.*)   We hate to do this. You've brought us to this. We've got to make you see things our way. We are all one. All is one. We are all brothers. We love you. We're doing this because we love you. We want you with us. Try to understand. You'll never understand. We hate to use force. I didn't want this to happen.

MEDIA   (*entering center.*)   Oh, we're all together. Wonderful.

Stunned silence.

CANNY   Media. We forgot all about you.

Robert Patrick · *The Golden Circle*

ERGO   Media, tell them—aren't all men brothers?

FISHY   No they're not, no they're not—we're all part of one great being.

MEDIA   Of course. Two different ways of saying the same thing.

SAGE   Media. Media. Where's Leo?

MEDIA   He's surveying the fire. Don't you know there's a fire? He'll be here soon to lead us all against it.

FISHY   The fire—no wonder we were angry. All that red light. . . .

MEDIA   Angry?

BULL   Media, they've been awful.

MEDIA   They? Who?

BULL   Well, someone.

CANNY   They hate us.

MEDIA   Who?

EGO   We told them we loved them.

JUSTINE   You *yelled* that you loved us.

CORNY   With rocks in your hands.

EGO   Well, you wouldn't accept it.

BULL   Well, of course not.

SAGE   You see?

BULL   I mean we *would*.

SAGE   You said you wouldn't.

BULL   I don't know what I'm saying.

SAGE   Well, if you don't know, how can we know?

MEDIA   Well, whatever this is, it can wait. Leo is coming.

CORNY   We've heard that before.

BULL   But they won't follow him.

SNAKE   We will, but if we do, you won't. And if you do we won't, so there.

They start again.

BULL   You *yelled* that you loved us.

CANNY   With rocks in your hands.

JUSTINE   Well, you wouldn't accept it.

SNAKE   Well, of course not.

JUSTINE   You see?

SNAKE   I mean we *would*.

BULL   You said you wouldn't.

SNAKE   I don't know what I'm saying.

CANNY   Well, if you don't know, how can *we* know?

MEDIA   Well, whatever this is, it can wait. Leo is coming.

JIMINY   We've heard that before.

CANNY   But they won't follow him.

SAGE   We will, but if we do, you won't. And if you do we won't, so there.

MEDIA   Good heavens. What on earth. You're fighting. I don't believe it. Not after all the trouble it caused last time.

EVERYONE   You started it. They started it.

JUSTINE   We weren't we when we started it, only we didn't, whoever we were—*you* did.

CANNY   Who were we, then?

ERGO   Who are we, now?

MEDIA   Well, isn't that question silly enough to stop you? Have you all forgotten? (*Sings.*)

This spinning world we live in has a tendency to leaven
everybody's urge to get along
until we tend to give in to thoughts of hell and heaven
and break up into teams of right and wrong.—
But we're all on every level
both the god and devil
that we dream of and we scream of to the skies.—
In the woozy alternation
of conception and sensation
we forget we're different, just like the other guys
in that:
Everyone's a world,
disconsolately hurled
into an orbit that they can't define.

Robert Patrick • *The Golden Circle*

Intellect and feeling
instead of just congealing
either arbitrate or intertwine. . . .
You can't do it that way—
you've just gotta say,
"I know what I know and see what I see"
but this has to be your song:
"The other fellow gets along—
so he has to know just as much as me.
(He's something else
but he has to know just as much as me.)"

Moving them all to their proper places in the circle.

The fellow with sad eyes (CANNY.)
The most cynical of guys (CORNY.)
The one with vision of the earth (SAGE.)
The one who sees just what it's worth (JIMINY.)
The one in love with power (SNAKE.)
The slave that makes it flower (BULL.)
The fire that wants it all (EGO.)
Or the one whose demands are small (JUSTINE.)
Can only live like animals out in the wind and weather,
but haven't you found, by fooling around,
you cannot live like animals together?
And aren't you happy underneath the cosmic rays
to know there's someone else to help you count the days?
Aren't you happy just to be together?
Remembering to forget everything that's happened, yet
remembering how and why and when and whether—
remembering at the start how it felt to be apart
aren't you happy just to be together?
When your combined desire can set the world on fire,
aren't you happy just to be together?

MEDIA *stands in* LEO's *place as the group sings "Together, to-gether, together. . . ."*

ERGO   You see, we *are* all brothers . . .

FISHY   No, we're all one thing . . .

EGO   If we just pull together . . .

JUSTINE   AND DON'T GO OFF ON MAD TRIPS . . .

SAGE   If you could all take care of yourselves . . .

JIMINY   But help each other . . .

SNAKE   Someone has to be in control, obviously . . .

BULL   Not over me.

CANNY   How come we're all fighting?

CORNY   Because you let everybody in!

ERGO   There has to be an order . . .

FISHY   There is one if only you're open to it . . .

MEDIA   (*panicked at this new dispute.*)   What is going on?

LEO   (*entering, center.*)   What's going on? What are you doing?
   Don't you know the world's on fire? (*Exits.*)

ALL   Leo! (*Instantly and happily they organize.*)

MEDIA   Get moving.

SNAKE   Now! Now!

EGO   Come on!

BULL   This way!

JIMINY   Here's what to do . . .

SAGE   Follow them, everyone.

ERGO   Yes, that's right. Get buckets. You take them. You hand
   them out, yes, yes, that's right.

*Trees dismantle into buckets and they all efficiently and joy-
ously go off chanting directions to each other.*

CANNY   This way. To save our homes. Off to fight the fire.
   (*Exit.*)

FISHY *is spinning, watching everyone. At* CANNY's *last line, he
is left staring at the fire.*

FISHY   The fire. Yes, yes, the fire. We shall fight the fire and
   we cannot fight the fire. We are the fire and we are not the
   fire. We shall defeat the fire and we can never defeat the fire.
   We are within the fire and we are without the fire, and with-

221

out the fire we are nothing and within the fire we are everything. We began the fire and we shall end the fire—together
. . . (*Sees that he is all alone.*) together . . . together. Together! (*Exits after the others.*)

The flames, offstage and on, grow to gigantic size.

Curtain.

An American Playground Sampler

MARC ESTRIN

"MARC ESTRIN in 30 words

1. microbiology
2. theater
3. head-stuff
4. cello
5. institutions
6. crap
7. looking
8. plays
9. Artaud
10. Nona
11. professional
12. bullshit
13. politics
14. Mario
15. Brecht
16. muckraking
17. alternatives
18. Hans
19. communications
20. improvisations
21. group
22. co-ops
23. services
24. streets
25. infiltration
26. help
27. total
28. community
29. responsibility
30. integration"

An American Playground Sampler

The American Playground is a group of socially concerned, politically active artists committed to the use of theater as a medium for confrontation and discovery. We are not primarily involved with theater which takes place in theaters, but with extending the legitimate domain for theater action. Anywhere there are people and a willing imagination there is the potential for theater. The stimulus may be a place (the White House), an occasion (a speech by Melvin Laird), a prevalent emotion (spring-feeling), or a commemoration of some event (the Wright brothers' flight). The where, the when, the how, what, and why are all open. The one requirement is a potential for human interaction and communication. One of our major concerns is in shifting the burden of the performance to the "spectators," providing them with a chance to examine their own acts instead of the acts of others.

What follows are examples from a spectrum of radical theater activities, beginning with a standard street theater piece, working through various levels of audience participation, and ending with a piece which is indistinguishable from real life. The latter end of the spectrum represents what I conceive of as "guerrilla theater"—that theater which becomes a manifestation of reality itself.

I   *The Military Execution of the Bill of Rights on the Steps of the National Archives*
   (Done in conjunction with a rally in support of the Fort Jackson Eight)

1. A crowd gathers in front of the Archives, waiting for the rally to begin. They have been leafleted with details relevant to the rally.

2. An army drummer in dress uniform appears on the marble steps and begins a funeral beat. The crowd quiets down.

3. A black-draped stake is carried by two soldiers in dress uniforms who march up the steps. They are followed by three other soldiers in dress uniforms who bear machine guns. The proceedings are (actually) covered by a closed circuit television cameraman in army fatigues. The TV picture is played in the street on a large monitor.

4. The stake is set up high on the steps. The gunners take their positions. The drum beat stops.

5. One of the stake carriers pulls away the drape to reveal a parchment copy (the kind sold in the Archives) of the Bill of Rights nailed to the stake. He stands to one side, holding up the reverse side of the drape which is lettered in white: "MILITARY EXECUTION OF THE BILL OF RIGHTS ON THE STEPS OF THE NATIONAL ARCHIVES."

6. A drum roll begins and stops.

7. The second stake carrier, provided with portable loudspeaking equipment, announces: "Article One, United States Bill of Rights. Congress shall make no law abridging the freedom of speech or the right of the people peaceably to assemble and to petition the Government for a redress of grievances." Drum roll.

8. A loud blast of fire from three machine guns. The TV

shows close-ups of bullets ripping through the First Amendment.

9. The speaker continues: "Article Five, United States Bill of Rights. No person shall be deprived of life, liberty, or property without due process of law." Drum roll.

10. Another burst of machine gun fire. This time the TV scans the faces of the soldiers firing the guns.

11. The speaker continues: "Article Eight, United States Bill of Rights. Excessive bail shall not be required, nor cruel and unusual punishment inflicted." Drum roll.

12. A third blast of machine gun fire. This time the camera pans the faces of the crowd.

13. The sign-holder walks to the stake and pulls the pin holding the Bill of Rights to the wood. The camera watches the paper fall limply to the ground.

14. The sign-holder covers the paper with the black cloth. The drum resumes the march beat. The soldiers march off.

15. The first speaker of the rally retrieves the dead Bill of Rights and uses it in his address to the crowd.

This piece is a simple, effective way of getting attention when beginning a rally, and of announcing its major theme in a way which will attract the media. It is designed to be communicative as a one-minute news clip, the point being to get the message into sixty million homes. It represents a type of street theater which, while functioning as part of a rally, is basically media oriented.

The next piece, on the contrary, is entirely independent of the media and was done solely for the benefit of the spectators present. Since it is illegal to demonstrate on the Capitol grounds, it was definitely a hushed-up, hit-and-run affair. The time: two days after Robert F. Kennedy's assassination, in the midst of the Poor People's Campaign. The piece developed out of discussions with Wolf Lowenthal, who was living at Resurrection City at the time, and who organized the Poor People's contingent of actors.

II   *On the Capitol Steps*

At precisely 1:00 P.M. a group of thirty poor people converge at the bottom of the main steps, all humming.

Simultaneously, four men dressed as congressmen in blue suits and Stetsons, carrying attaché cases appear at the top of the steps.

The poor people begin to slowly climb the stairs, always humming. They extend their hands toward the congressmen, the way one would ask for a hand getting up.

The congressmen reach into their cases and withdraw handfuls of pennies, which they begin to toss lightly to the poor people, the way one would toss feed to chickens. The congressmen chant, "Here you go, here you go," as they throw.

The poor people keep advancing.

The congressmen change their chant to "Careful . . . careful" as they begin to throw the pennies overhand to the advancing crowd.

The poor people keep coming.

The congressmen begin to feel threatened and slowly increase the viciousness with which they throw the pennies. Eventually the chant changes to a cacophony of "Stay where you are!" "Why don't you work for a living?" "Die, scum, die!" etc. They throw the coins with the intention of killing. One by one the poor people drop on the steps, assassinated by pennies. The steps are draped with bodies. The tourists scramble for pennies. The Capitol police arrive. Everyone splits.

The piece functioned as a graphic summation of the situation. It is not only the rich and famous who are assassinated; the poor are assassinated every day by a corrupt and brutal Congress. I spoke to a few spectators afterward. The message came across. I like to think that the pennies the tourists retrieved as souvenirs will serve to remind them of the event and its meaning. In general, it's a good idea to give the crowd something they can physically relate to, or even carry away with them. This idea was one of the keys to the success of the next piece, an audience participation spectacle.

III   *A Passion Play at the White House*

1. *Gathering.* Two hundred people gather on Easter Sunday at a park three blocks from the White House. I talk to them about the piece we are about to do, emphasizing:

   a. It's always Good Friday, never Easter Sunday.

   b. We will approach the source of death (the White House) in the spirit of ritual recognition.

   c. They, the marchers, will feel *real pain,* carrying the Cross and the Saigon regime. They are to concentrate on the physical reality of the pain which will enable them to reach the emotional reality of a constant crucifixion.

Vietnamese and American military hats are given out. Masked figures of Ky, Thieu, Lodge, and Abrams are raised on a litter to shoulder height. A five-hundred-pound, thirteen-foot cross is picked up and the procession begins, to the slow beat of a drum.

2. *March to the White House.* The Cross leads. Next, the figures of the Saigon regime, waving slowly to unheard cheers. Following these, the rest of the people. They all concentrate on feeling the death gradient increase with each step. They bear the pain of their burdens. People in the procession stop passers-by in the street and ask them the ritual question, "What is the President's plan to end the war?" These are the only words spoken.

3. *In front of the White House.* The Cross is set up and the procession continues around it. After some minutes the first protester, a Vietnamese, is raised above the crowd. He displays a large sign reading "RISING DEATH TOLLS." Holding the sign to one side he moans, "What is the President's plan to end the war?"

Upon hearing this, the Saigon Quartet freezes, then makes a gesture of shaking rage, pulling their masks away from their faces. In unison, they slowly point their rolled-up signs, first at the protester and then at the Cross. The Vietnamese and American soldiers raise the protester onto the Cross, high above the crowd. He slumps over one of the arms, his sign dangling beneath him. The procession continues.

The crucifixion is repeated three more times, with Vietnamese who outrage the regime by holding up signs reading: "PEACE LEADERS IMPRISONED," "NEWSPAPERS CLOSED," "GOVERNMENT BY TERROR," each time moaning out loud, "What is the President's plan to end the war?"

After the last criminal is up on the Cross, the Quartet freezes, and then goes into its Obscene Last Supper Comedy Routine. They slowly unroll their signs.

LODGE VERILY I SAY UNTO YOU THAT ONE OF YOU SHALL BETRAY ME. (*All mime hearty laughter.*)

THIEU YE HAVE THE POOR ALWAYS WITH YOU BUT ME YE HAVE NOT ALWAYS. (*All mime riotous laughter.*)

ABRAMS MY GOD, MY GOD, WHY HAST THOU FORSAKEN ME? (*All mime obscene laughter.*)

KY THE SPIRIT IS WILLING BUT THE FLESH IS WEAK. (*Freeze. Silence.*)

In the silence a single voice is heard in the crowd of Vietnamese: "Where is the resurrection?"

This is picked up by a few more people in both groups: "Where is the resurrection?"

The spectators begin asking the police, "Where is the resurrection?"

The question grows. Little by little it is picked up by each of two hundred people until it is heard as a deafening wail as far east as the Capitol, as far west as the State Department, as far north as the National Cathedral, and as far south as the Pentagon. The crowd allows the question to rise and fall as it will, much the way the chant of *OM* does. When it ends, the silence echoes.

The corpses are taken down from the Cross and the procession returns to the park.

For the rest of the afternoon the participants speak no words except to ask strangers the ritual question, "What is the President's plan to end the war?"

This piece was well covered by the media and also experienced intensely by the many participants and spectators. However, as involving as it was it was still experienced by all as "theater," and, as such, was muted in its effect by the "aesthetic distance" with which we view such phenomena. It is at this point that "guerrilla theater" enters the radical theater continuum. When aesthetic distance breaks down, emotional breakthroughs occur. If these are handled correctly they can lead to new insights for the spectator-performers.

IV   *A Unitarian Seminar on Guerrilla Theater*

We were asked by a Montgomery County Unitarian Church to present a seminar to their members on guerrilla theater (which meant to them any form of radical political theater, rather than the specific kind of infiltrative theater I am talking about). Now, Montgomery County is currently practicing a brutal repression of its kids, including arrests and school expulsions for possessing or selling the *Washington Free Press.* The liberals (including these Unitarians) had been notably silent about it all. So we got together with some people from the *Free Press* and the church and planned the following event, a guerrilla-ing of a "guerrilla theater" presentation.

We began the seminar with an apology for what would probably be the ineffectiveness of the puppet pieces we were going to show them. After all, they were made to be done at supermarkets to support the grape strike, and really could function only in that atmosphere. We also hoped they didn't mind some friends (the *Free Press* people) we brought along who wanted to see the supermarket pieces. The liberal group sincerely welcomed them—all the more, since some of them were long haired and some were black.

As the first puppet piece came to an end, one of the *Free Press* people called out, "Man, this stuff is irrelevant. You've got incredible problems right here in D.C., in the county, and you're worrying about the California grape pickers." American Playground people hushed him up and informed him and anyone else who had comments that there would be a discussion afterward.

When the second puppet piece finished, Becky, a black girl with us, interrupted the proceedings. She agreed with the first guy that this stuff was bullshit and that blacks were being shot in the street by racist cops and that *that* was what she wanted to talk about. This provoked some hostility in the audience, but nobody told *her* to keep quiet since she was black. She was answered by a Spaniard from the *Free Press* who, in a thick Spanish accent, talked about how it *was* relevant, about how the working class was through taking shit, about how it was all the same thing nationally, even internationally.

By this time, people in the audience were supporting one or the other side of the relevancy debate, even over the objections of the minister (who was in on this with us).

One of the *Free Press* people argued that not only were people uninterested in getting involved with problems of ethnic minorities, but that they weren't even interested in listening to their own kids, or caring about what was going on in their heads. This provoked an extremely defensive reaction: "Of course we're interested in our kids, of course we listen to them."

We escalated the violence of the argument, each of us dealing with the group of people immediately surrounding him. The emotional level was peaked by an argument between a respectable-looking elderly man from the congregation who had previously agreed to go along with our plan and Dennis Livingston, one of the directors of the American Playground.

They got into a vituperative shouting match which ceased to have any political substance and became entirely personal. At a key moment Dennis turned to the man's seventeen-year-old son (who had also agreed to work with us) and asked, "What do you really think of your father?"

"I THINK MY FATHER'S FULL OF SHIT! HE NEVER LISTENS TO WHAT I SAY, HE NEVER HEARS ANYTHING EXCEPT WHAT HE WANTS TO, HE HAS NO IDEA WHERE I'M AT, AND I'M SICK AND TIRED OF ALL THIS SHIT!!" And he threw a glass ash tray to the ground and smashed it.

At this cue we all fell silent, but the emotional momentum of the audience impelled them to keep going, screaming and gesturing.

They began to look at each other: civilized, white middle-class liberals, with red faces and clenched fists, screaming "dirty hippies" and "commies" at people they had welcomed half an hour ago. One by one they fell silent. One woman kept on screaming for a long time, alone.

We let the silence sink in. Then we began to talk gently to them, even whisper in their ears, things like:

"What's going on here?"

"What just happened?"

"Have you ever seen each other like this?"

"Have you ever talked to each other before?"

"You really *don't* listen."

The kid who smashed the ash tray walked to the front of the room and said, "You really *don't* listen to your children."

One of the *Free Press* people talked about how there had been no attempt to defend the kids against the oppression of the authorities at school or on the street, about how parents were only interested in kids telling them what they wanted to hear, and doing things they wanted them to do. It was inevitable that one of the congregation should ask, "What can we do?"

At that point a discussion began with suggestions both from

us and from the audience. People were really talking—beyond the shattered liberal bullshit.

One of the conclusions arrived at was that a parents' group should be formed to distribute the next underground paper that was banned. One man wanted to know if they could read it first and then decide. The group concluded that if they were *really* interested in freedom of speech, if they were *really* interested in what their kids were thinking, they should distribute and defend the paper *no matter what* it contained. The evening ended amicably and all felt that the experience had been constructive. Since then, these people have been involved in the formation of a Montgomery County Citizens Committee to combat oppression of the county's youth.

It is clear that the use of guerrilla tactics here opened this group up to feelings and insights they would never have had were the discussion to have remained on an intellectual level. That is the major strength of guerrilla theater: no aesthetic distance, catch by surprise, and go for the guts—avoid the trap of being "an entertainment." The next piece sits far along this road. It has not been done, but could be and will be. Some might feel it is not the responsibility of theater to get into such things, that there is some ethical failing here, that one has to draw the line somewhere. I, myself, am ambivalent. It's clear to me, though, that guerrilla theater, followed to its logical end, should be involved in a piece like this. It is, after all, no more than holding the mirror up to nature.

V   *A New Family Moves In*

I conceived of this piece while I was watching the Living Theater's *Paradise Now.* A group of actors were standing around in a circle. Two began accusing each other:

"You're old."

"You're young."

"You're old!"

"You're young!"
"You're OLD!"
"You're YOUNG!"
"YOU'RE OLD!"
"YOU'RE YOUNG!"
Another two began:
"You're tall."
"You're short."
"You're tall!"
"You're short!"
"You're TALL!"
"You're SHORT!"
"YOU'RE TALL!"
"YOU'RE SHORT!"
A third couple began:
"You're fat."
"You're skinny. . . ."

I realized that there is really no end to potential divisions among people, and how hopeless it was for people to order their lives along such divisions. It used to be that if the countryside was American Gothic, at least there was a healthy heterogeneity in the cities. But ghetto-izing seems to be getting worse, and people are growing more xenophobic. Communities, black and white, are becoming more exclusive; and the lines are being drawn: black-white, redneck-hippie, Christian-Jew, peacenik-patriot.

This piece is intended to explore and perhaps break down these divisions. The outline of the piece is not clear—only the intention. The working out will have to be improvisation.

Two families—one from each side of a conflict—are needed to co-operate in the making of this piece. Each must agree to move into the other's home. The experiments then proceed simultaneously.

Seen from my side of a redneck-hippie experiment, the scenario might run something like this.

A battered '37 Chevie van, painted in psychedelic colors,

covered with peace slogans, pulls up at a recently vacated home in the midst of a lower-middle-class white suburban community outside Arlington, Virginia. The new family, a bunch of weird-looking people carrying nonstandard belongings, move in. Since it is Saturday morning, the neighborhood takes note. From then on the family proceed to adopt the most open and communicative life style possible. They might call on their neighbors often, let their kids run naked on the front lawn, sit out on the front porch a lot, join the church, the P.T.A., go to all town meetings, subscribe to radical publications and leave them lying in the back seat of their car, use buttons and bumper stickers. Maximize talking with cops, store owners, people on the street, keep their curtains open, etc. *Threaten no one, be very friendly and open,* and just make sure that the neighborhood has to deal with their being different.

Now this might be an enormously difficult task. How the game is played would have to depend on the circumstances. The ultimate intention would also have to be flexible. Maybe the hip family would

1. love it and want to stay (if the original family didn't want to come back);
2. be run out of town after a week (but not if they were sensitive to the limits);
3. make a candid camera documentary of (suburban) prejudice;
4. write a book;
5. really change people's heads.

The time scale of the piece would relate to the intention. Whatever happened, life would be different afterward for all concerned.

Blacks in a white neighborhood, Catholics in a Jewish neighborhood, executives in a working-class neighborhood. Each would have to maximize in their own way the openness of their life styles and make them interact with the surroundings—not enough to destroy the experiment, but always enough to move things along.

If all this smacks of "I led three lives," let me observe two important differences:

1. No one is misrepresenting his position.

2. The goals of this infiltration are constructive and life-oriented, not destructive and death-oriented. The responsible artist merges with the responsible human being.

The King of Spain

BYRD HOFFMAN

For Laard Novak

Ann Pearson

"ROBERT WILSON, Director of The Byrd Hoffman School of Byrds, has presented dance and theatre performances at the American Theatre Laboratory ('68), Bleecker Street Cinema ('67), Peerless Movie House in Brooklyn ('66), Pratt Institute ('65), at the New York World's Fair ('64–'65) and at The Byrd Loft. He has designed sets for a number of Off-Broadway productions, including the first production of *America, Hurrah!*, and also for the Open Theatre. National Educational Television has filmed his work with children. Last summer the Grail School commissioned a huge outdoor pole structure, an architectural (or sculptural) monument consisting of six hundred telephone poles in an open field at Grailville, in Loveland, Ohio. Presently he is a special consultant and teacher for Headstart; in the past he has held a broad range of teaching positions, including the following: Special Instructor for the Department of Welfare, The New York Board of Education, at schools and art centers in the New York and New Jersey communities, in addition to lecturing at Harvard ('66) on the subject 'Schools, a Laboratory Situation.' "

The King of Spain was first performed January 30, 1969, at the Anderson Theatre, New York City. The cast was:

Arden Anderson—*Prince*
Liba Bayrak—*Royalty, Drawing room*
Bernice—*Runner*
Karen Birnbach—*Pile person*
Cedric—*Candle boy*
Hank Derrico—*Runner, Pile person*
Joseph C. Drexel—*Grass man for Cat*
Rose Dreyer—*Drawing room*
Carroll Dunn—*Game player*
Chris Haile—*Runner*
Sara Kate—*Pile person*
George Klauber—*Game player*
Hope Kondrat—*Old woman, Drawing room*
Alan Lloyd—*King of Spain*
Mateo—*Pile person*

Audrey Monk—*Woman with feathers, Drawing room*
Mary Peer—*Woman with mike*
George Phillippi—*Drawing room*
Dallas Pratt—*Royalty, Game player*
Raymond—*Child leaning into wire*
George T. Resch—*Drawing room*
Saito—*Nude runner*
Adrienne Scott—*Drawing room*
Scotty Snyder—*Drawing room*
Bill Stewart—*Usher*
Robyn Stoughton—*Pile person*
Robert Wilson—*Runner, Mammy*

Stage manager: Richard Nelson. Set: Fred Koluch. Sound: Hampton Sailor. Lighting: Peter Egan. Props: Adrienne Scott. Cat legs construction: Philip Haight. Sponsors: New York State Council on the Arts, Lena Robbins Foundation, Dr. D. Pratt, R. Dreyer.

Production Notes on *The King of Spain*, a play presented by the Byrd Hoffman School of Byrds

. . . She saw the flyer and she knew she says right away that it wasn't ballet. "Oh," she said, "this is just for a *very* limited audience." I could tell—about the flyer—she hated it! But she was just trying being very polite, but I know; she hated it. Well, uuuuuhhhh, then she said something about uuuuuuuuuummmmmmmmmmm I had definitely labeled it how it was.

What did she think it was?

Not what she thought dance was.

And she was really crazy because she had another image of *what* dance was cause Jerome Robbins had told me to go see her . . .

In Grailville, Loveland, Ohio, it was late one night last summer. I had been working very hard and was very tired. I would start off working by standing in the room for a long time without moving. The first movement I thought about after my body was relaxed was a feeling that I was going up. I started jumping and jumping. There was laundry that had been left

in the space, in the barn that was more like a chapel, and I
got into all this laundry and there were a lot of sheets and
clothing that belonged to the people at Grailville and I began
tying them all on me. It was like—I've never had that kind of
experience before—like a bright light, like two very strong images springing up. Oh wait—before that I had been thinking
earlier about . . . no, before that I had been lying on the floor
thinking about the time when I was in the second grade I had a
teacher by the name of Mrs. Weebush and she said to us, SUE
What would you like to be when
you grow up? And she said,
A NURSE.
She says JOE,
What would you like to be when
you're big? And he says,
A FIREMAN and she says SARA,
What would you like to be when you grow up and she says,
A HOUSEWIFE.
And then she says BOB what would *you* like to be when you
grow up and I said, I said
THE KING OF SPAIN
And she said now *this* child's got problems and she wrote
that on my report card and I remember that my mother kept
that card and I remember thinking at that time that it was
too bad she didn't see it that way.

Anyway this was last summer and then when I started jumping
all around I had all these clothes on that weren't mine and
I saw these pictures in my mind and the pictures were: an
interior of a room, a Victorian room—it was all grey and
musty and also I kept, I kept hearing drinking glasses and
people; people like at a cocktail party and chairs moving.
And the next thing that I kept seeing were these enormous cat
paws. And I was remembering too that when I was in the sixth
grade I had won an Art Contest cause I had drawn a magnolia
in chalk and it had been placed in the library in a children's

Art Show and I had won First Prize and the Waco *News Tribune* was interviewing me and they said, "Now tell us, Bob Wilson, What do you think is the Nicest Thing in the Whole World?"

And I said a big thick cat paw!! And that was printed in Texas in the Waco *News Tribune*. It was crazy—I was thinking that same night in the barn that it was strange about me wanting to be "The King of Spain" and that that was important its origin probably going much further back than the second grade. And then the weirdest thing happened just before Christmas. A very good friend of mine who is in California sent me some pictures. I hadn't heard from him for a year and he sent me some pictures in the mail of a Victorian room with all these strange people sitting around. And also a picture of a baby's face and sort of superimposed on the baby's face was a catlike image. And he didn't know that at about that time I had decided to do *The King of Spain* and I thought about it and I wanted to get a lot of people together and I had been looking and specifically noticing different people for, oh, I guess about the last year or so and had been thinking specifically about using them in something . . . in a large theatre piece . . . and so I got a lot of them together but the way I started getting them together was to think about them first of all clearly I guess—now let's see now—clearly about what they were and then I'd think about each one individually —that any one was so different from another so totally different and I thought that *was* especially curious. That was nice—I liked any two of them being together at different times.

And then I kept thinking too that certain people I knew had never just uuuuuuuhhhhhhhhhh seen a different kind of people (or persons)—other than themselves. Then I also kept thinking about what I've done at parties—getting different people together—and it's curious how at parties totally dissimilar persons get together unexpectedly like so I guess maybe that's really how I got the idea for my play.

So then most of the people—the cast—came from classes—awareness classes that I teach in a community center in New Jersey and the interesting thing especially about one of the classes—one of the adult classes—was that one of the members kept telling me, reminding me about all the tensions—unseen tensions that nevertheless could be felt (and experienced differently too) or expressed differently by all the members of that class and in their everyday life. And a whole lot happened in this class like after working a while we didn't see those tensions—and one of the things that I think is very important about working this way is first of all just getting people to relax and to be comfortable with their bodies and know just a little about what their bodies are like and be able to use just the smallest amount of energy to express whatever they wanted to—or whatever was necessary in those circumstances of being with each other. I found you could work with people several ways (at once); first of all uuuuuhhhhhhh by getting the people to move so that they know they can move and I do that by turning out the lights so they can't see themselves seeing one another or so they can't see anyone seeing themselves. And then I have them just move and try to feel that experience of their bodies moving and then think how their body is special—it's not like anyone else's—and also to pay attention to what's happening when their body is moving. At the same time trying to be aware as much as possible to be aware about what's happening too as a whole group—being sensitive to the energies of the other people and how they're moving and what they're doing in relationship—*not* trying to design it or anything, just trying to be aware of it. Then, uuuuhhhh, the second thing that really is like the *most* important thing is that I try to be superaware of what the people are and I try to have some insight or something that can help—some insight or something that I can tell the group on an individual basis—and I try to encourage them or compliment them so that whatever they begin to do will be done because they are beginning to have confidence in themselves and in their movements and then they naturally can relax and then you can *see* them better.

And the reason then for (later) presenting the results of these really very basic processes and exercises on a stage or in a theatre is that you can't even see the people (or the whole of it) unless they're totally relaxed. It's difficult to see the persons if they're not relaxed—to look at them; have an exchange with them.

The third thing then is to try and build a (group) energy level that is very high. And in order to do this we'd have a warm-up just before rehearsals or performances where we'd run and jump, stretch and shout until the energy was very high and then I'd say to "Sit on it"—like to hold it, sustain it once you have raised it, until the energy endures and yet remains relaxed, contained. And then I'd say that the piece is going to work because the people are so very different. That is, even though there isn't much action going on the people all being themselves and being very different construct of their own accord a context, or their own play, by presenting themselves as they are, then (theatrically) no more is necessary—I mean that's what any professional director tries to create only it's in the context of an imposed structure, not one that is drawn from within and generated of its own accord. Because I did the initial work (as such) of structuring the sequences of the stage action and activities, that is, the order of their entrances, the huge Victorian set and backdrop and the slow, modulated game the three elderly men play throughout, the "plot" in that sense became a loose, open-ended structure—or a non-structure in that it freed the people in it, enabled *them* to step out, step outside of themselves naturally by stepping into the context of *The King of Spain*. Now that refers to the people.

249

But the "activities" (the play) were all set as a general kind of framework to guide the people in it, even though probably most of the audience wouldn't see, or consider it to exist. And this in turn set up a series of theatrical contradictions that didn't seem arbitrary, say, but that arose spontaneously *and* visually in the performing situation.

That's how I started working with the people and got them through the performance. And the most important thing in this piece, that which even superseded the doing of the activities, was simply staying on top of the piece—on top of the energy of the piece as a whole and not within the (mechanical) confines of the activities. As I said the activities weren't arbitrary, but the encounters of the people within were flexible and immediate in relationship to the being of each person and to the group—sort of like an incalculable margin, a kind of human consideration that usually never has a chance to erupt in most traditional theatre.

We started off like a game. As a matter of fact watching it I was constantly reminded that the piece looked like a big game. (Suspended over the audience's heads in the front section of the orchestra was an horizontal cable containing chrome rings —markerlike—that were occasionally strategically repositioned. See diagram page 251.)

As the audience enters, a rehearsal tape of Mary Peer's is amplified over the loudspeaker:

. . . Now broadcasting from Terra Firma . . . I'm now upside down; I think. Yes. Now I'm testing the earth in back of my head. Tap Tap, or is it the cat feet? . . . I prefer to wait a minute. Doesn't it seem a shame to waste it? Oh in the fog? Well if I can only think of something funny, you know that's in juxtaposition to some other things that are paradoxes or what are seemed to be defined as paradoxes.

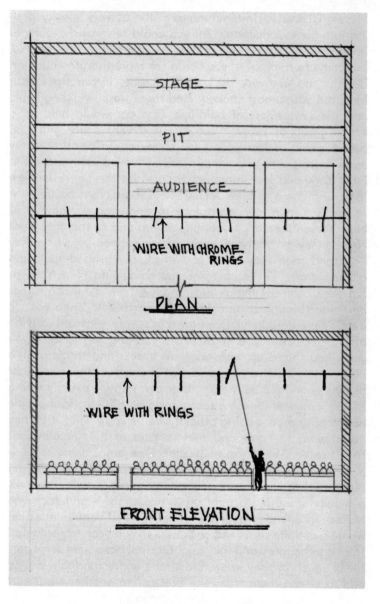

STAGE

PIT

AUDIENCE

WIRE WITH CHROME RINGS

PLAN

WIRE WITH RINGS

FRONT ELEVATION

Places. UUUUUUUmmmmmmmmm. It was very spooky driving into New York today. All you could see was the bumper ahead of you. And it was romantic looking on each side. No, but come to think of it, you could see more than the bumper. But the fog was very thick on each side. If you stuck your head out you almost choked. And there were twinkling lights and there were lots of hold-ups. One car would hold up a whole group of people. But it was a very polite group of people going to New York, for some reason or other. They seem more polite when they work in New Jersey and go to New York and less impatient than when they work in New York and come to New Jersey. . . . I suppose maybe New Jersey is a more peaceful place to work and so they go to New York after work to get pepped-up and so the ones from New Jersey go to New York to get pepped-up *while* they work and then they come to New Jersey pepped-up to get calmed down. I'd much rather be going into New York at 5 o'clock than coming away from New York. I'd much rather be going through a tunnel, from west to east, than east to west. Very definitely. Downtown it's very pleasant driving after 5 o'clock if you know where you're going. Course you get kinda mixed-up with one-way streets and that's a little bit——a little bit of an impasse. But if you pass the most least likely person he'll be the one that can tell you exactly where to go. Somehow for some reason or other. The official people are so busy maybe being official I don't know what it is they don't seem to know and they're kind of not impolite but they fluster. They kind of bluster. One day I came to New York and it was on Saturday and I guess they were trying out a whole group of new policemen on mid-corners. It wasn't a regular stand and I went up to two of them and each one looked frightened to death when I asked 'em a question where a definite street was so I guess they'd been transplanted from another area and they might as well have been Jerseyites for as much as they knew, but that's understandable if they had to switch them from one precinct to another——but sort

of gave me a little bit of a peculiar feeling. So now I take another tackle. I don't approach them and ask them a direct
question that's embarrassing to them and they don't have to
get on the defensive. Actually the best way to do it now-a-
days if you have to do it is to stop being on the defensive
yourself so as not to put the other person on the defensive,
cause that's, oh, oh, that's impractical. I guess that's the best
word for it. It's impractical. Cause the results don't seem to
be helpful. So with people on the defensive, you can kind of
start a little conversation and then sort of if you need to know
something important you kind of get around to it indirectly
so if they know it they can answer it or if they don't know it
they can't/don't answer. Well, now, wait a minute; does that
make sense? Well it works anyway; you get talking see, chat-
ting a little bit. That's how it works. Well, let's see now, I was
in the fog, before I digressed I guess. In the fog we fought our
way over to the empty theatre. But I'm not saying anything.
I'm not saying anything. . . . So then I went out again to go
swimming at 10:30 I put the back of the car window down
for something, I shut it went up and turned the dial and
something "schwunched" but the man standing there didn't
have sense enough to listen—I was so whiggly trying to get
swimming. But I was coasting along the street and everyone
was tooting but I had to coast and pray so I coasted and
prayed and prayed and coasted and I finally found an empty
space on the side of the road and I pulled up and thought well
nobody is stopping so nothing is broken. I couldn't believe
what I saw. The back of the car had somehow gotten loose—
the tailgate and there was this mirror this lovely thick glass
mirror with not a crack in it. I can't understand how it ever
could have happened. So I just had to heave it over and drive
very slowly so I dashed into the pool and one of the smartest
people in the Y is there and I said I've got problems I'm gonna
swim two people abreast will you help me? So he said yes he
would. So we swam and swam and got another quarter of a
mile and put it down on the chart which is always such a satis-

faction and dashed out to the car and then my helper Mr. Hamilton who's a School Principal on the side didn't come, so a tall swimmer we had been bumping into each other for weeks cause he has wide arms see and I seem to swim with my feet up so that's all we knew each other from bumping in. But anyway he said his name was Manager and he'd help me if he could and I said well I think you have to unscrew the thing so the poor man got this tiny, tiny I guess you call it the Star Screwdriver and he's tall in the arms and he's swinging around trying to do it and he got six screws out and kept talking all the time and he gets to laughing and Mr. Hamilton comes along and he's roly-poly with dimples and five of his children clustering around him and he said, Holy Goodness All we need to do is get the key out of the lock. Just get the key outta the lock. So this nice big swimming companion just laughed. I thought he must have a good disposition. So we got the key outta the lock and the glass window on the back of my station wagon went back squeak squeak but it went back very slowly, very slowly . . . (*Mrs. Peer now sits down to the Grand Piano with all her sheet music and begins playing softly.*) . . . I don't know . . . The piano doesn't *feel* like Mozart today. Of course it isn't I. You don't mind do you if I blame you? Well. . . . That's the end of something (*piano music is falling on the floor*). Oh dear . . . I just have to laugh in a situation like this and, and, Clair de Lune certainly isn't going to be any good in a situation like this, is it? Quiet! Do you have a *philosophy* about this? Oh dear it didn't stay together but that's all right. Stars. Now I'm playing a Greek Ceremonial Dance. Somehow I can't talk while I'm playing—it's so, so *involving.* . . . The only time I can play is when I'm at home at night alone. The only people I can play for are the artists and the people in my awareness group then the music doesn't stick in my fingers or in my head. You think you know it and you don't. Darn it that other flat keeps popping

up! People don't waltz very much any more, do they? Everything that's flat isn't regular. But it sure is a pleasant feeling
to play it. Da da da duuuuummmmm . . .

Mary is a unique, but puzzling person to work with. During
our concentration exercises Mary couldn't be quiet. She couldn't
sit still in her chair like everyone else. She had constantly to
get up and move around and, of course, to go in the corner
and change her clothes, which she wore in layers. She said it
was terribly convenient. And because she naturally talks in-
cessantly (and concentratedly) there was not an alternative but
that Mary talk and tell her stories, several of them going on
automatically, and eventually they get connected up. After she
says that about people not waltzing very much any more an
announcer announces: "The Byrd Hoffman School of Byrds
proudly presents *The King of Spain.*" A solitary "prince" in
a royal white jacket enters the box by the stage and bows to
the audience. The curtain goes up. We see a drawing room—
an old musty Victorian drawing room. In the center, back
facing the audience, a highback armchair. After a long long
pause the hairy head of an undistinguishable, beastlike creature
slumps sideways becoming visible and remaining immobile with
its back to the audience until the end, when . . . (Also casually throughout the performance an usher, kind of seedy, slop-
pily clad in oversized tuxedo, attends to sweeping the aisle.)

A very stout elderly man enters and studies a game table
located stage right containing on top a variety of very differently, almost enigmatically shaped geometrical objects—cubes,
etc. For a very long time he contemplates the pieces. A small
black boy enters and standing and moving a ladder carefully
lights a row of candles along a shelf positioned on the rear
wall (stage right). Then a second player and a third appear
and stand on each side. Like a giant game that requires all of
one's powers of concentration. Infrequent moves.

Byrd Hoffman • *The King of Spain*

In the back wall of the grey drawing room there is a floor-to-ceiling slit through which one sees a sunny Moroccan landscape. (See drawing room diagram page 259: one of the primary conceptions behind the piece was filling the space through an additive or cumulative process—layers of activity.) In traditional theatre the focus of the action of the "plot"—the words, dialogue, or reason for things happening—rather than a visual focus, and basis. My idea in part was a visual collage of images and activities occurring in layers, or horizontally in clearly defined, stratified stage zones that, from time to time, are juxtaposed with regard to focus and, thereby, thrown into relief. For example, a runner clad in red shorts and T shirt races back and forth throughout the play appearing whenever he passes the rather narrow slit. Also he changes his clothing throughout. Even later a nude man, a large white Saint Bernard dog, and even another man on roller skates pass by at time intervals. Also later, after Mary Peer has begun her piano-playing and more stories, two downstage vertical piles are set up—one of hay, the other of objects and people forming another, an intermediary "layer" (or horizontal stage zone) between the contents of the drawing room (upstage) and the passage space for the giant cat legs.

The "plot" then becomes all the actions, entrances, and gestures which take on proportions of minute concentration—even the most seemingly irrelevant activity is suddenly blown out of, or beyond proportion—no matter how it happens it becomes more captivating, noticeable because one is seeing the "stage business" *as* what it is (as "business") and it becomes primary—primarily of interest or the center of (visual *and* theatrical) focus . (The Still-Life is a Real-Life.)

Two hidden microphones picked up the inconsequentially necessary noises of the chairs moving and creaking when sat in and the clatter of ice cubes and liquids being poured in glasses on the serving table.

The game table and the three players serve as a sort of minia-ture interior representation, or model that reflects the larger stage patterns but that remains, instead, the same throughout— at a contained pace with an unmodulated rhythm.

After one of the women enters (left), mixes a drink, and after she begins her long cross to stage right a chair moves backward five feet as she approaches and sits on it. An invisibly controlled rope mysteriously slowly begins a vertical ascent out the top of the King's (beast's) head and disappears into the ceiling.

I LIKE TO LOOK AT IT.

—Gertrude Stein

When we started working on the production one of the first, and biggest problems was that a very large theatre was necessary. People would phone and say they found a theatre but it would always be too small. I said no, like a *really* big theatre. I knew that was important because part of the original thinking had been to have a big enormous space, with a lot of people and with almost Nothing Things (like when you're a child and your parents ask what you are doing and you reply, "Oh, just noth-ing") —just sitting there and whatever they did was very small (secondary things). They'd just be doing little things.

Details, you mean.

Yeah, details. Just doing detail things. Like the lady in black boots, cocktail in hand, who seats herself stage left and begins in front and to the stage left of the entrance an inarticulate mono-logue with indications of discontent and empty gestures intended for, perhaps, some invisible guest. Another imposing visitor takes a seat beside her. A chair suspended by a thin wire descends suddenly through the ceiling stopping at the top of the pro-scenium. Later it descends slowly and steadily into the pile of objects and people stage left.

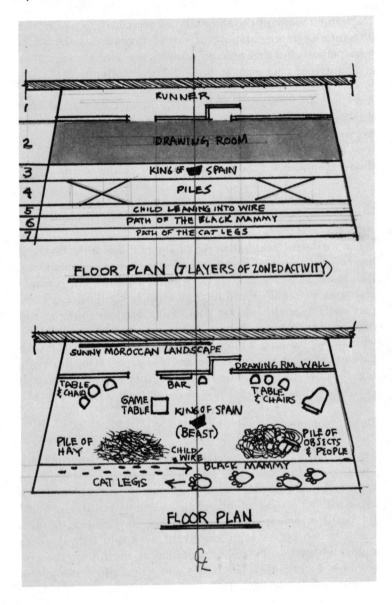

FLOOR PLAN (7 LAYERS OF ZONED ACTIVITY)

FLOOR PLAN

ELEVATION SHOWING DRAWING ROOM

ELEVATION SHOWING THE TWO PILES

ELEVATION SHOWING CAT LEGS

Yeah, cause like on Broadway they always do the big huge obvious things and I thought wouldn't it be Fantastic if there was a superbig space and a huge cast doing tiny but projected little things little individual things so then I called up the Riverside Church and thought maybe oh God maybe they'd be interested in sponsoring the Byrd School's new production so I talked to the guy and he said they were pretty scheduled-up oh G O D doing Real Plays and Operas and Modern Dances and Things so I'd havta wait till summer but then, then they just had had a cancellation and perhaps there was now a last-minute possibility that I'd get the Riverside Church but I didn't. Cause I'd already learned of course that in the last few years here you don't dare count on anything so I G O D I started checking out all sorts of things and places calling up everyone I knew and saying how I was looking for a really big theatre and the kindest person was Jerry Robbins who immediately gave me all sorts of leads and suggestions and had his secretary sit down and go through her files and help the Byrd School find theatres.

When I told him I was going to do *The King of Spain* he was kind—unlike the lady who made the comments about my flyer that I told about in the beginning; Robbins not asking about the particulars and not making me defend myself, which I really appreciated because I know his tastes and beliefs in theatre are so very different from mine.

Then I checked out zillions of theatres and rehearsal halls and so of course Riverside Church fell through and there was so little time left I said GOD this is already (another) Disaster there's no way, it looks, to do it. But then I went over to the Anderson Theatre since I had been trying all along to call a Mr. Barouk who worked with the Raines Reality Company and I understood that it had been the Anderson Yiddish Theatre for years and their not being able to renew their lease and they were inconveniently angry because of it. But I persisted in trying to get it for just two nights. Two nights. That's all I needed. It *was* really big and I *had* to have it. There was something special about it. Maybe cause it was old, big, and musty. And it seemed to be in a good location after all—on the fringes of the Lower East Side on Second Avenue and Fourth Street near where I used to live once and I really liked the whole aesthetic of the theatre. I couldn't get it out of my mind.

What's the "aesthetic" of that theatre, Byrd?

Well, it was very grand and had huge chandeliers hanging all over the place. All over. They were a little dirty though.

A little?

Well, actually they were filthy but somehow it *looked* grand and sort of fitted in—into my scheme for the Victorian drawing room the whole room of course being the whole thing, the walls the extension of the play and the theatre the extension of the game and it being the people inside. Everything in the Anderson Theatre at one time you see had been painted with gold leaf paint that was now sort of, sort of well . . .

Rancid, Byrd?

Yeah, I guess it *was* a little rancid. But there was definitely something nice about it. I can't explain it but it seemed to me to be just uuuuuhhhhhhhh

Just Right?

Just the right feeling for *The King of Spain*. But that was before the Disaster.

The Disaster, Byrd; which one?

Cause after we got the theatre—I paid for it on a Friday, $400 which was every cent I had in the whole world, not knowing how I was going to get another nickel to go on another day and I thought well, I'll just write another check; that's all. That's how I did *Byrdwoman* you know. Just wrote checks and they of course all bounced but *after* I got the materials.

Oh GOD. A Disaster. Another Disaster. Sunday see I go to the Anderson to sign the lease and the Manager says to me Oh GOD we've had a Tragedy.

A Tragedy? Waddayoumean a Tragedy? He said that the night before the theatre burned and I had put down my money, my rental money on a Friday and it burned on Saturday and I said oh my god this is a Disaster what are we going to do? The posters were already printed. Well, how bad was it?

He said the fire burned the stage floor pretty badly and the whole theatre had been flooded—all the carpets soggy wet and we're still not sure just how much damage had been done. Luckily though they had put it out before the whole theatre was destroyed. So, on that note we go into the theatre.

Well, actually I'm remembering now the Disaster was sort of beautiful. The lights were turned on on the stage and one quarter—the whole left-hand side—of the proscenium curtain from floor to ceiling was burned and charred and in back of it you could see the drops and scenery that had also been scorched from floor to ceiling and the theatre was entirely smoked and had the bitter, pungent scent of fire. It was an incredible theatrical thing in-itself and my friends said why Byrd why you should just do it like it is. This *is* fantastic I said of course but no, no cause I had a very clear, a very certain, distinct and sort of special idea of how it was, or should be and this would suggest, definitely suggest, something else. Something almost defiantly expressionistic and unwarranted although the effect *was* spectacular. Spectacular and devastating. But the Byrd School had *another* idea after all so I said yes it is it is very definitely theatrical but we intend another thing. Another thing than this entirely.

By the Monday now before we were to do it on Thursday the Manager said don't worry *everything* will be taken care of by next Monday—repaired and in working condition. We're going to put a new floor on this stage and we're going to have a new house curtain so don't worry, cause we know Mr. Hoffman you are a dancer and the Lena Robbins Foundation is sponsoring you. It'll be ready. Believe me. Don't worry your head useless about it he said it will all be taken care of. You've put down your deposit and we'll be ready to go.

Of course not having a whole lot of experience I'm remembering too now with theatre managers (mongers) I didn't know any more than to believe the man. Later, someone mentioned quite casually that it'll never, never be ready in time and I said G O D what do you *mean* not ready in time? Now I *knew* it was a Disaster. A Disaster *after* a Tragedy. G O D.

"Why," they said, "it'll take ages. Ages to repair all the damage."

You mean getting it done, don't you, Byrd?

Yeah, ages getting it done. In time. But the Manager promised me and so I thought surely we'll work something out. When we came into the theatre Monday practically nothing had been done and so naturally we were delayed and, in fact, the curtain was patched with an old faded piece of a different color velvet safety-pinned very awkwardly into position. Someone said later it very definitely fitted the Byrd School.

Then we go and have to raise money and that's the really big insoluble problem see . . .

You mean get sponsors?

Yeah, get sponsors. The first project we thought of was having a dance at the loft to raise money so again we call up everyone we know and have them call everyone they know for the benefit for the Byrd School's new production, *The King of Spain* at the Anderson Theatre.

So we bought lots of beer and chips. Records too. People had a good time and even though someone stole pocketbooks and flushed them down the toilet which got jammed. We charged a dollar admission which was put in the pot at the door. Only the person minding the door had to suddenly go to the bathroom and when he did the money got stolen and so another oh God another Disaster and we're back where we started—*before* the beginning. Broke. Reminds me of the time I worked G O D in a bank once and lost all the money from my drawer. It disappeared somehow. That's cause I made mistakes. I never could do figures but I did all the figures, and the budget too for this show. But I forgot to include some things it seems . . .

You mean, don't you Byrd that you lost another fifty-thousand?

No, oh no. We lost only $960 and it all ended up costing over thirty-four hundred dollars L O R D I've never spent that much on a show in my life.

Certainly sounds like *the* most expensive, avant-garde extravaganza of all time.

Well. Well it cost far more than I estimated. Or imagined. A Disaster. All the way. In fact at one point in my donations I thought wow I may even make $500 but of course I didn't. I lost much more but it was worth it. People had a good time. We had so many unscheduled expenses . . .

Like what?

Like the cat legs. They were the technical impossibility. In the beginning of the play all the people come slowly in one at a time and then sometimes together all sorts of different people elegant people and awkward people, middle-aged people and old people. Finally, after Mary Peer sommersaults in with microphone around the neck and tells all at once her daily bizarre stories that automatically all at once naturally come into her mind, bales of hay are loosened, scattered and stacked downstage right. Another rope rises out the peak of the haystack. Meanwhile, a tottering old black mammy in limbo-trance crosses the drawing room arms adumbrating revivalist gesticulations accompanying herself with muted wailing sounds, a fragmented, guttural melody. The lady sitting upstage holding one of her boots in hand (after arranging feathers in her hair and clothing) takes another sip of her drink. The mammy's hands grabbing continuously but gently for some invisible threads, or cobwebs. Then, suddenly, four giant cat legs begin descending into the space and walk in the opposite direction across the stage.

There was the problem. First we couldn't figure out how to do it. We needed miles of fur that was very expensive because the legs had to be really gigantic and then we didn't know whether to stuff them but we found that Macy's had giant Slinkeys kids play with that would be perfect but it being just after Christmas they were naturally totally out and so we have to call the factory but by this time already it's too late we have the Anderson and the date is set for January 30th and 31st and there's only two and a half weeks left and my friend Philip Haight started cutting and sewing all the fur and finally we find out that Playland on Twenty-third Street has a stock of giant Slinkeys. Then we couldn't figure out how possibly we could hang the legs and cinch them up to cross with those with some semblance of cat coordination. In fact, Anthony Jones who is a professional stage designer came over to the loft after we finished stitching the fur and he looked at our pencil sketches and said no, no it's definitely absolutely *imp*ossible to do what you want to do. Oh no I thought, the Final Disaster. Technically Impossible. But we, being the Byrd School are used (by now) to the impossible and to being told we can't do what we plan but somehow we do it anyway and again in this case we did it, we built a track and arranged somehow a system of pulleys and ropes devised inside the cat legs hidden and manipulated from the wings with sandbag weights and it was really Super all those people sitting so long like at a party see having drinks and then suddenly a pile of hay and a royal carpet of green grass for the giant cat crawling through the drawing room.

> AND THE FOURTH; THE DIMENSION OF STILLNESS,
> AND THE POWER OVER WILD BEASTS . . .
> —Ezra Pound

Then the stage empties, except for an old woman still sitting attentively as the stage darkens throwing the Moroccan landscape into superrelief. The runner continues on his race: back and forth, endlessly. A special spot on the highback chair. The tilted head of the creature quickens and the figure rises majestically. It's the King of Spain. The beast turns facing the audience in a final moment of suspense as the curtain falls rapidly.

Then I had to call the Lena Robbins Foundation still not believing we were being helped. But I had to go see Robbins because we were already in debt and had to have money immediately but I was nervous because I had never done this before. So I go up to his offices. Another Disaster. Also see I had been having trouble sleeping I had so much organization work to do and I had all these papers my flyers under arm and was *very* excited having just been to the printers and having just picked up the flyers—the ones the woman I told about in the beginning part said she thought couldn't possibly be for a *dance* program. I was very excited too because some aesthetically interesting typographical errors had occurred in the printing process. I go into Robbins' office and his secretary see says "Oh yes" and takes me into his Inner Office and I'm nervous even though I know him I mean this is the Byrd School now and Oh GOD oh no and as the door opens I see him speaking with his stage manager and I cross to shake his hand and then it happens.

Oh no, what happens?

I don't know how I did it. I was holding on I thought tight but I dropped all my flyers all over the floor. GOD! All over. Another Disaster. GOD I was so embarrassed. Everything all over. All over the place. Of course all of his staff came rushing forward trying to help me which made me even more embarrassed here I am seen barging unexpectedly in on a professional dancing conference a real one to get my dance grant and I blow it. My stuff. All over. I've always been awkward and self-conscious and I just couldn't that afternoon get it together. But Mr. Robbins was very kind and understanding. Even he got down and helped pick up my flyers and then he gave me a check; the grant. In fact, I was invited that evening for dinner because, after all, this was *an* occasion. I said yes when he asked (not really thinking—just anything to get out of this predicament) I'd love to come of course. Especially after I had come in, tripped in his office, and made such a fool of myself. Certainly I'll come to dinner. When? I planned to get home really early that evening to have enough time to get ready—change my dungarees see and put on a tie and get myself together for dinner. But I didn't get time at the last minute and Oh GOD another Disaster yeah two in one day. It happens the very same day and only two weeks before performance. First I was late. Then I arrive in my work clothes. *Then* we're eating dinner in a large room but at a very small (but comfortable) table and I think we were eating chicken when I got laughing, carried away telling a story and I went to cut my chicken with the knife and fork and somehow, somehow everything slipped and knocked my chicken on the floor! God, now I'm really awfully embarrassed so embarrassed you can't believe it see in this giant room and the small table and he looks over and God my plate's empty and then his eyes catch the heap, the mess on the floor. I didn't know what to do. I just kept wishing myself somewhere anywhere else and we're still laughing over the story I was telling before and the chicken's on the floor. GOD! And the rice sprinkled all over the tablecloth and the gravy on the carpet.

And you mean this is the Celebration Dinner for your Dance Grant, too, huh?

Yeah you hit it here I am trying to get my first Dance Grant from the Lena Robbins Foundation. L - O - R - D!! I didn't know what to do. So what else, I started picking it up. I mean I had to do *something* so I started picking up the chicken. Jerry said just leave it and we're now really in convulsions both of us and then the servants come out to help us pick it up and by this time we're on the floor again just like in the beginning and I said this is Oh GOD just another Disaster the Byrd School does it again. Here I'm thinking I walked in this morning and dropped my flyers all over the floor and then tonight now here I am all over again mopping up the chicken. But then (somehow) we got through that.

Where else did you get money, I mean, it was a really expensive production and as an Unknown didn't you have trouble but finally find other sponsors?

Yes, Mr. Gross of Multi-Amp, Dr. Dallas Pratt, New York State Council of the Arts, and Rose Dreyer. Well it was very interesting, and fortunate. See I had been working remember in my classes in New Jersey that I explained earlier and one of the sponsors became interested because of my working with an exceptional child who had motor difficulties in performing certain skills basic to elementary education—an impairment of body coordination and spatial (depth) perception—in spite of the fact that the child was unusually gifted with an advanced ability to comprehend and conceptualize pretty advanced material. We worked with basic body extensions after school and making connections between movement, and, say, these skills such as writing—it grew out of the work I did in class similar to the adults—getting them to relax so that by working on essentially one thing (the class itself) we were concurrently working actually on several processes at once—physical and psychological. I guess what I want to say is that what was specially interesting in this child was that the psychologists had no way to "reach" him—that is, the child obviously needed a special approach and further, was able to conceptually grasp what other children don't until their teens if they're pretty bright, and maybe an ordinary child would never perceive the scientific principles that young Jimmy could at twelve. Yet he had trouble, for instance, writing (which is usually taken as major proof of mental growth) because of not being able to execute circular patterns and ovals necessary in cursive writing. Actually he had devised a compensatory form of writing himself—a kind of private code only he could read. In fact, because of these special problems I included young Jimmy in *Byrdwoman* and wanted to have him be in *The King of Spain* but he couldn't and another child who was almost totally deaf and who had been given up as hopeless had rather remarkably been gradually learning to accommodate himself to the kind of classroom situation I always try to set up—that is, an open-ended, so to speak environment where there is minimum tension, judgment, comparison of work, or competition. Anyway this young boy obviously possessed a genuine talent for painting which has developed, in fact so much so that he seems to be able to transfer his feelings and his understanding of say color to the social transactions of the group. That is, in spite of his near total deafness and virtually no vocabulary he immediately became a jovial, outgoing, convivial, and even communicative member of the group. For instance, the movement sections—he is more lively in them and often more imaginative in demonstrating an ability to be exceedingly and exceptionally sensitive to the feelings of the others, only he "perceives" (and transmits) this through kinetic, or kinesthetic awareness rather than through discursive, or verbal dialogue. But he can establish a ready rapport or dialogue with movement. And this came about first through simple running exercises and feeling a confidence in his painting and then later through tying strings to both our bodies and to, say, the walls and maybe even to one another— sort of a connective playing and exploring just the nature of the material; the material between us.

In both these children I sensed not only a deep, special talent but channels usually unknown for establishing lines of communication. Sometimes we even ran with the strings tied to us. Because of a bodily maladjustment in a certain sense there was an extended range of feeling or, even, sensibility that, once *un*covered meant an expansion of awareness and communication. And that *is* most mysterious of all—not only can our psychologists not explain what "creativity" is, they can't really provide a program where each specialized ability can be cultivated— especially in an environment relying more and more on programmed textbooks. Mysterious too a bodily (or psychological) maladjustment because it makes any "sane" or conventional approach to education all the *more* problematic; impossible. It means that the teacher has to find a way to adjust to the vocabulary or sets of gestures the child sets up—in some cases, that is, even though it goes contrary to educational theories and institutionalized rules you have to do it—accept the child on his terms, on his set of symbols, even though of course the psychologists with their Ph D's say no no it's impossible and even though the head of the school calls you into the office and accuses you of all sorts of things like psychological heresy and fraud. That is one of the really interesting and maybe even radical realizations I've had in a broad set of experiences working with children—maybe you just *can't* demand, even like in theatre, too, any of the usual standards. You have to be prepared to float for a while and accept whatever happens. You have to let the circumstance work *itself* out so that whatever exchange or dialogue is possible *is* permissible. Sometimes that means making a lot of concessions, or even, even making enemies with the faculty, I mean you can't always expect the child to actually accomplish something concrete, like an object or a lesson. Sometimes we can't measure how much, or even *if* a child is actually learning. Once the Director of the school where I teach called me in before all the parents to demonstrate what I was trying to do in my classes. I would leave the class sometimes and I wouldn't "play" Teacher and the children would be left up to themselves. They devised their own plays. And those plays baffled some of the parents and, luckily, surprised others. Maybe I mean something like what a friend of mine told me about that psychiatrist in London, R. D. Laing—his approach is to the total situation, to the individual in the context of his environment and the circumstances of his actions and behavior. It was specifically because of these special cases and of my work in children's theatre that these very basic (felt) processes which I observe everyday in the classroom became also relevant to an understanding of self, or character, or theatre: a child is always presenting himself; nothing more or less. An observant person, or one who is "creative" or sensitive can contact the special, positive side of the personality—that is, as long as you don't oppose, impose, or make demands on the kids. You can't teach Art to children just as you can't define, specify, buy, or mass produce it for adults. Sometimes art is nothing and sometimes it's knocking around in swamps instead of singing Christmas carols and sometimes it's allowing for all possibilities and sometimes it's taking exception. Anyway, perhaps I've gotten side-tracked, but, maybe for a good reason. All these kinds of things are happening, that is, entertaining, arresting, educational; and hence, theatrical.

DRAMABOOKS
(Plays)

WHEN ORDERING, please use the Standard Book Number consisting of the publisher's prefix, 8090-, plus the five digits following each title. (Note that the numbers given in this list are for paperback editions only. Many of the books are also available in cloth.)

Christopher Marlowe (Tamburlaine the Great, Parts I & II, Doctor Faustus, The Jew of Malta, Edward the Second) (0701-0)

William Congreve (Complete Plays) (0702-9)

Webster and Tourneur (The White Devil, The Duchess of Malfi, The Atheist's Tragedy, The Revenger's Tragedy) (0703-7)

John Ford (The Lover's Melancholy, 'Tis Pity She's a Whore, The Broken Heart, Love's Sacrifice, Perkin Warbeck) (0704-5)

Richard Brinsley Sheridan (The Rivals, St. Patrick's Day, The Duenna, A Trip to Scarborough, The School for Scandal, The Critic) (0705-3)

Camille and Other Plays (Scribe: A Peculiar Position, The Glass of Water; Sardou: A Scrap of Paper; Dumas: Camille; Augier: Olympe's Marriage) (0706-1)

John Dryden (The Conquest of Granada, Parts I & II, Marriage à la Mode, Aureng-Zebe) (0707-X)

Ben Jonson Vol. 1 (Volpone, Epicoene, The Alchemist) (0708-8)

Oliver Goldsmith (The Good Natur'd Man, She Stoops to Conquer, An Essay on the Theatre, A Register of Scotch Marriages) (0709-6)

Jean Anouilh Vol. 1 (Antigone, Eurydice, The Rehearsal, Romeo and Jeannette, The Ermine) (0710-X)

Let's Get a Divorce! and Other Plays (Labiche: A Trip Abroad, and Célimare; Sardou: Let's Get a Divorce!; Courteline: These Cornfields; Feydeau: Keep an Eye on Amélie; Prévert: A United Family; Achard: Essays on Feydeau) (0711-8)

Jean Giraudoux Vol 1 (Ondine, The Enchanted, The Madwoman of Chaillot, The Apollo of Bellac) (0712-6)

Jean Anouilh Vol. 2 (Restless Heart, Time Remembered, Ardèle, Mademoiselle Colombe, The Lark) (0713-4)

Henrik Ibsen: The Last Plays (Little Eyolf, John Gabriel Borkman, When We Dead Awaken) (0714-2)

Ivan Turgenev (A Month in the Country, A Provincial Lady, A Poor Gentleman) (0715-0)

George Farquhar (The Constant Couple, The Twin-Rivals, The Recruiting Officer, The Beaux Stratagem) (0716-9)

Jean Racine (Andromache, Britannicus, Berenice, Phaedra, Athaliah) (0717-7)

The Storm and Other Russian Plays (The Storm, The Government Inspector, The Power of Darkness, Uncle Vanya, The Lower Depths) (0718-5)

Michel de Ghelderode: Seven Plays Vol. 1 (The Ostend Interviews, Chronicles of Hell, Barabbas, The Women at the Tomb, Pantagleize, The Blind Men, Three Players and a Play, Lord Halewyn) (0719-3)

Lope de Vega: Five Plays (Peribáñez, Fuenteovejuna, The Dog in the Manger, The Knight from Olmedo, Justice Without Revenge) (0720-7)

Calderón: Four Plays (Secret Vengeance for Secret Insult, Devotion to the Cross, The Mayor of Zalamea, The Phantom Lady) (0721-5)

Jean Cocteau: Five Plays (Orphée, Antigone, Intimate Relations, The Holy Terrors, The Eagle with Two Heads) (0722-3)

Ben Jonson Vol. 2 (Every Man in His Humour, Sejanus, Bartholomew Fair) (0723-1)

Port-Royal and Other Plays (Claudel: Tobias and Sara; Mauriac: Asmodée; Copeau: The Poor Little Man; Montherlant: Port-Royal) (0724-X)

Edwardian Plays (Maugham· Loaves and Fishes; Hankin: The Return of the Prodigal; Shaw: Getting Married; Pinero: Mid-Channel; Granville-Barker: The Madras House) (0725-8)

Alfred de Musset: Seven Plays (0726-6)

Georg Büchner: Complete Plays and Prose (0727-4)

Paul Green: Five Plays (Johnny Johnson, In Abraham's Bosom, Hymn to the Rising Sun, The House of Connelly, White Dresses) (0728-2)

François Billetdoux: Two Plays (Tchin-Tchin, Chez Torpe) (0729-0)

Michel de Ghelderode: Seven Plays Vol. 2 (Red Magic, Hop, Signor!, The Death of Doctor Faust, Christopher Columbus, A Night of Pity, Piet Bouteille, Miss Jairus) (0730-4)

Jean Giraudoux Vol. 2 (Siegfried, Amphitryon 38, Electra) (0731-2)

Kelly's Eye and Other Plays by Henry Livings (Kelly's Eye, Big Soft Nellie, There's No Room for You Here for a Start) (0732-0)

Gabriel Marcel: Three Plays (Man of God, Ariadne, Votive Candle) (0733-9)

New American Plays Vol. 1 ed. by Robert W. Corrigan (0734-7)

For a complete list of books of criticism and history of the drama, please write to
Hill and Wang, 72 Fifth Avenue, New York, New York 10011.